MIGHTY
BE OUR POWERS

MIGHTY
BE OUR POWERS

How Sisterhood, Prayer, and Sex
Changed a Nation at War

A MEMOIR

LEYMAH GBOWEE
with Carol Mithers

New York

Copyright © 2011 by Leymah Gbowee

Published by Beast Books
Beast Books is a co-publishing venture with the Perseus Books Group

Books published by Beast Books are available at special discounts for bulk purchases in the United States by corporations, institutions, and other organizations. For more information, please contact the Special Markets Department at the Perseus Books Group, 2300 Chestnut Street, Suite 200, Philadelphia, PA 19103, or call (800) 810-4145, ext. 5000, or e-mail special.markets@perseusbooks.com.

Editorial production by *Marra*thon Production Services, www.marrathon.net

Design by Jane Raese
Text set in 12 point Bulmer

Family photos courtesy of the author.

Library of Congress Cataloging-in-Publication Data is available for this book.

ISBN 978-0-9842951-5-9
ISBN 978-0-9842951-4-2 (e-Book)

10 9 8 7 6 5 4 3

For my sister, Geneva

CONTENTS

PART THREE

PROLOGUE

ODERN WAR STORIES often resemble each other, not because the circumstances are alike but because they're told in the same way. Commanders are quoted offering confident predictions of victory. Male diplomats make serious pronouncements. And the fighters—always men, whether they are government soldiers or rebels, whether they are portrayed as heroes or thugs—brag, threaten, brandish grisly trophies and shoot off their mouths and their weapons.

It was that way in my country, Liberia. During the years that civil war tore us apart, foreign reporters often came to document the nightmare. Read the accounts. Watch the video clips. They are all about the power of destruction. Bare-chested boys on foot or in pickup trucks fire enormous machine guns, dance crazily in wrecked city streets or crowd around a corpse, holding up a victim's bleeding heart. A young man in sunglasses and red beret regards the camera coolly. "We kill you, we will eat you."

Now watch the reports again, but look more carefully, at the background, for that is where you will find the women. You'll see us fleeing, weeping, kneeling before our children's graves. In the traditional telling of war stories, women are always in the background. Our suffering is just a sidebar to the main tale; when we're included, it's for "human interest." If we are African, we are even more likely to be marginalized and painted solely as pathetic—hopeless expressions, torn clothes, sagging breasts. Victims. That is the image of us that the world is used to, and the image that sells.

Once, a foreign journalist asked me, "Were you raped during the Liberian war?"

When I said no, I was no longer of any interest.

During the war in Liberia, almost no one reported the other reality of women's lives. How we hid our husbands and sons from soldiers looking to recruit or kill them. How, in the midst of chaos, we walked miles to find food and water for our families—how we kept life going so that there would be something left to build on when peace returned. And how we created strength in sisterhood, and spoke out for peace on behalf of all Liberians.

This is not a traditional war story. It is about an army of women in white standing up when no one else would—unafraid, because the worst things imaginable had already happened to us. It is about how we found the moral clarity, persistence and bravery to raise our voices against war and restore sanity to our land.

You have not heard it before, because it is an African woman's story, and our stories rarely are told.

I want you to hear mine.

PART ONE

CHAPTER 1

THE WORLD WAS MINE

On New Year's Eve, 1989, all of us who belonged to St. Peter's Lutheran Church in Monrovia gathered in the churchyard for the Watch Night Service, when we'd see the old year pass and welcome the new one. Everyone got a piece of white paper. On it, you wrote down whatever you hoped for the coming year, then cast it into a big steel drum in the center of the yard. The pastor said a prayer and touched a lit match to the pile. The smoke would go straight up to God, who would make your wishes come true.

As a child I had often wished for health. I was sick a lot—measles, malaria, cholera. I'd also wished for good grades, and for things to go well for my family. This year, I was seventeen, finishing high school and about to start at the university. I made a teenage good girl's wish: for good grades, interesting professors and the right classes. And I asked that those I loved be kept safe from evil.

When it was my turn, I dropped my paper in with the others. The smoke curled and rose as the congregation broke into songs of praise and thanksgiving, and I tilted my head back to watch it vanish into the warm starry sky. A feeling of safety enveloped me. God was good. I knew He heard all my prayers.

IT'S VERY HARD, NOW, to remember being that girl. So happy. So ignorant of what was coming.

A month later, my family gathered for a celebration. My sister Josephine, two cousins and I had all graduated from high school, and my parents threw the biggest party our neighborhood had ever seen. More than a hundred people came to our small house, so many that the festivities spilled over to my grandmother's next door, and then out into the neighborhood. No one minded. Though we were in the nation's capital, in some ways the cluster of houses on Old Road, near Spriggs Payne airfield, was like a village. The half-dozen homes, modest but of sturdy cement with corrugated metal roofs, were so close together that you could stand on your porch and sniff and know what your neighbor planned for dinner. Kids were always roaming the dirt paths and playing games in the sandy open spaces between them. A feast was set up at our home—American fare, like salad and sandwiches, along with traditional Liberian fish soup and goat meat soup—and my whole family was having a good time, even my shy oldest sister, Geneva. The youngest, Fata, only twelve, danced around and pretended to be singing traditional songs from our ethnic tribal group, the Kpelle. She got the words all wrong, but the tune sounded good.

Dozens of friends from church and school had come: Margaret, Kayatu, Flomo, Satta, Kulah and Emmanuel—we called him "Ayo"—tall and dark, with fierce eyes. Koffa, the joker, danced with a silly smile on his face but as always he was perfectly dressed, his shoes polished, a folded white handkerchief in his pocket. His dad was in the military and in that family, staying neat was a rule. Koffa dreamed of emigrating to the United States and joining the marines.

"Hey, Red!" someone called—my nickname because I was so fair skinned. "We need more drinks!" I ran to fetch them. Our living room had been emptied of furniture but was still overcrowded, with more than fifty people jammed inside. This was our dance floor, and "Just Got Paid" was blasting. I squeezed toward the back of the house, smoothing the front of my new pantsuit; it was aqua blue and gold *fanti* cloth, made just for me by Kayatu's brother, who was a tailor. The 18k gold earrings, bracelet, chain and ring my parents had given me a few days before glittered. Everywhere I went, guests passed me envelopes with bills in them. Other presents piled up: clothes, shoes, and best of all, a beautiful pair of Dexter brand boots, made of patterned leather that looked like snakeskin.

"We need the graduates to come forward!" my father called out. The music stopped. Josephine was nowhere to be found, so I stepped up, along with my cousins Fernon and Napah. My father, dressed in his usual weekend wear of jeans, T-shirt and baseball cap, a broad smile on his handsome face, told me how proud he was of me.

"And I thank you for all the love and support you have shown me," I told him and my mother. She looked lovely in a traditional African *lappa* suit and gold jewelry, her dark hair up in a French twist. "And thank you all"—I gestured to the crowd—"for coming tonight to celebrate our joy!" Everyone applauded, and my parents looked pleased and happy, their own marriage troubles put away for the moment.

They'd both grown up poor and tonight everyone could see how well they'd done—two of their daughters graduating from one of Monrovia's best private schools and heading off to college; a party with such abundant food and drink that it would be the subject of conversation for a long while. For me, the night was the perfect end to one of the happiest times of my life.

I loved my childhood home. The settlement on Old Road wasn't luxurious; there were no paved sidewalks or air conditioners to break the constant, muggy heat. But our homes had televisions, bathrooms, modern kitchens; this wasn't a slum like Logan Town or West Point, whose ragged children I had seen begging or pressed against the gates at friends' parties, watching us eat. No one was homeless or hungry here, and our community was built on togetherness and sharing. The five of us girls went back and forth constantly between our house and our grandmother's; she was actually our great-aunt, but she had raised our mother, and we called her "Ma." Along with other traditional midwives in the neighborhood, Ma delivered babies for women who couldn't afford a doctor.

When the Muslim family I knew broke their fast at Ramadan, I ate with them. When a friend had potato greens for lunch, I traded her some of my cassava leaves. We were surrounded by space and freedom. An empty plot of land lay across the street that led to the airfield, where daily flights left for Sierra Leone and Guinea. We played there endlessly, and Mama planted a garden of greens, okra and peppers.

The rest of Monrovia was beautiful, too, a long narrow city of a few hundred thousand, framed by the Atlantic on one side, the Mesurado River and its mangrove swamps and creeks on the other. It was clean and modern; almost nothing but the enormous Masonic temple, with its ornate white columns, was more than a few decades old. John F. Kennedy Medical Center, where Geneva worked in the records department, was the most sophisticated medical facility in all West Africa.

In the center of town, where we went to buy clothes and shoes, white and pastel two-story apartments lined the narrow streets, their balconies decorated with wrought-iron railings. Roads ended at brilliantly white sand beaches with tall palm trees. The long sweep of Tubman Boulevard curved through Capitol Hill, past City Hall, the Executive Mansion, where President Samuel Doe lived, and the University of Liberia, which sat behind a canopy of tall trees.

On the night of the party, I was happy with myself, too. I'd been a little shy and insecure in my early teen years, always in the shadow of Josephine, who was just a year older and who I thought was prettier than I, with a better shape. But in high school, I came into my own. My shyness disappeared when I got up to speak, and I was elected a senator in student government. I spoke at other local schools and made the honor roll. Boys let me know they liked me, too, and I realized that I looked *good*, tall and slim, my long hair in a braid down my back.

At fifteen, I had my first serious boyfriend, though the relationship didn't last. One night I went to a school dance and afterward was sitting on the sidewalk with a friend. This boyfriend came up to me and said, "You didn't tell me you were coming tonight! You have to go home right now!" We went back and forth and he slapped me. That was the end of him. I wasn't going to put up with that.

By graduation, I was confident in who I was, a pretty girl who was smart; a smart girl who was also pretty. It gave me a kick to say I would be going to the university to study biology and chemistry, and I knew that when I was in college, life would get even better. My parents' strict control over me would loosen, I'd have an intellectual adventure, and I'd go on to become what I'd dreamed of for years, a doctor.

My life stretched out ahead: I would study, work, marry, have children, maybe someday live in one of the sprawling brick air-conditioned mansions that lined Payne Avenue. I was seventeen, and I could do anything. The world was mine for the taking.

Community. Connections. Confidence. Big plans. Within six months, all of it would be gone.

THE COMFORTABLE LIFE my parents gave my sisters and me was hard earned, a slow crawl upward from almost nothing. The story is impossible to tell without also explaining their history, and Liberia's.

My country was settled as a colony in 1822 by freed and freeborn American blacks and African men and women liberated from slave boats that had been en route to the New World. The connection between us and the United States remained vital, like a blood tie, long after we became a nation in 1842. Our constitution was modeled on America's; our capital was named after President James Monroe. Until the 1980s, our official currency was the US dollar, and even after we had a Liberian dollar, US money was both accepted everywhere and desirable. My friends and I grew up on shows like *Sanford and Son*, *Good Times*, *Dynasty* and *Dallas*. We cheered the LA Lakers. Going to the US for education or to live was many Liberians' dream, and those who emigrated sent back glamorous pictures of themselves standing next to big cars.

Your ancestors' origins determined your place in the social order. Settlers who came from the slave boats—called "Congo People"—and those from America, many of them of mixed blood and light skinned—called "Americo-Liberians"—formed a political and economic elite. They saw themselves as more "civilized" and worthy than the tribes of Africans who already occupied the land: the Kpelle, Bassa, Gio, Kru, Grebo, Mandingo, Mano, Krahn, Gola, Gbandio, Loma, Kissi, Vai and Bella.

For generations, the elite clustered in and around Monrovia or in suburbs like Virginia and Careysburg, where they built expansive plantations that recalled those of the American South. And they held on to power with a tight grip. The awful irony was that they did to the indigenous people exactly what had been done to them in the US. They set up separate schools. Separate churches. The indigenous became their servants. It's like you go into someone's house, accept food and drink, then box your host into a corner, saying, "This is my room now."

The social inequality, the unequal distribution of wealth, the exploitation—and the desire of the indigenous to take back what was theirs—are some of the reasons we had so many problems.

My father was a Kpelle, a poor rural boy from Sanoyea, Bong County, in Central Liberia. For a time, his father worked as a virtual slave in the Spanish colony on Fernando Po Island, just off the coast of Cameroon. Villagers accused his mother, whose babies always died at birth, of being a witch, and took my dad away from her. He stayed with nurses at the Lutheran mission house, then went to the Booker T. Washington Institute, where ambitious indigenous boys could learn a trade. He became a radio technician.

Mama, also Kpelle, was born in Margibi County, on the north-central coast. When she was five, her mother left her father for another man, and abandoned Mama. Her dad became so depressed that he couldn't really care for her, and he died when she was just nine. His sister, our Ma, took her in.

Ma had her own story. In the recent past, Americo-Liberians often went into rural villages looking for fair-skinned children to foster and "modernize." Because Ma's skin was light, she had been chosen and brought up in an elite house. She then married (and divorced) three times, coming away with a rubber farm in the country and a house on Old Road. She expected my mother to marry "up" to a boy with money or education. When instead she fell in love with my dad, a sweet talker who was ten years older, from a poor family and unemployed, Ma was furious.

My mother gave birth to my sister Geneva when she was only seventeen. At first Ma took the baby away from her to raise, but she soon relented and let my parents move in with her. Mama went to pharmacy school, and one of Ma's influential friends found her a job at a drugstore; later, she was a dispensing pharmacist at several hospitals.

Mala was born next, then Josephine, then me. My mother had wanted a boy. "Leymah" means "What is it about me?"—as in "Why can't I conceive a male?" But my father called me his "luck child," because right after I was born, he was hired by Liberia's National Security Agency, equivalent to America's FBI. Eventually, he rose to become chief radio technician and liaison with the US, and worked at the big US embassy complex on a hilltop in the Mamba Point neighborhood, overlooking the ocean. His work was secret, and we never knew much about it.

One of Ma's friends owned the plot of land next door to her and agreed to sell it to my parents. They built our house, and when I was five, Fata came along.

If you had asked our neighbors on Old Road, many would have said we were the happiest family in the community. I know that from the outside we looked successful. Both my parents worked hard. A five-minute walk from Old Road there was a large dirt field that kids used for kickball and soccer games, and next to it was a market where women sold trout, snapper and salmon they bought from the local fishermen. We never shopped at the fish market because Mama said it was too expensive, but for years, she rose at 3 A.M. to make cornbread, shortbread and Kool-Aid to sell there at the end of the day, after she finished her pharmacy work.

All the effort paid off. My dad bought a car, a Peugeot. We kids went to some of Monrovia's best schools and were in the same after-school programs as the children of the elite—swimming classes, Girl Scouts, vacation Bible school.

But our life wasn't perfect. I don't think I ever saw my parents happy together. Papa went out to parties and clubs on weekend nights and was still sleeping when we left for church on Sunday. And he cheated on my mother—a lot. It wasn't at all unusual among Liberian men—some even brought home the kids they'd fathered for their wives to raise—but it hurt my mother badly. When I was growing up, she would say that she didn't know what love was. And that "man" was spelled "d-o-g." Every now and then, my sisters and I would be ordered to Ma's house or wake up to hear all the relatives and church elders gathered in the living room, and know there was a crisis.

"Who will you go with if they divorce?" Josephine and I asked each other gravely, because we could not bear the thought of being apart.

Mama stayed with our father because of us; later, she told us that she never forgot how she had suffered after her parents' marriage broke up. But she judged the boys we brought home with hard eyes, demanding, "Who is his family?" It drove me nuts that she, who came from a lowly background, would be so judgmental. And she was never physically affectionate with us; she didn't cuddle or say "I love you." By the time we were teenagers, she was always angry. Anything we did could set her off; if we didn't clean our rooms or get home on time—beatings! She would use a belt or a stick of rattan, and she left welts. She always told us, "If you talk back, I'll give you a slap, you'll lose a tooth." She was a hard woman. To this day, my sisters and I have a love-hate relationship with her; we can't stand her, but we can't do without her. There's a Liberian saying: "You're too greasy to throw away, but too bitter to swallow."

Now that I'm older, I understand her better. She had five girls to raise and a husband who often talked of us as "your children." (We were his only when we were successful.) She had to answer to Ma, who was quiet but very strong, and always the true boss. Ma was a member of the Sande, a traditional Liberian secret society, and almost a priestess, with the power to deal with snakes and snakebites. She was greatly respected, both in her village and on Old Road. She spoke with absolute authority; when she put her foot down, no one crossed the line. My mother also had her own private trauma. Only recently, she told me that when her mother left her father and she stayed in the village, something terrible happened to her. She wouldn't say what it was; she said she would keep the secret with her until she died.

Our house always felt full, with lots of relatives coming and going. Because my mother still longed for a son, we took in Eric, whose mother was one of the wives of my dad's stepbrother, a traditional village chief. And the children of my mother's cousins regularly came from their village to go to school in Monrovia. In return, they were our servants.

In Africa, that's the way it is. You might not have much, but there's always someone with less; when rural families send their children to city relatives for "opportunity," the relatives pay for school uniforms and copybooks, and in return the children work. When Papa grew up at the mission house, he had to sweep, fetch water and cut grass to earn his keep. (He rarely talked about his childhood, but sometimes when we complained about something, he told us, "I used to sit by the river and sew my pants with twine.") Ma took Mama in, but at ten, she was cooking for the whole household. Ma's biological son would come home from school and order her around, demanding, "Where's my food?"

Our village relatives resented that we had more than they did, and Papa could be really abusive, mocking their lack of education and shouting, "Dumb ass!" when someone displeased him. Sometimes, the girls who came to stay took it out on my sisters and me, spanking us when no one was looking or pulling our hair when they washed it. Few of them lasted more than a year or two; they got pregnant and my dad sent them back to the village because he didn't want them to be bad influences on us. Sometimes, I really wished I lived only with my nearest family.

My sisters all struggled in their own ways. Geneva, who was six years older than me, never played outdoors with the rest of us. She'd contracted polio when she was little and she was ashamed of her left leg, which was shorter than the other and a little twisted. Geneva loved Josephine, Fata and me, and we adored her so much we called her "Mammie," but with others, she was very withdrawn, so quiet that she was almost invisible.

Mala was darker than the rest of us, and always felt like an outsider in the family. She got poor grades and often was in trouble. While my friends and I spent time at places like King Burger after school, Mala favored the Monte Carlo Amusement zone, where she'd play pool and take a lot of pleasure in beating older boys and men. She ran away for the first time when she was only twelve. She would pick the poorest of the poor as her boyfriends, and by seventeen, she was married and pregnant. Her husband was an older Lebanese man. (Lebanese immigrants had arrived in Liberia in the late nineteenth century, and many were merchants and shop owners.) Eventually she had two children, and they both came to live with us while she stayed away, on her own. There was no shame in that for her; in Liberia, if someone is sick or having trouble raising her children for some reason, her family steps in. What's important is that a child is being cared for and loved, not by whom.

Josephine, almost my twin we were so close, was stubborn and strong willed. When we were young, she and I were partners in everything, including mischief, like ganging up on Mala. Later, when we were teenagers, my parents started taking the keys out of the back door when they went to bed, so anyone who sneaked out of the house would get caught out by daylight. Josephine learned how to open the lock with a knife. For a time, I liked to sneak out with friends and go to clubs downtown where we would drink and meet boys. I'd get home late and tap on the window, and Josephine would use that knife to let me in. If my parents got angry at her about anything, she'd stand up and never back down. Fata, born so long after the rest of us, grew up in our shadows, a loner who felt as if no one had time for her.

As for me, I was driven, ambitious, and most of all, eager to please. For the five years until Fata was born, I thrived on being the pampered baby, and to hold on to that attention, I tried to be perfect. I was active at church. Even in high school, when I was doing my sneaking out, I did all my schoolwork so well that my parents never knew. I always brought home good grades.

I struggle with my weight now, but back then I was skinny, never more than a hundred pounds, and would get so hyper and caught up in what I was doing, I'd forget to eat.

I also seemed to catch every illness. At thirteen, I developed an ulcer, as well as suffering bouts of cholera and malaria. I was in the hospital at least twice a year. That was why I decided to become a doctor; two young pediatricians cared for me during one of my illnesses, and they were so loving. I remember looking in their soft eyes and thinking, *This is who I want to be.*

Most of all, I wanted to please my father. I loved going with him on visits back to Bong County. We'd stay at his family's house, where he'd sit on the porch holding court and drinking palm wine with his step-brothers. The stares Josephine and I got—city girls with shoes! Relatives would laugh. "Joseph has brought his civilized daughters to see us!"

I feared his thunderous voice when I was a kid, but I never doubted that my father loved me. I remember being quarantined in the hospital when I was eight and had cholera. They gave me something for the pain and I drifted in and out of sleep, but it seemed like every time I opened my eyes, he was standing at the window outside my room waving at me. By high school, I would drop in at his office to talk. I knew he expected a lot from me.

"I don't want you to be like other girls, who don't pay attention to their lessons," he said. "I know one day you'll be great."

Life at home could be hard, but when I think back to the years before the war, more than anything else, I remember being happy. If we had two weeks of icy-cold atmosphere because my parents were fighting, the next week we'd all go to the beach together. When the village girls working in the house yanked my hair as they washed and braided it, Mammie Geneva sent them away. "Let me do it," she'd say, and she had the most gentle fingers. If my mother threw me off her lap after five minutes, there was always Ma next door, whom I could talk to about anything and who was always glad to cuddle. My sisters and I created our own world in the bedroom we shared, and outside was the warmth of Old Road.

During vacation time, sometimes there were power outages in the evenings, and all the children would come outside. The nights were warm, the moon up. My cousins would play drums and other girls would shake the *saa-saa* and everyone would try their hand at traditional ethnic dances, while the parents sat on their porches, looking on. It was my home.

CHAPTER 2

"WE'LL SOON PUT AN END
TO THE PROBLEM"

R IGHT AROUND THE TIME of my high school graduation party, a
group of armed rebels crossed the border from Côte d'Ivoire into
Nimba County, in northern Liberia. Their leader, Charles Taylor,
claimed they would overthrow President Doe.

My parents weren't concerned. Nimba County was three hours away,
and the group of rebels was small. Surely, the government would handle
the problem.

"Take it outside," my mother said whenever we had guests and the
conversation turned to politics. I didn't even pay attention; that kind of
talk was for old people.

During the months that followed, my classmates dispersed, some going to a school outside Monrovia, others to Ghana and Sierra Leone.
Josephine enrolled in a private Christian college to study accounting and
business management.

In March 1990, I started classes at the University of Liberia. After
years at B. W. Harris Episcopal High, with its well-stocked science lab
and library, I was not prepared for the chaos of a big, government-run institution, where you had to get to class early just to fight for a chair. The
students who had gone to public schools—where the underpaid teachers

were always going on strike, and sometimes there were no books—laughed at me. I knew at those times that I was a spoiled child.

In May, we moved to Paynesville, in the suburbs just outside Monrovia. Ma stayed behind in her house and we rented ours out. My parents were looking ahead: Josephine now spent most of her time with her boyfriend, also a Lebanese, who lived in a neighborhood that group favored; Mala lived on her own; and the rest of us would surely be leaving home soon as well.

The new place was on almost an acre of land, set off from neighbors and reached by an unpaved lane that was a twenty-minute walk from the main road. The house was small, but I thought it was beautiful, painted a clean, bright white and newer than Old Road, with paneling on the living room ceiling and wall-to-wall carpets. The dining room had a large window that looked onto a field full of flowers.

My mother planted more flowers in the front yard, and corn, peppers and other vegetables in back. Geneva, Josephine and I shared a bedroom that had been painted a soft pink, with a black and white linoleum floor and a light fixture that had the face of a clown. The Old Road house was often hot and stuffy, but here it was always breezy and pleasant. Except for a few hours in the morning and evening, when you could hear the muffled roar of cars on the main road, it was also completely quiet. This was my parents' reward for their years of hard work. They expected to retire and grow old here.

But the government had not put down the rebellion in Nimba County; in fact, it was growing. Each night when we turned on the BBC's World Service *Focus on Africa*, we heard reports about Charles Taylor and his rebel soldiers. They were attacking, capturing territory, moving south, toward us.

A kind of denial kept my parents complacent. They'd lived through instability before. In 1980, Papa had been working under President William Tolbert (as always, a member of the elite) when Samuel Doe, then an army master sergeant, had seized power. Tolbert was disemboweled and shot, and the next day, thirteen members of his administration were publicly executed on the beach. Papa spent nine months in jail. I was very young and my mother kept everything from us—somehow we imagined he was away traveling—and since Papa still won't talk about that time, until today I don't know why. But when he was released, he was offered his old position back, and he took it. He later said he was afraid to say no, but I also knew he valued his prestigious job, especially after having been unemployed so long as a young man.

Doe, a Krahn, was the first nonelite president of our country, and his coup was supposed to mean the beginning of a new era of fairness for the indigenous people of Liberia. *"The native woman has borne a son, and he has killed the Congo People!"* his supporters sang. (By now, "Congo People" referred to anyone who was elite.) Doe got generous financial support from Presidents Reagan and Bush, who wanted to keep Liberia as an ally during those Cold War days and who liked that he opposed the Libyan leader, Muammar Gaddafi. But Doe proved corrupt and violent: he stole an election, pocketed hundreds of millions of dollars, and tracked down and killed his political enemies. Some prominent Liberians fled the country. One was Amos Sawyer, a popular University of Liberia professor with a PhD from Northwestern, whom Doe had appointed to head Liberia's Constitutional Drafting Commission. Ellen Johnson Sirleaf, who had a master's degree in public administration from Harvard and had served as President Tolbert's minister of finance, was another. She ran one of Liberia's largest banks after President Doe took office but later stood up against his corruption. She was arrested twice, threatened with rape and being buried alive, and finally was allowed to leave for the United States.

It was during Doe's rule that tribal identity began to matter. Before Doe, the split was between the elite and the indigenous. All of us had our tribal identities: our dances and traditions, our native languages. But we were equal to each other, and tribal intermarriages took place all the time. Doe changed that, awarding all the jobs that came with money and power to his fellow Krahn. Some ethnic groups, like the Gio and Mano, were excluded from politics completely. Bitterness, then opposition, grew. Some of the exiled Liberians, including Sawyer and Sirleaf, formed the Association for Constitutional Democracy in Liberia (ACDL) to lobby the US government to put pressure on Doe. But the Cold War was ending, and with it, Liberia's strategic importance. The opposition turned to Charles Taylor. As he began his campaign, they raised tens of thousands of dollars to support him.

Still, as we settled into our new home, my parents were not worried. "We'll soon put an end to the problem," my dad said confidently.

Geneva didn't share his confidence. She had a boyfriend in the opposition movement and knew the depth of hatred many people felt for Doe. She'd also heard stories that when government forces went to Nimba County to put down the uprising, they'd gone crazy, indiscriminately raping and killing Gio and Mano, since those tribes supported Taylor.

"This government is wicked!" she burst out one day, arriving home from her medical records job. She sat down on the porch with us, angrily pulling off her shoes. Someone had come into the office that day, she said, looking for the records of four hundred children who supposedly had been evacuated from a village in Nimba County and sent to her hospital. "But we'd never seen them!" Later, she had heard that hundreds of sick and wounded children had been in transit to Monrovia, but government troops had instead dumped them in wells to drown.

"Nobody is that evil!" my mother said, horrified.

"Shut up about things you know nothing about!" my dad shouted at Geneva.

There was no way to prove or disprove the story. So much of what we heard from now on would be like this, information or rumor passed from one person to the next till it came to you.

"We should leave," my sister said. "Now."

"And go where?" said my dad.

"Sierra Leone. Anyplace. The embassy could get us visas. War is coming. We should get out of Monrovia."

I waited for Papa's answer. I knew that some of my high school friends had already left the country. Some had gone to the US, which was easily arranged for Americo-Liberians; because of their ancestry, many had dual citizenship. Ironically, the rebel leader Charles Taylor was one of these. He had an Americo-Liberian father and Gola mother, and though his large family wasn't wealthy, he earned a degree in economics from Bentley University in Massachusetts. He later worked within the Doe government, but after he was accused of embezzling nearly $1 million, he fled to the US. He was arrested on an extradition warrant and jailed in Massachusetts, but escaped with four other inmates by sawing through the bars in a laundry room and dropping down a knotted rope. (Later, he claimed that his cell door had been left unlocked and his escape had been arranged by US agents who got him out of the country.)

If you were indigenous like us, or didn't have a lot of money, fleeing Liberia was a different story. Papa rolled his eyes. What would we do in Sierra Leone? We'd never even been there. He knew Geneva had always dreamed about going abroad to study, and now he protested, "I promised to send you girls to school, not to pay for travel!"

That was enough for me. I trusted my dad, and I didn't have much sympathy for the people of Nimba County. If they allied themselves with the enemy, I thought, then they deserved whatever they got.

In July, my mother's real mother, whom we called Ma Korto, showed up to stay with us, because there was fighting near her village. She brought along her husband and several of my mother's half-sisters and their children. Still, we didn't imagine we were in danger. There were no cell phones then, no Internet; Paynesville didn't even have a regular phone line. News of the outside world was distant and removed. Information arrived sporadically, from TV or radio reports or from someone passing by to deliver a message.

So there was no way we could have known, when we came to a particular midsummer Monday morning, that it would be the last of our old life. Papa, Mama and Geneva left for work as usual. I had late classes that day so I stayed back with Fata, Eric, Mala's kids and the other relatives. I ate a lazy breakfast. And then I heard a strange sound in the distance, like a popping: Pa-*poom*. Pa-*poom*.

"I know that sound," said Ma Korto's husband. He froze. "The rebels are here."

Pa-*poom*. Pa-*poom*. An explosion—*boom!*—then *pop, pop, pop*, like a hard surface being hit. The children were playing outside! I ran to grab Mala's four-year-old son as her three-year-old daughter rose from the sand and raced for the house. She reached the porch just as Ma Korto did, carrying one of the grandchildren she had raised, and whom she favored. In a second, they were all inside the screen door—and then I saw

Ma Korto push Mala's daughter back out. An aunt screamed, "That's wickedness!" and I froze, because the sight was so shocking I almost could not believe it.

Then the moment ended. The noise stopped and no one passed by, so we didn't know who had been shooting. We stayed inside for the rest of the day. At 5 P.M., I closed my eyes, imagining I would soon hear cars on the road. My parents and Geneva would come home, and the radio would announce it was all just a scare.

But the evening passed, then the next morning, and no one returned. Friends of my parents, people who also worked for the government, began appearing at the door with bundles on their heads, holding the hands of children exhausted from walking for hours. The rebels had taken over their communities. Soon, there were more than thirty people in our house, filling the bedrooms, living room, hallway.

Another day passed without word. The grown-ups who had fled sat in the living room exchanging stories. *"We were walking . . . Government soldiers stopped the group and asked everyone for their national identity cards. Anyone from Nimba, they pulled out and shot! Right in front of us!"*

Two more days. Three. Official broadcasting stations announced that the government had the situation under control. On *Focus on Africa*, Charles Taylor bragged that he was taking Monrovia and that his National Patriotic Front of Liberia (NPFL) would "get that boy Doe off the backs of the Liberian people!" The radio announced a 6 P.M. to 6 A.M. curfew. As the eldest family member, I took care of the guests, assigned them to bedrooms, cooked meals for everyone, and made sure my parents' belongings were safe.

I wasn't afraid; I was angry. I was a girl who'd never before had to take any responsibility or make an important decision, and this should not be my job! And it was hard for me to look in Ma Korto's face. I had always believed that adults gathered children to protect them, especially in times of danger. But I'd seen her push Mala's little girl out the door. *Into* harm's way. The scene would not leave my mind. Until today, I have few memories of that week, but during it, I grew up fast, and the world started to change for me.

On the sixth day, Mama and Geneva came home, limping and covered with mud. On their way to work they had stumbled into a gun battle between the rebels and Liberian army. They had been diverted from the main road, they said, then soldiers had appeared, shouting, "Out of the car!"

"We ran into a nearby house and lay on our bellies while bullets were flying," my mother said in a flat voice. "We stayed there day after day . . . Soldiers would come to the house and the owner would give them money or food or whiskey . . ." During a break in the fighting, they had escaped and walked home the long way, through the swamp. Mama looked old and confused, as if she'd been to a place she'd never known existed.

Another week passed. We heard nothing from my dad. The grown-ups stayed close to the TV and some days someone would walk twenty minutes to the main road and just stand there, seeking news from anyone passing.

"Where are you coming from? Have you seen my cousin?"

"I'm so sorry, your cousin was killed a few days ago."

"Have you seen my neighborhood? What about my house?"

"The soldiers have looted everything . . ."

At twilight, we turned off all the lights, so no soldiers—government or rebel—would spot the house. Our distance from the main road might keep us safe, but if anything happened, there was nowhere to run.

One afternoon, Fata, Geneva and I were on the road when we saw a cream-colored van flying the US embassy flag and waved it down. We knew the driver, who rode with two US Marines. "I've been looking for you!" he exclaimed. "I've come to collect you on the orders of your father."

There was no time to think about what to pack. Mama, my sisters and me, Eric, Mala's kids and a cousin pulled open drawers, grabbed a few things, and threw them into bags. Then I stood in my bedroom, looking at its beauty, at all the new clothes I had gotten for graduation, my wonderful Dexter boots. My mother ran to her bedroom to pull out important documents and some cash she'd stashed away. She gave handfuls to the people staying behind. "Take care of the house," she said. We left them our pantry full of food, taking only one bag of rice. I was so happy to be getting out and so sure we'd soon be back that I didn't even turn around for a last look at the house as we drove away. If I had known what was coming, I would have taken those boots.

When we got to the city, Geneva said she wanted to stay with Josephine. The marines took the rest of us to the Sinkor neighborhood, where our church, St. Peter's, had a guest compound on a residential street not far from Payne Avenue. It was just a simple and spare two-story building, with offices downstairs and a chapel and dormitory-style bedrooms above, but the large bare yard was behind a high, gated wall. It wasn't too far from the church itself, and the congregation had come here for picnics.

There also were several small cement houses in the compound; the bishop lived in one, the church treasurer in another. The treasurer's family had fled to Guinea and he said we could stay with him.

That night, I couldn't sleep. In the distance, I heard shooting. Church had always been a place of comfort for me. I loved St. Peter's high, wood-covered ceiling, the arched windows of pale blue and red colored glass. Since I was ten, I'd served as an acolyte, marching to the altar in my gown each Sunday to light the candles. I would turn to the congregation and see my mother, who was an usher, standing in the aisle, and pews full of my neighbors and cousins sitting under the slowly turning ceiling fans. Children squirmed on the hard, narrow seats next to men in suits and women in bright African dress and their best jewelry. From the rear balcony, Geneva's voice would ring out with the rest of the choir: *On the solid rock of Christ I stand / All other ground is sinking sand!*

All I wanted was to go home.

God is ever faithful, ever loving; he listens to our prayers. "Please, God," I prayed. "Make this stop."

TWO MORE WEEKS PASSED, and the compound dormitory beds filled with other members of the congregation who'd fled their homes—most of them, like us, people with connections to the Doe government.

Charles Taylor continued advancing toward Monrovia. When he came on the radio at night, he called himself "the president of this nation," and from the United States, his supporter Ellen Sirleaf told a BBC reporter that if Taylor destroyed the Executive Mansion trying to oust Doe, "We will rebuild it."

"What if Taylor wins this war?" the reporter asked. "What then?"

"Well, we are nearing July twenty-sixth [Liberian independence day]," she said. "On July twenty-sixth, we'll drink champagne."

One of Taylor's commanders, Prince Yormie Johnson, had defected and was also moving toward the capital with a rebel group. (In Liberia, "Prince" is a common first name.) The streets grew full of government soldiers manning checkpoints. Ethnic tensions rose even higher. Doe's soldiers went after the Gio and Mano, Prince Johnson targeted the Krahn, and Taylor's men singled out both the Krahn and the Mandingo, a Muslim tribe also known to support Doe.

Papa managed to see us once, but he had to remain at the US embassy. He thought it best that we stay in the church compound, since the intelligence he had was that Taylor's troops had infiltrated Paynesville. But the city began shutting down. Schools closed, electricity went out. Food was harder and harder to find; rice, our staple, was so scarce people were calling it "gold dust." Friends passing through often came by hoping I could spare a bit. My fear grew. I tried to avoid going outside— "Ummm, mama," the checkpoint soldiers would hiss whenever a young girl passed, "you gonna be my wife"—but we had to venture out if we wanted to eat.

We bought food from anyone who had something to sell. Often, it was soldiers. At night, you'd hear gun battles that were just cover for looting. The next morning you'd pass by a market to find the soldiers had taken what they wanted, and some of the lower-ranking ones would be standing out front hawking wilted greens or sausages whose packaging dates had expired.

One morning, my cousin and I left the compound on our usual quest. Two teenage boys passed us on the road, wearing jeans and red T-shirts. One rumor being passed around was that red T-shirts were a rebel "uniform." Suddenly, a pickup truck roared up behind them and came to a screeching halt. Soldiers jumped out and fired at one of them. He fell dead in the street and the other began to run frantically with the soldiers in pursuit.

I couldn't even scream. I had never seen someone killed before. The dead boy's bloody body lay where it fell, and I was frozen. That night I lay awake wondering if the other boy had made it to safety.

At seventeen, you're not used to thinking about death, especially your own. But now it was all around and I was forced to realize that it could come at any time. I heard from friends passing by that one of my professors had been killed, along with his entire family. That daughters of family friends had been raped. That another boy I knew had been passing through a checkpoint when one of the soldiers decided he wanted his brand new sneakers and killed him on the spot.

And I heard about Koffa, my high school friend, the joker with the perfect handkerchief, who dreamed of becoming a US Marine. His father had enemies who were also in the military, and under the guise of war, they came for him one day. He hid, so they killed the rest of the family and laid their bodies in the street. Koffa's body. He had been such a clown. When we were in school, there was a silly TV jingle about a fruit drink—*"Disco drink comes from an orange!"*—and every time our teacher, Mrs. Jones, came to class, Koffa would rap on the desk and sing out, *"Disco drink comes from . . . Mrs. Jones!"*

"Outside!" she would shout while all the kids giggled. "Koffa, outside!" But nothing stopped Koffa. One night, on Old Road, he'd nearly driven one of my favorite uncles crazy by making fun of the way he pronounced "malaria." I thought of my friend's laughter. And I had darker thoughts. Which parts of his body had the bullets penetrated? Had his blood stained the white handkerchief? If I were shot to death, how would it feel?

Some of the boys staying in the dormitory and I had debates about the future. "I'm looking forward to going back to school," one told me. "Put this nightmare behind me."

I shook my head bitterly. "What's the point of education when one bullet can undo it?"

The violence increased. At six in the evening, we gathered for prayers in the big room of the treasurer's house, away from the windows and doors. *Please God, end the war. Please, God, let us go home soon.* After, my mother would tell funny stories to try to make us laugh. Then, outside the walls, the shooting would start. Every morning, there would be another store stripped bare and men in government uniforms at the side of the road selling whatever they had stolen. Just two blocks away was the beach, where soldiers held executions, so sometimes I could hear crying and screams. "I beg you, please don't, please don't! . . ." We knew that soldiers left the bodies of those they killed, because eventually the smell would reach us.

I was afraid, especially at night, but I also got more and more angry. *They say God responds to our prayers but we have been praying for deliverance and nothing happens. The war is not ending. We are not going home. He is not listening to us.* I was starting to understand that I was trapped—and that things were not going to get better.

CHAPTER 3

I AM TOO YOUNG TO DIE!

M Y COUSIN AND I HAD GONE OUTSIDE the compound to look for food. My mom was sitting in the empty space behind the treasurer's house and got up to stretch. Beyond the fence, she saw a ragged man rummaging through mounds of garbage on the street.

She put her face to the wire. "What are you looking for?"

"Palm kernels," he said.

"*Palm kernels?*"

"Yes, ma. There is no food and this is what we live by."

In the Liberia my mother knew, this made no sense. "Wait a minute," she said. She went inside, poured a few cups of rice into a plastic bag, then pushed it to him through the fence. As he walked away, a pickup truck full of soldiers roared up beside him and stopped.

"What do you have?"

"Rice . . ."

"Who gave it to you?"

"I . . ."

The soldiers passed rumors that whenever rebels entered a community they distributed rice to the people to win their support. Anyone who had the precious "gold dust" was suspect. My mother tried but couldn't speak. The soldiers grabbed the man's bundle of rice, then calmly shot him dead, threw his body into their truck, and drove out toward the beach. When I returned to the compound, Mama was still wailing.

"I've killed someone!" she said again and again. The soldiers were from the government she supported. The government my father worked for. After that day, it was hard to persuade her to do anything, even to eat. "Give it to the children," she said.

Fear was the first feeling when I opened my eyes every morning. Then gratitude: I'm still living. Then fear again. While you're thankful for being alive, you worry about being alive. People said the rebels were merciless. But all around me, the government forces were killing, too. Our connection to the government was less important than our ethnicity—we weren't Krahns. We were sitting ducks, caught in the middle.

We pray and pray and nothing changes. No one can save us because no one is in control. Pieces of me were being stripped away, replaced by anger. I stopped talking to God.

And then one day, Doe's soldiers heard there was food at the compound, and goods to loot. They came for us. It was a Sunday morning. My mother was in the upstairs chapel at a church service, and the kids were having Sunday school. I was cooking when the treasurer pulled me aside and took me to look out his bedroom window. Soldiers were pushing their way through the front gate.

I came outside to look. They had already put one man staying in the compound, the local director of police, into their pickup truck. Now they surrounded the main building.

"Everyone downstairs!" the commander, a man with ceremonial markings of the Krahn tribe drawn in chalk on his face, shouted through the front door. "Everyone outside!"

The children came down the staircase, frightened but chanting, the way they'd been taught to do when the war scared them: "Jesus! Jesus! Satan, we rebuke you!"

The words made me angry. *God won't help you*, I thought.

"Face the wall!" We lined up near the door. The wall was rough, bumpy.

One of the women could not stop crying. "Jesus!" she sobbed. "Satan, we rebuke you!"

"Shut up!" ordered another soldier. He also had chalk lines on his face and a thin cord tied around his forehead with a piece of coral in the center.

"Leave her alone!" The cry came from the woman's sister, Murtha, whom I knew as the girlfriend of a former teacher. The soldier slapped her across the face. Without thinking, Murtha slapped him back. He raised his gun as the man standing next to my mother switched the baby he was holding to his other arm, and fired. Pa-*poom*. The bullet passed through Murtha and hit the man's raised hand, which had just moved to block my mother's face.

"I'm shot!" he said, and Murtha dropped. She had two children.

Two soldiers carried off Murtha's body, and others pulled out the wounded man and the wife of the director of police. *We are dead,* I thought. I looked at the faces around me and realized that the church treasurer wasn't there. He had stayed hidden in his house and no one knew. Regret swept me. *I should have hidden, too! I am too young to die!*

"The couple has three children. Where are they?"

The police director's children were right there, but we knew that no one the soldiers took would ever be seen again. I heard my mother's quiet voice: "They are not here."

A moment, then he nodded and the other soldiers began to herd us back inside and into a small front office. "Go! Go!"

"I have money tied around my waist," whispered my mother when she got close to me. "If I am killed, ask for the body."

"You!" the soldiers shouted, as they began to beat the older women with their belts and their rifles. "We know you've been saying 'The monkey should go.' You support Taylor! You support Sirleaf! We know!"

I wasn't afraid now, only numb. Stop. Go. Sit down. I was acutely conscious that soldiers raped young girls and I was wearing only a T-shirt and shorts. I pulled my nephew into my lap to cover my bare legs. *We will never leave here. We are dead.* Everything came to me from a distance. I was outside my body, floating, watching the soldiers hit my mother, waiting to die.

And then, the husband of one of my aunts, a physician's assistant, appeared at the office door wearing a white coat.

"What do you want?" the commander challenged him.

"My sister-in-law and her children are here." He gestured at us.

"What tribe are you?"

"Mende." He spoke a few words in Mende.

The commander smiled. "Take your people." To us he said, "Don't come back. Those who are coming next are even more wicked. They will do terrible things."

My mother hesitated at first, arguing for the rest of the women. I pulled my niece onto my back, grabbed my nephew's hand, and ran out. My mother was old—if she wanted to stay and die, I would not join her. We took nothing with us and made our way across Tubman Boulevard to Josephine's boyfriend's small first-floor apartment.

It was 3 P.M. by then, not long until curfew. Geneva, my mom, cousin, all the kids and I moved into one room, putting pads on the floor and pushing mattresses against the windows to shield us from bullets. When it grew dark, we went to bed. The city was completely, utterly still and quiet—no sound of cars, generators, voices from the street. Then, in the night, we suddenly jerked awake to terrible screams.

"Help! God! Please help us!" Shrieking. Wails. I could hardly breathe. I heard Mama moving around, her low voice reciting the 91st Psalm. *"He who dwells in the secret place of the most high shall abide under the shadow of the Almighty—"*

"Dear Jesus!"

"—I will say of the Lord, He is my refuge and my fortress; my God; in Him will I trust—"

"No, no, no! Help us!"

It went on and on and on. We were all awake. At dawn, when curfew lifted, we ventured out. The street was full of people, passing fragments of information. *Massacre . . . butchered . . . the church . . .*

Soon we saw. When President Doe's army had begun going after members of the Gio and Mano tribes, the Liberian Council of Churches made a conscious decision to offer asylum to people in danger. They believed that although the soldiers were brutal, they would fear to commit violence in a house of God. Close to a thousand men, women and children had ultimately taken refuge in St. Peter's chapel and the adjoining high school. But on that night, the ones "coming next who are even more evil than us," a different government battalion that carried machetes and machine guns, had pushed their way inside. Among the pews where we sang and prayed, where on Women's Day husbands and children pinned flowers on their mothers' clothes, they raped, slashed, shot and hacked.

The Gio and Mano inside had pushed open the doors and run out into gunfire, and there were bodies on every street corner. Men, women, *babies*. I saw dead and bloody pregnant women. A dead man lying with his dead child in his arms, the baby bottle still in his hand. My sisters went inside the church to see, as if without that final proof they couldn't believe. I couldn't bear it. Not far from Josephine's apartment, Geneva and my mother encountered Mala and Ma, who collapsed, weeping, at the sight of them. Ma had heard we were among the dead at St. Peter's and was on her way to identify our bodies.

THERE WAS NO WAY NOW for anyone to deny what was happening. Charles Taylor had spent time in Burkina Faso and Libya, where he'd received military training, and his NPFL fighters were getting arms from allies in Burkina Faso and Côte d'Ivoire. They handed them out to anyone threatened by government forces. In the countryside, Taylor's troops also recruited male children, many of them orphaned by battles, and organized them into special forces called Small Boy Units. The children called Taylor their "Papay."

Taylor's troops massacred hundreds of Krahn and Mandingo in Lofa County, in the north, and the coastal city of Buchanan, south of Monrovia. These forces and Prince Johnson's men were soon within a few miles of the capital. As they advanced, they cut water, electricity and phone lines and blocked the escape route to Sierra Leone.

Just as it happened elsewhere in the world—in Bosnia, Rwanda, Kosovo—some balance had shifted, and decades of repressed rage poured out. From now on, nothing would be the same.

Foreigners began to flee. Four US warships full of marines anchored off the coast and evacuated American citizens but made no move to intervene. Not long after the massacre at the church, Iraq invaded Kuwait, and the US government turned its attention elsewhere.

We didn't know what to do or where else to go—the Old Road neighborhood was too near Payne Spriggs airfield to be safe—so we stayed at

Josephine's apartment. When battles raged and mortars fell near the house, we ran to a neighbor, who had a basement, and huddled on the dirt floor listening to the booms and screams coming from above. It was rainy season and the rain fell endlessly. It was possible to find drinking water if you took care—there were stories of bodies in the wells—but the port was being controlled by Prince Johnson's forces, and they blocked food from reaching our part of the city. Sometimes my mother would ask one of us to go out in search of food. It was very dangerous and my other sisters said no, but I was still the pleaser. I carried money wrapped in a cloth between my legs, like a sanitary pad, and went to find what little I could. We might try to feed twelve people on two cups of rice.

I was so shut down I didn't even want to eat. But it was hard to watch the children grow so thin and weak that all they wanted to do was sleep. I carried them on my back when I could, to soothe them. My nephew, who was six, a big boy used to eating a lot, would cry and shake from hunger.

My mother seemed broken inside. She still wore the green and black suit she'd had on the day the soldiers came to the church compound. Each night, she washed it and hung it dry; she said she would wear these clothes until the war ended.

The dead from St. Peter's lay unburied, and the stench began making the children sick. Eventually, all of us but Josephine, who was pregnant, decided to leave Sinkor and risk crossing the Gabriel Tucker Bridge to Bushrod Island, Prince Johnson's territory, in hopes we'd find food. It took us all day. We walked through main town. Stopped and scattered to hide behind buildings because there was shooting. Stopped so Geneva could rest her swollen leg. Came to a checkpoint, were herded into lines and told to identify ourselves to the soldier at the table.

"What tribe are you?"

"Kpelle."

"Say something in Kpelle."

"Bá ngung, ku me ni ná?" said my mother in an even voice. ("Hello, what news is there?")

"Go ahead."

The checkpoint soldiers always looked carefully at men's bare feet for signs they'd been wearing boots, which meant they were fighters. Behind us, someone was pulled off the line. We heard "No! Please!" then *pop-pop-pop*. We kept walking. On Mechlin Street, near the Waterside Market area, where Mama would take me to buy school shoes, I saw the body of a woman lying in the road. She wore a dress and stockings as if she'd just come from church. A dog was pulling at one of her legs. Eating her.

We were in another world now; we had crossed a line. I saw dogs eating the dead at other times during the war, especially when there was a lot of fighting in the center of the city and bullet casings and bodies filled the narrow streets. I can tell you this: you never get used to it.

We found shelter in the Logan Town slum, where Mama knew of a relative who had a tiny room. Again, we waited. One day, I was standing outside when a convoy of Prince Johnson's soldiers passed. Suddenly, a huge fighter broke away and grabbed me in his arms. I panicked, but then I saw his face: Ayo, my friend from school.

"Don't worry, Red," he told me. "I'll look after you."

I soon learned that he had a reputation for being merciless. Koffa was dead. Ayo was a killer. Nothing made sense.

After about a week, Josephine arrived to tell us she'd made contact with our dad, who was still at the US embassy compound. Without any way to reach us or get news, he'd been convinced we were dead. "He said I should bring you to him," Josephine said.

We made our way slowly to the embassy and Papa. They had food, and we ate all we could. But what I remember most clearly was seeing a big, pale, soft sofa next to a living room door. "Henceforth, this will be my bed," I announced, dropping onto it. I would lie on that couch for hours and let the numbness that began at the church compound grow until it filled me and pushed out everything else. My eyes stayed closed, my mind shut down and I floated away into another world . . . Empty. Blank. Peaceful.

We stayed at the embassy for three weeks. My dad said he couldn't leave his job but the first week in September, he got Mama, Geneva, Josephine, Fata, all the kids, and me places on the *Tano River*, a Ghanaian cargo ship that had come to evacuate West African foreign nationals. At Monrovia's Freeport, the piers and docks lay behind a ten-foot-high wall with only three entry gates, and the day we left, there was so much fighting and pushing to get to the boat that a soldier had to help us get through.

The *Tano River* held thousands of people. We took our place among them in a huge space below the deck. Some people were sitting, some lying down; families clustered in small groups. No one in my family had been on the sea before, and when we moved into open water, I got so seasick I wanted to die. Some wives of fishermen who sat near us advised my mother to feed me dry food, but nothing helped. We were short on supplies, and after the first day, Mama had to cook our rice with seawater. In exchange for a bit of food, boys on the boat would help you lower a pot into the water by rope. The children ate because they were hungry; I turned away. I remember lying there, Mama's voice in my ear, "You *have* to eat." I couldn't hold anything down. After three miserable days we reached land.

We'd thought we were going to Sierra Leone, but we found ourselves in Ghana. We had no way to reach Papa, and so for months he had no idea how or even where we were. He had everything in his embassy apartment—electricity, water, plenty of food—but his family had gotten onto a ship, sailed into the distance, and vanished. Outside, the city descended into a whirlpool of violence. He did his job, he later told us, and then simply sat in his rooms, staring out the window at the sea.

OUR NEW HOME was the Buduburam refugee camp. It was 144 acres, bleak and isolated, a former prayer camp about thirty miles from Accra. There were only a few hundred of us at first, though eventually the camp held fifty thousand Liberians. My family moved into a partially built cement house with no furniture, window glass or running water. The first day, even Mama cried.

I was happy to be away from all the shooting and death, but Buduburam was grim—smelly, full of mosquitoes, with almost no shade to block the blazing heat. Water came from hand pumps, and church aid groups handed out rations of maize meal, oil, milk and sugar.

Mama quickly pulled herself together. "This is where we find ourselves," she told us. "We will have to make the most of it." She hired boys to build us a palm-thatch hut to shield us from the midafternoon sun, and dig a hole for our toilet, and then she cut the tall grass growing around our "house," to stuff into vegetable sacks so we could have mattresses. She searched out some seeds and put in a garden, planting greens that we couldn't find or afford locally.

Weeks passed, then months. I got up early every day to fry doughnuts that we'd sell to make some more money. Geneva went to work managing medical records at the camp's small clinic. A school opened, and Fata began going to class. Josephine, now four months pregnant, was sick and miserable and missed her husband, who as a foreign national had been airlifted out of Monrovia.

In the mornings, she'd say to me, "Leymah, I need a bath, so please carry my bucket."

I would answer, "You're pregnant, not handicapped."

Her response was always, "In my condition, I shouldn't lift something heavy!" and it always worked on me. I'd carry the water, take Josephine to see the doctor at the camp clinic. We talked about the coming baby; although I already had a niece and nephew, Josephine's child would be like mine. Time moved on, but nothing felt real to me.

Each afternoon, the adults gathered under our palm thatch to listen to radio reports of home. The news was always bad. Soon after we arrived, Prince Johnson and his men captured President Doe. For more than six hours, they tortured him to death—and everyone learned exactly what happened, because they filmed the execution and sold videos on the streets of Monrovia.

At first, there was jubilation in the camp. We all knew the evil things Doe and his men had done, and maybe with him gone, the situation would improve. Peacekeeping troops from the Economic Community of West African States (ECOWAS) arrived in Monrovia and installed a new government under the former professor Amos Sawyer, who'd returned from exile.

But the fighting went on, and Charles Taylor was gaining more and more territory. Although his brutality had cost him some of his support from the Liberian exile community—the ACDL, the group run by exiled Liberians, for instance, had cut him off—his control of everything outside the capital meant he held the keys to Liberia's timber industry, diamond and iron-ore mines, and the big Firestone rubber plantation in Margibi County. Foreign companies were willing to pay what he demanded for licenses to operate; Taylor used the money to buy more weapons. Prince Johnson's men were still waging war against him, and Monrovia was being torn apart by young fighters scavenging and looting.

When we finally established contact with home, we heard that there was almost no food and what little existed was beyond reach—one cassava might sell for five hundred Liberian dollars. Ma's flesh now hung from her frame like cloth, and my favorite uncle, the one Koffa had teased so terribly, had been stripped naked and beaten by a crowd on the road in Logan Town because someone accused him of stealing a fritter.

"I'm hungry but I'm not a thief!" he had cried. A few weeks later, he set out looking for food again, walked for hours without success, and not far from home simply dropped on the road and died. The family had no way to bury him properly, so they threw his body beside the train tracks.

"I'm going home!" he'd shouted at Koffa the night my friend mocked his pronunciation of "malaria," and we'd all roared and held our sides. Now they were both gone and I wondered if they were together. Had they greeted each other? Was there a special place where the dead could meet?

The boats from Liberia kept coming. One thousand refugees on this one. Five hundred on the next. At Buduburam, rows of tents stretched across the sun-baked ground. One thousand more. Peace negotiations were finally beginning at home, but that meant fighters from both sides who feared reprisals for what they'd done were fleeing to Ghana, too, and the camp became different, a place of bars and prostitution and sections where I did not dare to walk. I sold my doughnuts; I joined the other kids in games of kickball. And I kept company with a gentle young man who dreamed of being an architect. He said he loved me and talked about a future we might share.

But I saw no future at all; for me, time had stopped. When I closed my eyes, I was back on Old Road, seven years old and playing with Mala in the body of an abandoned car beneath a plum tree. She was the driver and I took the tickets. Neighborhood children of every tribe—all of us friends, then, all of us together—would climb on for pretend rides to our ethnic homelands. "Bong County!" I'd call—that stop was for the Kpelle. "Lofa!" The Loma and Mandingo would jump off. "Cape Mount!" Now the Vai were home. "Bomi!" That was the Gola.

And over and over, ever more clearly, I saw myself leaving this barren, ugly place and going home. I would get off the boat, climb into a car, and drive straight to Paynesville to get the house ready for my mother and sisters. I could feel the way the cool, breezy air would touch my face, see the beauty of the trees and flowers. I'd walk up the path to the house; I'd see my dad and call a joyful hello. I'd open the front door, shaking my head at the mess we'd left behind. And then I'd go in, and put it all away—the clothes, the shoes, the cups and plates, hanging and arranging, until everything was just the way it had been before.

In May 1991, the ECOWAS peacekeeping force (known as ECO-MOG) moved into Monrovia, a new interim government formed, and the fighting came to a stop. I begged Mama to let me go home, and she agreed. I traveled on a Ghanaian navy vessel, courtesy of her negotiations and some "emergency" money we'd had no idea she possessed.

Almost as soon as I arrived, I knew I had made a mistake. Of course I'd heard that what was happening at home was terrible, but no amount of description could have prepared me. The port smelled of death and destruction, and my first glimpses of Monrovia almost took my breath away. Whole blocks of the city had burned down. Buildings stood with their roofs blown off and walls half crumbled and pocked with huge blast holes. Families were living in the wreckage. The John F. Kennedy Medical Center had been vandalized and closed. The University of Liberia had been commandeered by Taylor and used as a base for assaults on President Doe's Executive Mansion, which stood across Tubman Boulevard. Now, my university was destroyed.

There was no electricity, running water or working toilets. People used plastic bags, the beach. The air stank.

My dad was still in his apartment at the embassy.

"Your mother told me you wanted to come back, but honestly, I can't have you here," he told me. I didn't ask why. Josephine's Lebanese husband had returned and was renting a tiny apartment in a Central

Monrovia neighborhood that had suffered less destruction than others, and he said I could stay in one of the bedrooms. When two of my old friends also returned to the city, I invited them to share the room and we all crowded in together.

Around us, others began trickling in, coming back as they'd left, with bundles on their heads, emptying out rubble, trying to resume life. Lebanese merchants began to reopen a few stores that carried forgotten luxuries like shoes, clothes, perfume and cosmetics.

I enrolled in a typing school with some thought of going on to learn about computers so I could get a job, but I never did. There was nothing I really wanted to do, and my friends and I just drifted. We had almost no money; often, we'd wake unable to buy breakfast. Whenever we could, we'd pay a local boy to bring us a five-gallon container of water—we didn't ask where he got it—and share it to take a bath. I always felt dirty. At night, everyone would come out, looking for company and alcohol, but except in those few areas with generators, the streets were pitch black. We would drink until eight or nine, then everything shut down. My life was as temporary as it had been in the camp at Buduburam.

Three weeks after I arrived, I took a bus back to Paynesville with a man my father sent along to keep me safe. We got off at the main road and walked down the smaller lane toward the house. The nearby communities, once bubbly and filled with activity, were deserted. It was too quiet—not peaceful, just still.

We walked. Nothing . . . nothing. Houses stood with their gates open wide, their windows broken or torn off. My parents' beautiful white house came into view. At first, it didn't look too bad. An aunt was staying in the outside quarters in the back, where the village girls had lived. She'd kept the yard neatly swept and had been trying to revive Mama's garden.

But inside the main house, wreckage. Ruin. The carpet was stripped from the floors. The glass on the dining room table was gone. The china cupboards were empty. My parents' bedroom was empty. The pink bedroom was empty, the bed smashed, the louvered windows broken, the closet stripped bare. There was a gaping hole in the ceiling where the looters had broken in. There was a smell, male and sweaty.

I spent the night with my aunt, and in the morning, as I was walking back to the main road, I saw one of my neighbors. Everyone around Paynesville had fled, leaving their homes to the fighters, and anyone who returned to find their possessions gone went through the homes of others taking whatever was left to grab. My neighbor was dressed up, clearly heading to the city. On her feet were my Dexter boots.

I'd been dreaming of a place that no longer existed. My home was gone. The people I'd loved were gone—refugees or internally displaced or dead. My life was smashed to nothing, stolen from me, and all I could feel was rage. At my parents, for being too foolish to get us out of the country in time. At Doe's government soldiers and the rebels, all of them murderers. At the people around me, for taking whatever we might have salvaged. And at God, who let all of this happen. The girl who had laughed and danced at the graduation party not even two years before was completely gone.

When you move so quickly from innocence to a world of fear, pain and loss, it's as if the flesh of your heart and mind gets cut away, piece by piece, like slices taken off a ham. Finally, there is nothing left but bone.

CHAPTER 4

TRAPPED

HELLO, YOUNG LADY! I know you from the camp in Ghana."
It was July 1991. I had been back in Monrovia for two months. I stopped on the sidewalk outside the apartment where I was staying and studied the man who'd greeted me. He was about ten years older than I was, dark skinned and slender, with a long, narrow face. I remembered him: Daniel, a Ghanaian who had lived next to us at Buduburam with his Liberian wife and son. The boy was two and very cute. I'd played with him from time to time.

"You're the little boy's father."

He grinned and nodded. "Where do you stay?" His eyes never left my face.

I remembered that Daniel had always stared at me when he saw me around the camp. "That man really likes you," my boyfriend had said. I also remembered the stories I'd heard about him. Daniel had come to Buduburam with his wife and child, and she'd fallen sick there, with tuberculosis and pneumonia. A woman had come into their lives, supposedly to help. She bought Daniel's wife antibiotics and took care of her. Then she and Daniel began a relationship. After a while, we still saw the sick girl, but Daniel was gone. We heard that he'd abandoned his wife for this "helper," and we never saw him again.

"I live . . . around . . ." I said warily. I knew enough about this man to know he was trouble.

That day, he just laughed and moved on. Then one evening, I saw him on my street again. "Do you live here?" he asked, pointing to my building. I nodded and soon after, returned home to find my roommates eating from a huge bag of sandwiches, more food than we'd seen in a long time.

"Some guy came and brought this for you," they told me.

Daniel. He asked me to have lunch at one of the few nice restaurants that was open in the city. As we talked, he watched my face closely; it was like there was no one else in the room. Going out was fun, I told my roommates afterward, but I would never have a relationship with this man. I should have known better; we have a saying in Liberia: "'Never' belongs to God."

I got a really bad bout of malaria—constant pain in my fingers and joints, unbearable headache, high fever. I couldn't stop throwing up. I needed medicine, but there were only a few doctors left in all Monrovia. My friends took me to a local clinic. I had no idea how I'd pay for treatment, so after I'd been there a few days, I decided to send them to ask my father for help. But I was told there was no bill—a man had paid it for me. Daniel again.

And so we began. It's been nearly twenty years since I met Daniel, and it's still hard for me to think and talk about him. I know this: The children we had together are the center of my world. I wouldn't be who I am today if I hadn't been their mother, and if I had my life to do over again, I wouldn't change a thing if it meant not giving birth to them. I also know that being with Daniel nearly destroyed me. I never was in love with him, so when I look back now and try to understand the choices I made, I'm lost. I honestly don't know what I was thinking.

Financial security was part of it. At a time when almost everyone we knew was out of work and struggling from day to day, Daniel made eight hundred US dollars a month—the equivalent of tens of thousands of Liberian dollars—working as a logistics officer at the American embassy complex, and he spent it freely on me: gifts of jewelry and perfume from the Lebanese merchants, meals at Angel's, his favorite restaurant.

Intense and passionate sex was also a part of it. And then there was the war. Without it, I would have been in school and living at home, sheltered by my parents, not shifting for myself in a city where nothing functioned, surrounded by young people who were as lost and confused as me. And rebellion had its part, too: I was tired of being the good girl who took care of her parents' house when relatives crowded in, who went out into dangerous streets to look for food so everyone could eat, and carried hungry kids on her back. I'd seen so much destruction and death, felt so much rage and misery . . . I was only nineteen, and I wanted to have a little fun.

For nearly a year, I continued my involvement with Daniel, without planning, worrying or thinking, not even about something as basic as biology. I wasn't a virgin, and of course I knew very well where babies came from, but I had pushed my luck before without consequences. One of my aunts was unable to conceive, and I let myself believe I was like her. By the time I realized that I was fooling myself in a lot of ways, it was too late.

Daniel wanted to do everything together, but one afternoon I told him I was going to sit with a friend who had lost her brother. When I got home, he said he'd seen me in a car with a white man. And he hit me. I was frightened, then outraged, then confused when he made love to me, apologizing over and over for what he'd done. "It's just that I love you so much . . . " Then I found out that a few times when I'd gone out with other friends, Daniel had followed us. *I should end this*, I thought. Two weeks later, I discovered I was pregnant.

WITH THE PROMISE OF PEACE (and the presence of ECOMOG troops to enforce it), my family had returned from Ghana seven months earlier, in late 1991. My parents, with Fata and Geneva, had returned to Paynesville to try to repair and refurnish their looted house. Now, they were furious when they learned my news. Part of me expected—wanted—them to insist that I come home immediately. When Josephine had first taken up with her husband, they'd threatened to cut her off for being with a Muslim. But the war had upended everything, including the power parents felt they had over their children. Mala had divorced her first husband and was involved with a Swedish engineer who'd come to Liberia as part of a relief effort. We knew a wealthy man who cried helplessly when friends asked him how he tolerated his daughter's relationship with a non-Liberian. "Do you think I don't hear when he comes at night? But what can I do? I rely on her to bring us food."

Josephine, who was living with her husband again and had given birth to a son, was more positive. "Have the baby," she told me. "For all you know, this will be the only one you'll ever have."

I didn't see another option. Even if I'd wanted to end the pregnancy, having an abortion in Liberia in those days was so unsafe I'd be risking death. In July of 1992, Mala married her Swedish engineer and the two left for Sweden (although for the time being, her kids were staying with my parents). She offered me their apartment on Front Street, in the heart of the city with a view of the ocean, and Daniel and I moved in together.

As I would later learn about domestic violence, pregnancy never solves anything, and more often, it makes things worse. Now that I was "his," Daniel's need for control tightened. He didn't like my friends visiting. "Which boyfriend are they bringing a message from?" If we needed food, he had me wait for him to come home from work so we could shop together. A moment of rebellion, and now I was caught. It's hard to explain. You start with fantastic sex; you give another person that power over your body, then gradually, you give him other powers, too. I'd always vowed never to be like some of the women I'd seen when I was growing up, who had babies with multiple fathers. The father of my children would be my husband, and I would stay with him.

Sometimes, I told Josephine how miserable I was. I never told anyone that Daniel was hitting me.

For months, it was possible to go about your business in Monrovia and believe that the war was over. But outside the city, the rebellion was fragmenting, widening and gaining strength. An exiled journalist, Alhaji Kromah, called on Muslims to launch a jihad against Charles Taylor's NPFL; and Albert Karpeh, a Krahn and US-trained special forces officer, joined with him to form a new rebel group, United Liberation Movement of Liberia for Democracy (ULIMO), which began pushing into the diamond fields of Liberia and Sierra Leone. Taylor made, then broke, an alliance with Prince Johnson. The interim government, meanwhile, was backed by the national army, the Armed Forces of Liberia (AFL).

There were differences between the groups. The NPFL attracted young men who wanted to avenge the deaths of family members or get rich; Prince Johnson's men were older, often ex-soldiers. And during the first part of the war, at least, when the AFL wore uniforms, it was possible to tell them apart from the rebels. (Later, all the fighters wore the same basic uniform of jeans, T-shirts and bandannas—either looted or stolen.)

But Taylor was the name you heard most often, and in such contradictory ways. Taylor was the rebel who sounded reassuring and rational on international news shows, while he was at the same time encouraging his men to dress in bizarre costumes meant to inspire fear: wigs, wedding gowns, decorations made of human bone. Taylor's forces were terrifyingly wild and unpredictable, and their commanders kept them high on cane-spirit alcohol, marijuana and speed.

By the fall of 1992, there were rumors all around Monrovia—*I hear Taylor's planning something*. Most of us shrugged them off. If you believed every story you heard, you couldn't live, and we often heard similar warnings. But this time, they were true. After controlling the countryside so long, Taylor was determined to take the capital. NPFL fighters headed toward the city, killing, raping and looting as they came, then moved through the swamps and surrounded us: the tentacles of his "Operation Octopus" were meant to strangle and conquer the city.

A high-pitched whistle, then SLAM! Right next to our apartment, a building was shattered and pouring smoke. Someone was screaming, "My baby! My baby's in there!"

As Taylor's forces began their offensive, ECOMOG hit back with shells, missiles, heavy artillery. Suddenly, out of nowhere, fighting was everywhere. The battles moved around—different places, different times—but our apartment overlooked the Ducor Palace Hotel, once one of Africa's fanciest and now home to the interim government, so we were often in the line of fire.

You'd hear the whistle signaling that a missile was coming and run outside, not knowing where to go, then SLAM!—the earth was shaking, buildings were punctured, people were running by with bloody wounds. Sometimes we'd go home, our hearts pounding, once the bombardment stopped; sometimes I'd escape to Josephine's, whose neighborhood was quieter.

But the rebels were firing mortars at the airfield near Old Road, so Ma and the family members who hadn't gone to Ghana were at Josephine's, too. Then there was fighting in Paynesville, which brought Mama, Papa and Fata into the city. There were too many of us with too little room, and when we opened windows against the heat, rats crawled in. They were fearless, used to feeding on human flesh.

The battles started and stopped and moved around and started again. It was chaos. City people seeking safety tried to flee; rural people seeking safety from other outbreaks of violence flooded in. Tubman Boulevard was barricaded with concrete blocks and car-bomb barriers, and there were soldiers everywhere—some of them little boys in baseball caps, even Donald Duck masks. Anyone who broke the 6 P.M. to 8 A.M. curfew could be shot on sight.

In the end, ECOMOG held off Taylor's troops without really defeating them. In two months, more than six thousand people died, most of them civilians. Somehow, in the midst of it all, in the moments of peace, life went on. My belly grew. I had a dream one night: I was teaching school and a little boy came, put his arms around me and wouldn't let go. I knew I was carrying a boy.

And one night, when I'd left our apartment but couldn't stand the crowd at Josephine's or the coldness with which my parents still looked at me, I went looking for Daniel, whom I knew sometimes went to a tiny rented room he'd kept from before we were together. When I got there, he had a woman with him. He grinned at me, unashamed.

"The president said that every Liberian should help as many of the internally displaced as possible," he said. "I'm just giving this poor girl a home for the night."

MY SON JOSHUA WAS BORN on February 9, 1993, in an old warehouse that Swedish relief workers had turned into an emergency hospital. The day was bittersweet. My mother and Josephine were with me while I went through labor, and I was sure that afterward, my mother would ask me to come home with her. In the African tradition, when a woman gives birth, her family takes her home and cares for her, and everyone has a shift with the baby so she has time to rest and heal. I wanted to go home, wanted to be with Mama and Ma, to have them fuss and bring me tea and pepper soup. Instead, after my father visited, my mother left without saying a word, and I went home to Daniel, alone.

It hurt. *They hate me,* I thought, and then I got angry, too. I've been so good, and now you do this? Even if I'd done the worst thing in the world, I'm still your child. Daniel saw how bad I felt, and because men like him always want you to believe no one else wants you, he was fast to use it against me.

"These are the people you say love you?" he said of my parents. "They treat you like shit."

I adored my baby, whom I nicknamed "Nuku" after the brand of his favorite baby bottle, but I was so lonely. Geneva had returned to Monrovia, but she was busy with a daughter of her own, from a man she'd gotten engaged to at Buduburam and who was now in the United States. Josephine was my only regular visitor, and I lived for my time with her.

My life with Daniel continued to deteriorate. Once, he brought a girl home and slept with her in our house. The intense sexual pull between us had died for me, but not for him. Sometimes after he hit me, he'd want to have sex, then that struggle would get violent, too. One night, I ran from the bedroom, my nightgown in pieces, grabbed my Bible and shut myself in the bath.

"God," I said, "Guide me with a verse." I let the book fall open: Isaiah 54. *"For the Lord has called thee as a woman forsaken and grieved in spirit . . . O thou afflicted, tossed with tempest, and not comforted, behold, I will lay thy stones with fair colors, and lay thy foundations with sapphires. . . ."*

The door banged open. Daniel looked at the open book, read the passage, and laughed in my face. "This is written for a barren woman! God isn't saying this to you, young girl!"

I didn't listen. *Stones with fair colors. Foundations with sapphires.* I came back to Isaiah 54 again and again over the next decade. I knew it was my promise.

Sex was not something I could negotiate or avoid, so I went back to the emergency hospital and asked for a contraceptive injection.

"Not while you're still breastfeeding," the medical worker told me. "Come back once you've stopped, and once you've gotten your period again." By July, I still was breastfeeding and I still hadn't menstruated. But suddenly I started feeling completely exhausted, ready to go to bed every day by 4 P.M. I recognized the sign—I was pregnant again.

Around that time, Josephine's husband got a job transfer, and the whole family moved to Holland. My sister said she had given up on our country, the capital quiet under yet another ceasefire and transitional government, even as battles broke out and massacres continued in rural counties.

"You should get out of Liberia," she told me. "Nothing good can happen here."

I was losing my main source of comfort and solace, and she was never coming back. I couldn't bear to go to the airport to say goodbye to Josephine, but stayed at home and cried for days. I was so tired, so sad. It was hard to care about anything. Two babies. Now I really was trapped.

I dreamed I was somewhere, my home, though it wasn't my apartment, Paynesville or Old Road. An old woman brought me a girl of seventeen or eighteen, with long, flowing hair.

"This is your daughter," she told me.

I was heartsick. "I don't want another child!"

"That's sad, because your name is written on her grave."

The girl looked at me.

"If you don't take me, someone else will."

The old lady shook her head. "She will take you. She doesn't have a choice."

My parents still disapproved of my relationship with Daniel, but for the sake of Nuku and the coming baby, they offered to let us move to the Old Road house, which we could share with the aunt, uncle and children who'd been staying there. Of course we said yes.

My daughter Amber was born on the last day of April 1994. Not long afterward, I went back to St. Peter's for the first time since the massacre. The Sunday service felt like a funeral. The congregation had spent months worshipping in a tent while the chapel was rebuilt, but it was hard for me not to have visions of bodies in the aisles and on the altar.

There were mass graves both in front of and behind the church, and that month, the congregation voted to build a memorial. The bones in back were dug up and moved to the front with the others. Large white stars mark the two graves. I eventually learned to walk by them, and to push away thoughts of what I'd seen. The war touched everything. If you allowed yourself to be overcome every time you revisited a place where something terrible had happened, you wouldn't be able to move.

Around that same time, Daniel lost his job. He'd been promoted into the embassy's investigation office; when people applied for visas, he went out to verify the information they'd given. Because of the war, everyone wanted a visa to leave, and Daniel began suggesting that, with a payoff, he could help. He was caught and fired, and afterward no one would hire him. I tried to earn a few dollars by making cakes and pastries to sell, but not being able to support his family as he thought a man should put him in a constant rage.

"Read the Bible!" he'd shout at me. "*But if any provide not for his own, and especially for those of his own house, he hath denied the faith and is worse than an infidel!*" Anything could set him off, anything could bring a slap.

Rise each morning, bathe the kids. Make pastries. Daniel and I bought a bed and dresser, and I hung curtains in the creamy pink-brown bedroom that all four of us shared. We had a radio, so Amber could listen to soft music in her white crib. My aunt cared for Amber as if for her own child, and Nuku began saying that he had two mothers. I was grateful, and more and more, I invited God back into my life.

I decided I didn't want to stay at St. Peter's and be part of my parents' church world, and instead I chose a newer, evangelical congregation. There were many women there from the Old Road community who were struggling with various hardships, and we began to meet for Bible study. That time became one for talking and sharing, and during it, I felt a real sense of peace.

In some ways, Daniel was a good father. He loved to carry Nuku on his shoulders and watch him play ball. Everything his son did was exciting to him. He was always patient and gentle with Amber. But for me, there were daily humiliations, and they were especially painful because we were living among people who'd known me as a child. A card game Daniel played with an uncle turned into a fistfight because he thought he had been insulted. He would disappear for days to the place he kept in town. He rarely touched me, though every now and then he still wanted sex. I would go numb and let him do what he wanted. At least with my family members around, he had mostly stopped hitting me.

As the war subsided, there was time to think about the concerns of normal life. When Amber was four months old, I learned about a program run by UNICEF, the Ministry of Health and Mother Patern College of Health Sciences, training people to be social workers who would then counsel those traumatized by the war. I'd never had any ambition to do that kind of work, but it was a way to get out of the house, and I fought for it. You had to be recommended by an organization, so I asked my pastor to write a letter for me. I needed money for fees, so I looked past my pride and asked my father. With their help, I was accepted.

The program began with several months of classroom training at Mother Patern, which was part of a walled compound shared by St. Theresa's Convent, where Fata went to high school. Some of it almost lifted my head off. In one class on marriage and family life, the teacher talked about the cycle of domestic violence: how in an abusive relationship, there was a romantic honeymoon period followed by hitting, which led to apology and making up and another honeymoon period. *This is me,* I thought. *They are talking about my life!* In another class, we talked about trauma, and how to be a social worker you had to "train for transformation"; that is, deal with your own issues before you could learn to help others. I had a first glimpse, a first awareness of how bad my situation was.

In small ways, I began to fight back. During the week of "training for transformation," we weren't allowed to miss a single day or we would have to start all over. Amber was running a slight fever, and Daniel insisted I stay home with her. I wouldn't do it. I left my daughter in the care of my aunt and went to school. When I came home that night, he hit me. But I went back in the next day. Now when I got up, I felt a sense of purpose. Trainees earned a small stipend, so I was contributing to the house, and that felt good.

Next came fieldwork. I was assigned to work at an orphanage, but when I arrived, the state of the children paralyzed me. It was breakfast time, and I had never in my entire life seen people cooking baking flour—just flour!—to make porridge for the kids to eat. The women in charge were hitting the children, all of whom had skinny little limbs and swollen stomachs. There were flies everywhere. You might think I had seen worse things through the war, and I had. But I had children of my own now, and the suffering of children was personal to me. I sat in the corner and didn't move. The next morning I went back to campus to debrief and told the instructor, "I can't do this." And so I was assigned to work with a group of refugees from Sierra Leone.

Liberia was enjoying relative peace, but Sierra Leone's civil war had been raging since 1991. A former army corporal turned radical, Foday Sankoh, whom Charles Taylor had met in Libya, was leading a fearsome force called the Revolutionary United Front (RUF). Its fighters were known for hacking off villagers' arms, legs, lips and ears. Just as people from my country had fled north during the fighting, Sierra Leoneans sought refuge in Liberia and despite our trouble, we were bound to help them. Even if you're poor and struggling, you don't kick out someone who comes to your house in need. There were about fifty women refugees from Sierra Leone in Monrovia, living in a displaced persons center, and I was to work with twenty of them.

We met in the unfinished building where they lived. It was perpetually dark inside, just one beam of sunlight coming through the open door. The women, in their thirties and forties, had tacked plastic bags over the windows to keep the rain out. They sat on the floor wearing blouses and old, torn *lappas*. They had been through hell. All of them had been raped.

My official job was to teach the women about sexually transmitted disease and HIV prevention, but I could see they needed a lot more in the way of help—clothes, food, sheets of plastic to cover the windows properly—and said so in my case report. The Lutheran World Federation had a relief arm, and one of my colleagues sent me to meet the boss.

"Push for what you need," my colleague said. "He'll tell you, 'We don't have it,' but he does. And I know he has a very keen eye for pretty girls."

The boss's name was Tunde. He was fourteen years older than I, and a big man, over six feet tall and heavyset. Just as predicted, he told me he couldn't help me. I went back to him for three days, and on the fourth, he gave me what I needed. After that, he started inviting me back to his office, and eventually he started coming to see me. I liked him, liked the talking, the breaking free of my isolation at home. Tunde was married, with two children, but he also had a girlfriend and endless complications as a result.

"Why is my wife never happy?" he'd ask me, smiling. "Leymah, help me, tell me what women want."

He made it clear he was interested in me, but when I told him I already had a relationship and it wasn't my nature to have more than one, we became friends. Sometimes, he brought little presents for Nuku. He was such a calm man, so patient and understanding, that I dared to be honest.

One day I came in with a sprained arm. "How did that happen?" he asked.

I took a breath. "Daniel and I had a fight." He was the only one I told about the violence at home.

"Why don't you leave him?" he asked.

"It's not as easy as that," I said. "I don't want to raise kids who don't have their father."

"Oh? So you're ready to die just so your kids have a father?"

"It's not *that* bad," I said quickly.

Not that bad. He just squeezed my hand so tightly that my ring cut my fingers. He just slapped me with his hand. And, every now and then, with his belt.

I continued working with the women from Sierra Leone. Over the days, I asked about their lives, but they also asked me about mine, and they saw my bitterness without understanding it.

"Have you been raped?" several asked me outright. When I said no, they shook their heads. "Then why are you so angry?"

I couldn't understand their *lack* of bitterness and rage. They still laughed. They still had hope. I would go home at night thinking, *What kind of people are these? How can they still have this zest for life?* All of them dreamed of returning to Sierra Leone. One woman in particular talked about how she planned to teach local children to sing and dance, and as she did, a peaceful smile spread across her face. The woman had only one breast. She'd been fleeing her home during the fighting and was stopped at a rebel checkpoint. One of the men had watched her nursing her baby and it bothered him for some reason. He gestured at her, "Come here!" And he pushed the child aside and cut her breast off.

"How can you want to go back?" I asked her, and she looked at me as if I were mad.

"What else should I do? Allow *them* to win?"

The words lodged deep inside me, and I suddenly thought of a song we sang at church: *"Count your blessings, name them one by one, and it will surprise you what the Lord hath done."* Compared with these women, I had many blessings. Yes, I lived in an abusive relationship, but I had two healthy children, a warm bed, a roof over my head. The understanding put a boundary on my own pain.

But there was a second lesson that I didn't see at the time. Each day, I'd been enduring and surviving the life in which I found myself. It was all I could do, all I could imagine doing. But this woman knew that her personal tragedy was about more than just her. It was national; it was political. I never forgot what she said, but I didn't understand what it meant for a long time.

Working with the Sierra Leone refugees made me believe I might have a future in social work. The three-month program I was in was meant to lead to a longer program with an associate of arts degree at the end. I saw the possibility of taking my life in a new direction. Daniel, meanwhile, had reacted to my growing independence by withdrawing. He was gone for days, even weeks at a time, and we barely had a relationship. The stronger I got, the more he retreated. I began to think that I might be able to end the relationship. *I could get more training and find a job. I could earn a living. I could take the kids and leave.*

And all that might have happened, but for two things. The first was that Daniel came home late one night, and he and I had a very bad fight. It had been a long time since he'd touched me, so I hadn't even been thinking about contraception, but when we stopped quarreling, he wanted sex. He wouldn't listen to my "no," and forced what he wanted. Within a month, I recognized from my body's signs that I was pregnant again.

The possibilities for change I had seen fell broken at my feet. *I have two children,* I thought. *I will not survive having another.* Then, on top of my personal nightmare came an even greater, public one.

A few months earlier, in the summer of 1995, Charles Taylor's NPFL and the rest of the warring factions had signed yet another peace treaty—the thirteenth of the war. It provided for a council of state in which seven different factions would share power. When Taylor arrived in Monrovia, dressed all in white, crowds cheered with the hope that real peace had come. But it was the same story as before. The new government quickly splintered into yet more factions, each grasping for political power that could in turn be used to generate riches. Each of the leading warlords—Taylor, Roosevelt Johnson, Alhaji Kromah—had his own forces in Monrovia. (Karpeh had been killed.)

By the spring of 1996, political parties were bickering on the radio, the streets were filling with large numbers of young men, and some of my male cousins told me they'd been approached and asked to fight for Roosevelt Johnson. The signs of trouble were there. Again, some people allowed themselves not to see. More, like me, simply didn't have the energy to respond. If you fled from the war, you ended up as one of tens of thousands in the limbo of a refugee camp, or you came home to nothing and struggled to rebuild, just to lose it all when you had to leave again. During the time my parents were staying with Josephine, a new set of looters had plundered their house.

You'd hear the weariness in people's voices. "I've been to Guinea. I've been to Sierra Leone and Ghana. I can't run anymore. I'm just too tired."

On April 5, Daniel came home after having been gone for two weeks. The next day was his birthday. That morning, the sixth, the forces led by Taylor and Kromah tried to arrest Roosevelt Johnson—who greeted them with an assembled army. On Old Road, we woke at dawn to the sound of rockets and guns. *Pop-pop-pop! Boom! Boom!* Bullets slammed into the house.

"Amber! Nuku! Get down!" I was sick with fear; I had lived through fighting before, but not when I was five months pregnant with two toddlers to protect.

"Here! Push!" Daniel grabbed a mattress, and he and I shoved it against the door, then we all raced to a protected corner where stray bullets couldn't find us. My aunt had already started to pack. Outside, people were screaming and running. *Boom! Pop-pop-pop.* My nephews and nieces were very quiet, but each time the guns roared, two-year-old Amber squeezed her eyes shut in terror and shrieked.

Boom! Boom! By noon, my uncle said we'd better run for it. Paynesville would be safer.

No time to think or plan, and you can't drive a car when you need to avoid the road. Travel light. Cousins had just sent presents for the kids, but we took nothing except their medications packed in a bright woven straw bag; even the little pillow that Nuku loved to sleep with was left behind. I was still in nightgown and slippers when we set out on foot for my parents' house. Fleeing from a battle that has suddenly overrun your home, running in terror under a hail of bullets: it was an experience Liberians came to call "Exodus."

Down the lane to the highway, off onto Samuel K. Doe Boulevard, the new road our president had built paralleling it. A young fighter was crouched by the river where the road crossed it; no military uniform, so we knew he was NPFL. He was covered in blood and washing a huge, bloody knife. We looked straight ahead and just kept going. The trip took seven hours in the sun and muggy heat. By the midpoint, I was so tired and full of despair I told my family to go on without me; just tell my parents I died on the way.

Then we'd made it, and there we all were once again—not just Daniel, me and the kids, but Fata, Geneva and her baby, Mala's two children, and a dozen other displaced relatives, all of us jammed together just as we had been in 1990. Tempers flared. Every day, my parents had something negative to say about Daniel. Food was scarce.

"Mama," Nuku said to me one morning, "I'm so hungry! I wish for a piece of doughnut this morning."

I looked at my son. It was so hot, sweat was pouring off him. Where could I find him a piece of doughnut? All at once, I was filled with rage and pain.

"Nuku," I said softly, "I don't have a piece of doughnut to give you."

"I know," he said with a resignation that broke my heart. "But I wish for a piece of doughnut."

Six years, so much suffering, and nothing had changed! My social work certificate was useless. The home I'd left behind would surely be looted. My babies had spent half their lives hungry and afraid. The city was burning again, descending into even greater madness. "Get out, get out," was all anyone could talk about.

Daniel's parents had divorced when he was a boy, and he was raised by his father, who had taken him from Ghana to the US. He came back to Africa in his early twenties because of "trouble" in America, though I didn't know what that meant. But before he met me, he'd reconnected with his mother, who still lived in Accra. He said if we went there, we could live with her. Looking back, I see that it was another chance for me to make a choice. I could have let Daniel go and gotten away from him forever. When the fighting died down, I'd start over. Just do my best. But at the time, none of it seemed possible. I still held to the belief that the kids needed their father. And I had no confidence in my ability to care for them. Where would I stay? With my parents? I saw the scorn in their eyes.

A cousin of Daniel's picked us up in a car and drove us to Bushrod Island. We stayed with him for two days and then made our way to the Freeport, where my family and I had left for Buduburam. Thousands of others had the same idea, and the empty warehouses along the main street were filled with families waiting and hoping to get passage out. The gates to the docks were guarded by ECOMOG soldiers. Each time one opened, a crush of people pushed in. We made it through, Daniel holding Nuku's hand tightly and carrying Amber on his shoulders, and found our way to the administrative office. There, I ran into Geneva and her in-laws. Her sister-in-law's husband was a well-known pastor, and through his connections, we managed to stay in that office for two days while Daniel went out in search of boat tickets. When he returned with them in his hand—I never asked how he got them—I said goodbye to Mammie. The boat she and her in-laws found took them to Nigeria. I wouldn't see her again for more than two years.

CHAPTER 5

HELPLESS IN A STRANGE PLACE

Our boat, the *Bulk Challenge*, was an ancient Nigerian freighter. We were all too desperate to notice or care how awful it looked. When it came time to board, the crowd surged forward again, pulling on the rope ladders hanging down the ship's side, climbing on each other's shoulders. I was too heavily pregnant to move forward up the steep ramp to the deck and fell farther and farther away from Daniel and the kids. I panicked as the ship began to move. "My babies!" I screamed and from behind, some men lifted and pushed me on board. As we moved out, the crowds were still screaming and fighting below us on the dock.

There were thousands of us on board—people squeezed on the deck, in the hold and the ship's corridors, without even space to lie down. The children and I found a spot outside. Behind us, a blind musician sang gospel songs. *"I'm learning how to lean and depend on Jesus, He's my friend, he's my guide . . . I'm learning how to lean and depend on Jesus, because I found that if I trust him, he will provide. . . ."*

Nearby was a Ghanaian woman with three children. She'd brought fish and dried *keke*—corn dough—and gave the kids some to eat. I wasn't hungry. At night, we heard terrible sobbing. The woman got up to investigate and came back with a girl and her two young children. Despite the crowding, the girl's husband had been pressuring her to have sex, and when she said no, he beat her.

Two days passed, the kind of time when you have to shut down and not allow yourself to think or you'll go mad. There was only one bathroom on the boat, so men peed over the side and women used bottles they'd throw overboard. Almost all of us got seasick, and everywhere was the stench of vomit and shit—people throwing up all over themselves, wetting themselves because they were too weak to get up, kids shitting in their pants. We were just off Côte d'Ivoire when I heard screams and cries. "Water coming in! We are sinking!" Daniel rushed below to help those who were bailing. A strange calm came over me: I knew somehow that my children and I would survive, even if we had to climb over the bodies of the others to save ourselves.

We docked in the Côte d'Ivoire port of San-Pédro for two days for emergency repairs. Some people got off. Two were women who'd been my classmates at social work school and they encouraged us to join them, but we had nowhere to go in that country. We set sail again, but when we got to the port at Takoradi, the Ghanaian government said it would accept no more refugees and refused us permission to land.

Again, we headed back to sea. By now we had been aboard a week, hungry, filthy and sick. Nuku was vomiting and had diarrhea, and both he and Amber were running fevers. We'd found a new place to sit, in an inside hallway, next to a door. We didn't know it led to the ship captain's cabin. He stopped the next time he came by and touched Nuku's forehead. "This baby is sick. Come inside." His girlfriend helped me bathe the kids and gave them something to eat. And we survived.

The voyage of the homeless *Bulk Challenge* made the newspapers around the world. When the international outcry for mercy grew strong enough, we finally were allowed to dock at Takoradi. I spent two days at a refugee camp, with pneumonia. Pregnant women and children had a room to themselves, so the kids would sleep with me at night and Daniel would come to care for them during the day. And then when I was well enough to leave, we boarded a bus that would carry us to our new home.

"I am a Christian, and I have compassion, so I am taking you into my house, but this relationship is sinful," Daniel's mother, Old Ma, told me the first day we met. She was in her sixties, a full-busted woman with long salt-and-pepper hair. "This man was married and left his wife. You have two children and are expecting another. You go against the will of God."

You. It was the only way Old Ma ever addressed me when I lived in her house. She never spoke my name.

Old Ma's house was in the coastal Nungua neighborhood of Accra, about fifteen miles southwest of the city's center. It wasn't exactly a slum but congested, rough and rundown—dirt roads of shacks and crumbling houses with hanging doors and stoops that were no more than a pile of rocks. Rents were cheap, so Ghanaians without money lived here, and nearby, a lot of displaced Liberians. Electricity came and went and the water was always cutting off. People built concrete tanks and for a thousand *cedis* (about fifty cents) a water truck would come and fill them. Old Ma's house was one of the nicest, made of cement, and large and clean. Relatives in the US paid the bills. There was a long hallway with bedrooms off it, also a washroom and separate toilet, and a kitchen. Along with Old Ma, three of Daniel's sisters lived there, plus a brother and sister-in-law.

I was grateful to have shelter. Josephine sent money, and Daniel and I bought mattresses, curtains, linoleum for the floor and a set of dishes for the room we had been given. But I was shocked by the coldness and distance in that house. In my home, and in most of Liberia, everything was shared. Especially in families, you always stepped in for those who couldn't afford. If you gave a hungry child a cookie, he would break it into pieces to share with his cousins. Here, everyone had his own cup, fork and spoon. The first time I used a bath bucket to wash the kids, I was told, "Don't use that again—it's mine and I don't share with other people."

Each family cooked their own food. Some days, Daniel's brother's wife would offer food to our children, but many days she didn't, and when they were hungry, I tried to keep them from the kitchen. In Africa, having a child so undisciplined he stands for food—begs—is a shameful thing. There was a wooden table in the kitchen, but it was mainly for my mother-in-law and her daughters. When I prepared a meal, I would take it into our room, and we ate sitting on the floor.

Hey. You. I was beyond exhausted those first months, and I couldn't seem to get well. Even though my pregnancy was advancing, I lost weight. I had constant bouts of malaria. The clinic that treated me in Takoradi had given me a referral to an Accra doctor, who told me I was so badly anemic I needed a transfusion. Daniel refused to give blood, and when I told the doctor, I cried.

"How old are you?" he asked, certain at first that I was a teenage mother because I'd gotten so thin. I said I was twenty-six. "What's the level of your education?" When I told him my story, he shook his head and told me he would give me some of the drugs I needed without charge. "I don't usually say this, but I can see you're smart. You need to leave this man and make the most of your life."

I wasn't yet ready to hear that.

"The real problem with you," Daniel told me when he found me in bed, resting, "is that you're lazy."

Hey. You. It was clear that Daniel's family thought I was nothing. I had come to Ghana with two pairs of underclothes and one green dress that I could wear to church. Every time they got dressed to go out, they would come before me and show off. Daniel's mother believed that somehow I had performed *juju* on her son and bewitched him into taking responsibility for children that weren't even really his. The terrible thing was I knew that Daniel shared some of her feelings.

"I'm gone for weeks, then after one night of sex you're pregnant?" he'd said to me when I told him I'd conceived. "How convenient. Maybe you should be telling your boss."

The girl I'd been at seventeen would never have tolerated this treatment. How can I explain the way confidence and strength can disappear? It wasn't about the war; it was what happens during a relationship that involves domestic violence. I knew those dynamics—I'd learned them in my social work class—but I couldn't help myself. The war had taken away my home, my family, my future, all my foundations and the faith that might have allowed me to find an escape route. I was alone and felt helpless in a strange place. It felt like my fate to be here, to stay, to live in this violent relationship, suffer and have a lot of children. I took two buses home from the hospital one day, in one of Ghana's worst rainstorms of the year. The wind was blowing hard, and I was so thin that it literally threw me sideways. I came home covered in mud, shivering, and ran to the bathroom to cry.

"I'm so fucked up," I told myself through the tears. "I'm finished. I'm done."

My third child, Arthur, arrived on June 23, 1996, two months early. He was the tiniest creature in the world, just two and a half pounds, with hair almost as soft and straight as a white baby's. He cried and suckled endlessly, his tiny mouth always open, like a baby chick looking for food. I called him "Birdie."

Daniel drove me to the hospital and told me he'd wait outside the delivery room, but after the birth, he was nowhere to be found. When the nurses said I needed to pay extra for Arthur to have special treatment, like an incubator, I didn't have it. Neither Daniel nor I had money for a cell phone and there was no phone line at Old Ma's house. I had no way to reach him. I wanted to go home, but it's a shameful fact that in Africa, if you haven't paid your bills, many hospitals literally hold you and won't let you leave.

I was given a blanket and told to wait in the hall. I stood for a while, then sat on the floor. Night came. It felt cold. I had nothing for Arthur, not even diapers. I could feel his tiny body shivering. I wrapped him in my *lappa* and held him close, next to my skin.

We stayed in that hallway for a week. Once Daniel came, told me he was trying to get the money together, and vanished again. I was still sore and bleeding from the birth and worried about my child who never seemed to get warm. And I was humiliated—I had fallen further than I could have believed possible. The pretty, smart Gbowee daughter, the promising student, the good girl who did everything right, was lying on the floor in public in a dirty nightgown. People who passed through the hall tossed me coins and bread as if I were a beggar.

Finally, a woman with a private room took me in and gave me diapers and a clean blanket. I couldn't stop crying.

"Shut up," she said. "Stop your crying. You can't give up. You may not have anything, but you can read and write. You can educate your children."

The next day, the doctor who'd earlier given me drugs arrived and paid my hospital bill.

These acts of kindness . . . We used to say to my mother, "Ma, you can melt." In Liberia, "you melt" means "you get into everyone's business." Growing up, if someone in my neighborhood was having a hard time, my mother always helped. If someone lost a relative, she was the first to make a contribution to pay for the funeral. I have a cousin a year younger than me, Small Moses, who was born sick. When he developed whooping cough as a baby, his mother said she couldn't handle it, and my mother took him in. She was caring for me, an infant of her own, at the time, but she and Ma nursed my cousin back to health. When I had an episode of false labor with Nuku, she paid the bill of an impoverished young girl she saw crying at the clinic. My sisters and I were always told that one day, when you least expect it, all the good your parents have done will come back to you. It did. When I encountered the ship captain and his girlfriend, the woman in the hospital, the doctor, I understood Ecclesiastes: that life is like a circle. And these moments offered me tiny pieces of hope.

I took home my fragile baby. Each time he ate, he struggled to catch his breath. But he held on. We had no money to buy him a crib, so he slept in a cardboard box.

Now there were four of us at Old Ma's. I stayed home with the kids and sang and read to them. They were my world. I hadn't wanted to get pregnant, but not wanting a pregnancy doesn't mean you won't love the child you bear. What my babies gave me, and what I felt for them was the reason I got up each day. Nuku entertained me a lot. He would go outside to play in the neighborhood, and he always came back with a story to make me laugh. On Sundays, we went to the local Lutheran church, where there were other Liberians in the congregation, and later in the week, Nuku would play preacher.

"And Jesus said I should tell you that everything will be all right!"

"Amen, Nuku!" I'd cry.

"Kneel down, let me pray for you. Thank you, Jesus, for Mama! Anyone doing bad to Mama, Jesus, punish them!"

We would laugh and laugh. At night, I slept between their small bodies, touching them, counting, even in my sleep, to make sure everyone was there and okay. But Nuku and Amber sometimes had questions that reminded me they carried their own bad memories.

"Where *are* we?" Amber sometimes asked. "Where is Grandma? Not *this* one! Where's my other mama?"

Daniel still didn't have a steady job, although he went out daily and was gone for hours. Josephine, who had moved from Holland to France, was going through a bitter divorce and couldn't help anymore. We were always short of money. I couldn't afford to buy gas to fuel the cooker at the house, so I used charcoal, as if we were in the bush. Sometimes the kids went hungry. We got by because at church, mothers would look at the braids I did for Amber and ask if I would do their daughters' hair.

This became my work. Every morning, by divine intervention, someone from the neighborhood would come asking for me to braid her hair and give me a dollar for it. With that dollar, I'd go out to one of the little neighborhood kiosks and buy breakfast. I would wash baby clothes, do another braid, go out for rice. Sometimes, all I could afford was an amount so small it was enough only for Daniel and the kids. I ate the crust left at the bottom of the pot.

In our frustration and poverty, Daniel began hitting me again. One afternoon, a woman had come to the house so I could do her braids. Her hair was very long and it took me hours. At dusk, I took a break to bathe Amber, feed her, Nuku and Arthur and put them to sleep. Finally, I was done. She paid me five dollars, enough to buy food for the week. But by then it was dark and she didn't know the neighborhood, so I walked her to the main road. When I got back, Daniel was at the door, holding Amber, and she was crying.

"What happened?"

"Your fucking ass, you don't know!" His face was twisted with anger. "You leave my daughter and go out walking?" He slapped me hard across the face. All I could do was go to the bathroom to cry.

Your fucking ass. Your dirty fucking ass. Lazy bitch. Liar. Whore. Even when there was no hitting, the words came at me.

"You never learn anything. Your head is hard as a rock so nothing gets in there."

"You're a stupid bitch and your mind is fucked up."

Stupid. Stupid. Stupid. He used the word so often that even the kids picked it up.

"I'm hungry, too," I said to Daniel one night when he was sitting with Amber and they were eating rice.

"I'll give you some," he said.

"Papa, don't!" said my daughter. "Don't give her any! She's a stupid girl."

When I couldn't stand it, I would cross the road to sit under a palm tree with a young girl who sold fruit. Or huddle in the bedroom and open the Bible to Isaiah. *"I will lay thy stones with fair colors, and lay thy foundations with sapphires."* Asking God—begging—"Where are you? Where is the promise you made to me?" I made a little money, bought enough food to get us fed and tried to get through the days without any sense of what might be on the other side of them.

"Mama, why are we here?" Nuku would ask me. "When are we going home? Mama, why are you crying?"

One day, there was so little rice that after the others ate there was nothing left for me. As I washed the dishes, one of my sisters-in-law came in. She had guests and began boiling yams for them. I was still breastfeeding Arthur and so hungry I thought I would faint. She ignored me. I watched her empty the yams into a big bowl, smelled the steam rising from them. She disappeared into her room and I heard her friends laughing as they ate, their spoons clinking. My mouth was filled with saliva, my stomach a small, painful knot. My sister-in-law opened the bedroom door, brought out the bowl, set it beside the sink, disappeared again. I rushed to it and, hunched over, gobbled what was left—then cleaned the bowl and kitchen from top to bottom so she would never know I had been reduced to eating her leftovers.

The shame of that moment was so deep I didn't tell anyone of it for years. The time I spent at Buduburam had been better than this. At least I'd had my family. Now they were scattered: Mama and Papa in Liberia, Geneva in Nigeria, Mala in Sweden, Josephine in France. Then I had felt

I was waiting for my life to resume. Now it was moving, but like a train that had lost its direction, and I saw no way forward.

Depression is a strange thing. You feel so helpless, so drained, that no matter how bad the place you find yourself, you sink into it, thinking, *It's too hard to move. I'll just stay here.*

More and more, I was in my own world. When I think back, it was almost as if I was on drugs. I couldn't change anything, so I had fantasies, and in them, I had a different life. Daniel was a loving man, attentive, caring, sensitive to my needs. He had a good job, so our struggles were over. We lived in our own home. He was patient and kind with the kids. I didn't let myself see the reality. And because of that, I didn't protect my children.

Daniel's family loved Amber. They said she looked like one of his sisters, and the two had similar personalities, slow, quiet and intense. Nuku was something else: hyper, feisty, a headstrong kid who was tough in his own way. Some of the neighbors laughed and called him "Charles Taylor." It drove Daniel crazy that he couldn't tell Nuku what to do. "Stop it! Sit down! You're so wild!" he would shout. And to me, "Why can't you do something with this boy? He's uncontrollable!" It was a terrible family secret that one of Daniel's close relatives was gay, and when he saw Nuku hugging anyone who was male, he grabbed him and shook him hard, shouting, "Don't do that!" Daniel's mother even said that my son needed to be taken to church for exorcism, because had a demon inside.

One afternoon, Daniel's sister complained again that Nuku was standing for food—staring at her longingly while she ate. I lost control and I hit him. Beat him until he was on the floor with his arms covering his face. He began crying. "Mama, you're going to listen to these people and kill me for nothing!"

I fell down beside him and we cried together. I never hit one of my children again.

Word came only rarely from home, but in the spring of 1997, Mala wrote to my parents from Sweden, asking them to help get her kids out of Liberia and to me, until they could get visas to join her. My mother brought them to Ghana, and the way the kids ate, whispering, "We were so hungry," gave a hint of the nightmare they'd just escaped.

Mama had little to say. "Everyone has their difficult experiences, and this is yours," she told me before she left.

Soon after, Daniel had a terrible fight with his family, and we moved to an unfinished house on a dirt lot that belonged to a friend of his. For three months, we coexisted. Then Daniel reconciled with his mother. He openly had an affair with a neighbor. I was finding it hard to maintain any fantasies about a life together or my belief that the kids needed him. Now my dreams were mostly about independence. At the school Nuku and Amber attended, the teacher had learned I had a social work certificate; she talked to me about childhood development and said, "You should come work for me." I dreamed that I would take that job and find a two-bedroom home without Daniel. I would go back to school. I would go back to Liberia, and in a few months return to Ghana, a success.

"I'm going to be a rich person in this life," I told the man who owned the unfinished house, and he laughed at me.

Mala's kids got permission to emigrate and left for Sweden. I felt very alone without their company. And just like that, it was over for me. Within a couple of days, I had packed things for the children and me. Daniel was gone when we left the house. I never said goodbye.

CHAPTER 6

A GLIMPSE OF PEACE

IT TOOK US OVER A WEEK to get back to Paynesville by bus; the driver let me ride on credit, because I didn't have a cent. We bounced and rattled through Ghana, Côte d'Ivoire, and into rural Liberia, Nuku hanging like a monkey on the bars. I hadn't told my parents I was coming, and I was sick and scared, wondering what would happen when we arrived. In villages we passed, men and women were gathered around the radio listening to reports of the death of Princess Diana, one of the few Europeans who'd cared about what happened in this part of the world.

And then I was back. I threw myself on my parents' mercy, not really seeing how I could go on. I was twenty-six, penniless, broken, and charged with the care of three utterly dependent toddlers. Soon to be four. One sad night on the mattress in that unfinished house . . . Now I knew what I'd suspected before we left. I was pregnant again.

No ONE IN LIBERIA wanted to talk about the last two years; they had been that bad. In late 1996, the warring factions had signed yet another peace accord, but by then, the country was in ruins. The industries that had sustained the economy—ship registration, timber, rubber, iron ore and diamond mining—were gone. There was still no electricity or running water; roads were impassable; hospitals and schools were closed. Even the poles that held the streetlights that no longer worked were chewed up; for sport, the fighters had turned their guns on anything standing.

Except for the US and Nigeria, every foreign country had closed its embassy. More than 80 percent of the population was living below the poverty line. Monrovia was bursting with families who'd come seeking safety and now squatted in bombed-out and bullet-ridden buildings, beside the road, behind stores in the city center, anywhere there was an open bit of land. Formerly stable communities like Old Road were filled with slum homes built of tarp, cardboard and salvage tin. In towns and villages where aid couldn't get through, men, women and children had cut off the tops of trees looking for edible leaves, then died of starvation.

In a survey of 205 Monrovia women and girls that had been published in the *Journal of the American Medical Association*, nearly half said they'd been the victim of least one act of physical or sexual violence by a soldier or fighter. A World Health Organization survey of 334 Monrovia high school children found that 61 percent had seen someone tortured, raped or killed. Those with education or means to flee and survive elsewhere had joined a great diaspora that stretched from other African countries to Europe to the United States. There was a pervasive sense of despair. It was hard to imagine that life here could ever be normal again.

In July 1997, the country held elections. Several candidates ran, including Ellen Johnson Sirleaf, who now spoke out against Taylor. Taylor won the presidency by a wide margin.

"He killed my ma, he killed my pa," chanted his supporters. "But I will vote for him." The Liberian people weren't crazy, just exhausted to the soul. Taylor had destroyed the country, so let him put it back together. Yes, he was a monster, but perhaps if he got what he wanted, he would become human again. All that mattered was that the fighting stop. Years later, when we knew what would come, we referred to this brief period of peace as the end of the first war.

Mama, Papa and Fata lived in the only partially repaired house in Paynesville. They'd never replaced the looted carpet. The chandeliers that had hung in the dining and living room were gone, though there would have been no electricity to power lights anyway. Papa, who'd survived prison and Samuel Doe, quit his government job the day Taylor took office. Working for that criminal, he said, was more than he could stomach.

I signed up Nuku at a local kindergarten, enrolled Amber in a pre-school, then collapsed onto a new version of the couch that had sheltered me at the US embassy, this one in my parents' living room. It was dark and quiet there, and I just lay still for hours trying not to think and letting Fata take care of the kids.

"What is she doing?" I'd hear my father demanding of Mama. "What is her plan?"

I had nothing to say. I had no plan at all. Look what I had done with my life. I had seen at the start that Daniel was bad news, but I'd gone ahead anyway. I really was stupid. I was paralyzed with shame and sadness.

"Tell me what was Ghana like," Fata encouraged Nuku. "Was it pretty? Didn't you have fun?"

"No, Mama always said she was sick," he whispered. "She just sat there and did nothing."

Days went by. Papa already had a new job, as head of security for St. Peter's, and my idleness drove him wild. "I need to know what you are planning to do!" he shouted at me. "At the rate you're going, you won't amount to anything. Get a job, go back to school, do something! If you can't put your life together, you will have to leave this house!" *Stupid, failure*, I heard in his voice, an echo of the names I called myself. Weeks passed. "You can't stay here! I won't have my house as a damned day-care center!" I hadn't even told him I was pregnant again, but he looked at me with contempt. "It's such a disappointment when you expect your child to make something of herself and she grows up to be a damned baby machine."

One night, I went out to rake the yard beneath the plum trees with my mother. She pulled the leaves into piles; I dumped them into a drum where we'd made a bonfire. It was a beautiful night—the big empty yard, the dark sky, the flickering of the fire. Nuku and Amber were asleep in the house; Mama carried Arthur on her back. Suddenly, she spoke very quietly. "Leymah. What do you want to do with your life?"

I froze. Had I known this moment was coming, I would have avoided it. I thought of what to say, then simply spoke the truth. "I don't know."

"Let me tell you something," she said. "I've endured these nights of listening to your dad say terrible things about what you've become. But I know that's not who you are, and I know you can do better. I want to make a vow to you. If you decide you want to do something for yourself, if you decide to go back to school—I will tie my waist." By now I couldn't see the beauty of the night, because my tears were flowing. When an African woman tells you she will tie her waist, it means she will do anything for you, give you everything she has. "I will support you, Leymah. I will help take care of your kids. Until you make something of your life."

Before you can take action, something must shift inside you. My mother's words should have been the start, but I wasn't ready yet. My sadness and self-hate still grew. It seemed that every page I turned was darkness. I was nothing. Soon, I would have four children, but no husband, education, no income or skills. I was a damned baby machine. What was the point? Maybe this life wasn't worth living; maybe it was time to leave it. If I died, people would feel sorry for my children and take better care of them than I could.

Then that weekend, my mother went to check on Nuku, because it was almost eleven in the morning and he still wasn't up. She found him lying motionless in bed, with his eyes open. He had wet himself, something that had not happened in many years.

"Grandma?" he asked in a frightened voice when she entered the room. "Is that you? Where are we?"

"We're in Liberia," she said, surprised. "Why do you ask?"

He pointed to the mosquito net above his bed. We had always slept under a net during our time in Ghana, but rarely did here at home; my mother had put one up the night before only because the house hadn't been sprayed as usual. Then he pointed at a pair of Papa's shoes, kicked off and left nearby. "I saw the shoes, and I thought they were my father's," he whispered. "I saw the net. I thought we were still in Ghana. And I didn't want to get up."

When I heard the story, I broke down and wept. What had I done? After so many months of retreat and telling myself stories and refusing to feel, it was a rough jolt into reality. I was not a seventeen-year-old girl who could afford to sit back, consumed with sadness. I was a twenty-six-year-old woman with children who depended on me. I had to take action. I had to stop blaming my parents, Daniel, single motherhood, the war, for what I was. I had to stop hating myself, find my strength again and step forward. My children had suffered so much, and they deserved so much more than they had. I was the only one who could give it to them.

PART TWO

CHAPTER 7

"YES, YOU CAN"

MORE THAN ANYTHING, I needed a job, and when I thought of where to turn for help, I remembered Tunde, the head of the relief agency in the days when I'd worked with the women from Sierra Leone. I asked around and learned that he still worked for the Lutheran World Federation, but their offices had moved to Bushrod Island. I couldn't call him—Monrovia still had no phone service—so one morning, in November 1997, I took the bus to his office. Through Gardnersville, change at Freeport . . . I was oblivious to everything but the fears racing and looping inside my head: *What's going to happen to me? Where is my life going? What should I do?* As we crossed the Gabriel Tucker Bridge, we passed near the spot where I'd encountered Ayo, my classmate who'd become a rebel fighter. Seven years had passed since that day. It was like looking back at someone else's life.

Tunde was in the office. His face lit up, and he pulled me into a hug. "I'm so glad to see you!" he exclaimed. "I've been asking people about you." I could see different emotions in his eyes, pleasure mixed with simple relief. I understood. When I'd thought of Ayo, I wondered where he was but also *if* he was. In those days, when you didn't hear news of friends, you knew it might be because they were dead.

I asked Tunde about his family—he said they'd fled during the fighting—and told him my news. "I've finally left Daniel."

He beamed. "Good for you. Don't worry, you'll find someone else one day."

"I don't want someone else," I said harshly. I told him about the kids, and that I was pregnant again. "I'm living with my parents. I have no work and no money. I don't need a husband. What I need is some man who'll pay me to have sex and then just be on his way."

He took me seriously and looked horrified. "No! You're too smart to lead that kind of a life."

I looked straight at him. "You don't know the kind of person I've become."

"I know you're discouraged," he answered. "But trust me, this time will pass."

It was still easy for me to talk to Tunde. He offered to drive me home that day and I said yes, but I asked him to leave me on the main road instead of at the house, because I didn't want any comments from my parents. But later that week, I saw his red car outside. I later heard he'd driven all around the neighborhood asking people where to find the young lady who'd just come back from Ghana.

Tunde's family had left the country because of the war, but his troubled marriage had also collapsed. He was separated, though not divorced, and soon was coming to Paynesville to see me on a regular basis. He was polite and respectful to my parents and even my dad refrained from negative remarks. Our relationship wasn't physical then—I was pregnant, after all, my kids were around and my parents were in the next room—but we spent many hours together.

Some evenings, he took me for a ride. Most of the time we would just sit on the porch and talk—about life, politics, current events, sports. Later, Tunde told me that he fell in love with me because we could talk about anything. What drew me to him was his quiet steadiness. He was a very different kind of man than Daniel. He'd grown up amid the worst kind of domestic violence: his father beat all the children, and his mother finally sent Tunde to live with a son from a previous marriage, a home where even more abuse occurred. He still bore the scars of whippings on his arms and back. But he was the gentlest person I'd ever met. He never even raised his voice. And he offered the kind of encouragement that chipped away at my feelings of being stupid and useless.

If I was silent, he pushed me to talk. "Tell me what you think." He listened to my opinions and told me they were valuable. "There's no level of conversation you can't have with me," he assured me. When I told him that thinking about the coming baby had me feeling desperate, he took my hand. "What if I told you that I would be there for you and this child? What would you say?"

"I would say that you're lying. Men are not to be trusted."

But Tunde was there. If he arrived in Paynesville to find me washing the kids' dirty clothes, he rolled up his sleeves and helped. He played with Amber, Nuku and Arthur, brought them small gifts and bought me baby clothes. After I got word to him that I'd given birth on February 14, he broke curfew and rushed through the city to where he knew a Lebanese family slept above their store, banging on the front door until they let him in. He came to see me at the clinic laden with shopping bags, most of them filled with sweets. "I didn't stop to think!" he told me. "I just grabbed things, I was so excited." *This gentle giant,* I thought. *This man is someone I could love.*

My new daughter was a pretty, chubby baby who curled up on herself, sleeping peacefully, until another infant in the clinic nursery let out a wail. Then she would cast her eyes up with an impatient, haughty expression that demanded, "Who is disturbing me?" The nurses laughed—"This one is a real princess!"—and "Princess" became her first nickname. But when Tunde and I were alone, I told him the real name I'd chosen for the baby: Nicole Lucy, after his most beloved cousin, Nicholas, and his mother. His eyes filled with tears. Tunde and I became lovers not long after Princess was born. I kept in touch with the one sister of Daniel's who'd at times been good to me, and every now and then I heard word of him. Once, he sent the kids birthday gifts. But Tunde was the man they turned to for play or advice or help with schoolwork. To Nuku, Amber and Arthur he was "Uncle Tunde." To Princess, he was "Dada."

My parents let Tunde know they weren't thrilled that their daughter, barely out of a bad relationship, had landed so fast in another. He told them that he, too, wanted me to do something more with my life—and he meant it. Finding a job wasn't what I needed to do right now, he said; I would find nothing with a future unless I got more education. The most important thing for me to do was go back to school. "Yes, you can," he countered whenever I offered a reason why that was impossible. "No, you haven't," he said when I told him I'd lost my old abilities. "Yes, you will," he repeated whenever I said there was no chance for me to succeed. "You have too much potential. Don't throw it away. You know this isn't the life you want for yourself."

I was afraid, but I also knew he was right. My parents had taken me in, but the price of their generosity was that they sometimes treated me like a child. And my father's description of me as a "damned baby machine" had lodged in me like a barb that still gave off poison. I ached to show him how wrong he'd been. Even my relationship with Tunde, good as it was, was based on dependence. One day, not long after he first started coming to see me, he had drawn out his wallet before he left and handed me two thousand Liberian dollars—about forty US dollars. "Get something for the kids," he said. "I know it's tough." Ever since, giving me money had been a regular gesture.

It wasn't that I didn't appreciate his help, and I needed it—having cash meant I could buy small things like diapers or soap powder without having to ask my mother for even more—but it depressed me, too. I was still trapped. I wanted to be able to take care of myself.

One Sunday, I ventured back to St. Peter's, although I rushed out through a side door once the service was over, so I wouldn't have to answer questions from people who'd known me before. My mother, as head of the church's women's division, was chairing a project to enlarge a bathroom. When she asked me for help balancing the books, I complained but I did it—and when I found some mistakes in the builder's estimate and called her attention to them, I felt competent. And that felt good.

What to do about school was a harder question. There was no way for me to resurrect my old dream of becoming a pediatrician. The university, repaired and reopened after the destruction of 1991, had been torn apart by looting in '96 and was closed again. Then I learned that

Mother Patern College of Health Sciences, where I'd gotten my social work certificate, once again offered an associate of arts degree program.

Because Mother Patern was in a walled compound and its Central Monrovia neighborhood hadn't seen much fighting, it had survived the war intact. It received financial support from the US embassy, so it even had luxuries like a fully equipped library and air conditioning. It was a "polytechnic" college, midway between academic institutions like the university and technical schools, like the one my dad had attended.

Mother Patern emphasized practical experience, so to be accepted for the fall term, I would have to show not only that I'd received my three-month certificate, but that I'd actively used it to do either paid or volunteer social work. Tunde found something that seemed like a perfect opportunity for me: the Lutheran Church in Liberia/Lutheran World Federation's Trauma Healing and Reconciliation Program (THRP) had just opened offices in the St. Peter's compound and might welcome a volunteer, especially one who'd already worked with war refugees. It turned out that my mother knew the pastor in charge, Reverend Bartholomew Bioh Colley, and when she spoke to him, he agreed to give me a chance.

The THRP's offices were new, but the program had a history. Liberia's churches had been active in peace efforts ever since the civil war started, and in 1991, Lutheran pastors, lay leaders, teachers and health workers joined with the Christian Health Association of Liberia to try to repair the psychic and social damage left behind by the war.

Trauma Healing was a little like therapy. Our goal was to do workshops with villagers who'd suffered during the war, get them to tell their stories so they'd gain awareness of where they were now and what problems they faced. Then we'd teach them conflict resolution strategies that would enable them to help their communities. *What is conflict to you?* we'd ask. *What is peace? How does your local language and custom define it? What are the national issues that affect your village? What do you see as the cause of conflict in Liberia? What do you have within your culture that can be used to resolve it?* The format was one that had been used mostly in the West, in places like Bosnia. As part of adapting it to the situation in Liberia, we were supposed to identify local leaders and groups

81

throughout the country and teach them how to teach others. By helping people and communities heal themselves, we'd be helping our fragmented, suffering country mend itself.

Volunteering for the THRP was my first introduction to being a peace-builder. When I use that word, I mean something much more complicated than negotiating, brokering or signing treaties. Peacebuilding to me isn't ending a fight by standing between two opposing forces. It's healing those victimized by war, making them strong again, and bringing them back to the people they once were. It's helping victimizers rediscover their humanity so they can once again become productive members of their communities. Peace-building is teaching people that resolving conflict can be done without picking up a gun. It's repairing societies in which the guns have been used, and not only making them whole, but better.

I didn't choose this role; I fell into it. I didn't expect to be at the THRP for long; I stayed almost five years. They were hard and often frustrating, but what I learned there, and the people I met, changed my life forever.

My mother went with me on the bus on my first day of work. Along Payne Avenue, the houses I'd once admired were burned out and destroyed. The roads had crumbled from the weight of ECOMOG tanks, and enormous potholes were full of water. We parked and she led me to a small first-floor office in the compound. It was the same room to which Doe's soldiers had herded us in 1990, the room where my mother had been beaten and I'd expected us both to die. Neither of us mentioned it.

"Reverend Colley? This is my daughter."

My boss-to-be, casually dressed and in his forties, turned to the room, which was threadbare and crowded with thirteen people sharing only six desks. "This is Leymah, a member of St. Peter's. She'll be volunteering with us as a means of enrolling in social work school. She'll sit with Jill." He pointed at a heavyset white woman, who moved a chair in front of her desk and gestured that I should sit down.

Then I tried to stay out of the way as everyone went back to work. I was nervous, and quiet-quiet-quiet. Were the others staring? Whenever I was in a group, I imagined all eyes on me in judgment. *That's the girl who was going somewhere but instead she had four kids.* I already could tell that one of the regular workers, an older woman with a nursing degree, didn't like me. (I later found out she was a friend of Tunde's wife.) The program secretary, Vaiba Flomo, all business in an African suit and glasses, was a Loma, like the other worker, so I avoided her, too. And I had no idea what to say to Jill Hinrichs, my desk mate. Jill was a social worker from Chicago, Illinois, who'd come to Liberia as a volunteer with Evangelical Lutheran Church in America. I'd never been in a close relationship with a white person before.

Within weeks, "BB," as everyone called Reverend Colley, asked me to lead a day of workshops for women brought in from Lofa County, far in the north, where there had been a recent ethnic clash. Jill, who was trained as a grief counselor, gave me a book on dealing with loss and grief to help me prepare. I don't remember exactly what I said or did that day; I just know I was thinking that because of my own experiences, I had some idea of what these women had been through during the war. To get them to open up and talk, I should ask questions that would work on me. The workshop was a great success: the women wept as they recalled the destruction of their villages, the death of children, the friends who'd been raped. Afterward, the coworker who disliked me was even colder, but BB was impressed.

That same month, a group from Manchester, England, came to Liberia to do research for a paper on what had happened to rural communities during the war, and whether and how they were consulted about postwar relief. They asked the office to suggest someone who could assist them on a three-week trip to the northern countryside. BB recommended me.

The job paid a stipend of two hundred British pounds—a relative fortune to me then—so of course I agreed to go, although I'd never been away from the kids for that long. Princess, whom we now called "Pudu" (when I wrote to Josephine, I joked that she was like a proud little French poodle) was still nursing. The night before I left, I put a clean sheet on my bed and gathered all my babies to sleep with me. In the morning, I packed the sheet, so I could take their smell along, and I slept wrapped in it every night I was gone.

Away from Pudu, my breasts leaked and ached, but by the time I came home, she turned away from me when I opened my blouse. It had been too long; she was weaned. It was the first time I chose the need to work over being with my kids. Not the last.

The trip was shocking. Humbling. We drove in jeeps down rough rural roads and for all I'd been through, I realized I'd never understood the full horror of the war. In the countryside, civilians had been caught between warring groups, with no safety, and everyone suffered. I saw the ruins of good cement homes, schools, hospitals and clinics. Where survivors were trying to rebuild, they were constructing houses of mud. Bridges had been blown up; we crossed rivers on rough planks or got out and walked. Fields of cassava had gone fallow. At first, villages often seemed empty; the memory of fighting was so fresh that everyone hid if they heard a car, because they didn't know who was coming and what the strangers would bring. The poverty was unspeakable—stunted, silent children; women dressed in rags.

In one region, where it was custom for girls to quit their education in sixth grade to marry, I met a slender, fatherless fourteen-year-old who was the laughingstock of her village because she was still in school. Once she understood that I was an educated woman, she began to shadow me. She was at my side the whole time I was there, watching me write, reading with me, even sleeping in my hut. The night before I left, her mother came to me.

"Take her."

"What?" I had seen the two of them together. Their love for each other was palpable.

"Take her with you! There's nothing for her here!" The woman's voice was filled with anguish. "I don't want her to be like the other girls, doing nothing but having babies. She should have more."

I knew what she was asking, but I had four children, no home of my own, no income. It was impossible. I avoided the mother's eyes. "I'll see when I get back to Monrovia. I'll let you know."

When I said goodbye, the girl's cry was a howl that tore through me. I never saw her again.

CHAPTER 8

TAKING ON "TAYLOR'S BOYS"

W HEN YOU'RE DEPRESSED, you get trapped inside yourself and lose the energy to take the actions that might make you feel better. You hate yourself for that. You see the suffering of others but feel incapable of helping them, and that makes you hate yourself, too. The hate makes you sadder, the sadness makes you more helpless, the helplessness fills you with more self-hate. Working at the THRP broke that cycle for me. I wasn't sitting home thinking endlessly about what a failure I was; I was doing something, something that actually helped people. The more I did, the more I could do, the more I wanted to do, the more I saw needed to be done. I couldn't get that young girl's wail out of my mind. Even though my volunteer agreement had been for only two days a week, I started going to the office daily, and looking forward to it.

In many ways, it wasn't what I'd imagined a working life would be. Monrovia was still so unstable you never knew what the day would bring. Pouring rain might make the roads impassable and no one would show up. We had to make do with nearly nothing—only one computer, no pencils or paper clips (but lots of mice). Power came from a generator that only sometimes worked; when it died, the computer went down and we did our best in the dark. There was no phone, of course. If you needed to see people, you walked through city streets still filled with trash and sewage to meet them, hoping someone would be there when you arrived.

We didn't even greet each other with "Good morning" but asked "How was the night?" If the answer was "Praise God," it meant "All right, considering." *Praise God: no one shot me or looted my house. We had something to eat.* "We're trying" meant "Not so good"—sickness, an empty wallet, a ravenous, wailing infant. There were only two others in the office who were raising young kids, both of them young men who did the cleaning, and sometimes they couldn't even afford to buy their babies milk. I often brought them something from home.

I worked at learning all I could, and more and more the THRP staff became like a family. Vaiba, the Loma secretary, whom I'd seen as serious and aloof, got picked up by an office driver each day, and soon began stopping for me. She came to know and love my kids and even invited Amber to spend weekends with her. Vaiba was traditional, secretive, strong. She'd grown up one of many children in a very poor family and had had to put aside her own dreams of education to help support the little ones. She did for others, not for herself, and openly yearned to do the same work I was now doing. "Tell me what you said," she'd demand fiercely whenever I ran a workshop. "Tell me what you learned! Teach me what to do."

Jill, the white social worker, was warm and motherly. We began sitting together at lunch and Sunday services, and in response to her gentle questions, I found myself telling her stories about Daniel, Ghana, even what I remembered of the war's early days—memories I usually tried hard to push away.

Our time together didn't last long. In September, just as I started classes at Mother Patern, President Taylor accused the former rebel commander Roosevelt Johnson of planning to oust him, and his troops moved in for an arrest. Johnson took refuge in the US embassy and a battle broke out. For a few terrible days, until Johnson was smuggled out of the country, it looked as if full-scale war was erupting again. All American citizens were evacuated, including Jill. I cried when she left.

"The mountains shall depart, and the hills be removed, but my kindness shall not depart from thee," God promised in Isaiah 54. A few weeks after my friend went home, I got a letter from Chicago. Jill had told some

women she knew about me, and they wanted to help me out. In the envelope was the money I needed for school fees. Jill's other gift to me was emotional. Our long conversations had been like a form of therapy. I hadn't let out all the poison in me—that wouldn't happen for some years—but it was enough that I felt a new ease, as if I'd been holding my breath for an impossibly long time and finally had dared to exhale.

When school started, my days fell into an exhausting pattern: I passed the morning working at the Trauma Healing offices, took the bus to school to attend classes from three in the afternoon to six or seven, then Tunde would pick me up and drive me back to Paynesville. Nuku wasn't yet six, Amber four and a half, Arthur two and Pudu only seven months old. My mother watched them during the day, but the nights were mine. My parents couldn't afford a generator, so while the kids slept in the room we all shared, I did my homework by lantern or candle.

The doctors had told me that because he was so premature, Arthur would never be normal. *He probably will never be strong enough to sit up.* He sat up. *He'll never be able to walk.* He walked. But he constantly suffered from fevers, malaria, outbreaks of rashes all over his body. Once, he and Nuku both came down with measles, even though they'd been vaccinated. Arthur got really sick. We had to take him to a clinic, and they said he needed a blood transfusion. Because my mother had worked in the government hospital, she had contacts and was able to get him blood. But we didn't think to ask if it had been tested for HIV. For the next nine years, I thought about that blood every time he got sick, until I finally had the money and the guts to get a test, which came back negative.

When I remember those three years of school, I see myself bent over a paper in the dark, then jerking to attention at the sound of a child's moan. Which one is it this time? There's vomit on the floor, diarrhea soaking through a diaper and running down the side of the bed. I get up, change the diaper, change the sheet, clean the floor, give medicine, rock whoever's sick back to sleep and get back to work. The alarm rang at five and often I didn't think I was going to be able to get out of bed.

But I loved learning, loved stretching my mind the way I had in those few weeks at the university before the war. When I got good grades, when Tunde read and edited my papers and told me how good they were, my confidence grew. My education continued at work—BB had decided to make me his improvement project.

BB looked like a simple, unassuming man. I don't remember seeing him twice in a suit and tie. But he held a degree from the university, where he had studied liberation theology and was a student activist. He loved to talk politics and he was radical to the core. Our mission at the THRP, he said, went far beyond the work we did on behalf of the office. "Every one of us in this country was victimized one way or another, and every one of us has to heal," he said urgently. "You tell your own story. Now you've survived, you've overcome your victimization. Then you need to help somebody else—and not just a person, you help the society!"

Why did he pick me? I had passion, enthusiasm—and I liked to talk as much as he did. BB had also rebelled against his own very traditional upbringing when it came to women. "Most African women never have the opportunity to work with a man who's open to whatever they want to do," he said. He was going to give that chance to me.

But first I had to become "academically fit." BB read my school papers and sought me out at lunchtime when I stayed in because I didn't have the money for street food. "Read this!" he'd command, tossing a newspaper story on my desk. "Tell me what you think!" When I'd venture an opinion, he'd scoff—"That's naive!"—then explain. Yes, the war was evil, but *why* had it started, Leymah? Liberia was a disaster, but *how* had we gotten to this state? Look at our history! Look at the centuries-long oppression of the indigenous by the elites! "Think who has power and how they're using it," BB urged. "Think, Leymah!"

At BB's prompting, I read books on social transformation. "You need to know about economics as well as politics," he said. "If you're going into the field, you must be armed with ideas." I read *The Politics of Jesus*, which talked of Christ as a revolutionary, fighting injustice and giving a voice to the powerless. I read Martin Luther King Jr. and Gandhi and the Kenyan author and conflict and reconciliation expert Hizkias Assefa, who believed that reconciliation between victim and perpetrator was the only way to really resolve conflict, especially civil conflict, in the modern world. Otherwise, Assefa wrote, both remained bound together forever, one waiting for apology or revenge, the other fearing retribution.

No teacher had ever challenged me so hard, and my brain was lighting up with the electricity that is a young person first glimpsing the true complexity of the world. I was nearly twenty-seven and old beyond my years when it came to knowing about death, but intellectually a child. The more I recognized my own ignorance, the hungrier I was to learn.

I made more trips into the countryside, this time to the southeast, where I saw farmers who no longer grew coconuts and fisher folk who couldn't sell what they caught because markets had collapsed during the war. I met families that had hidden in the forests during the endless fighting, trying to survive on wild roots, and whose children had the dead eyes and swollen bellies of kwashiorkor. I heard wartime memories, and I helped plan strategies for the future with community leaders and heads of youth organizations. Then BB told me I that while my trips into the countryside would continue periodically, I also would be overseeing a new category of trauma healing clients in Monrovia: disabled former child soldiers.

"Leymah!" BB announced as if addressing a large audience, "We are going to bring them back into society as responsible citizens of the Republic . . . of . . . Liberia!"

"WHY YOU COME HERE? You a spy?" Hostile eyes stared at me from a dark office in the National Veterans Assistance Program building just off Tubman Boulevard. The boy was no more than a teenager, but his voice was heavy with threat. There were about ten more young men like him in the room. They were a frightening-looking group, scarred, dressed in ragged, filthy clothes—for years, they'd looted whatever they wanted and never learned to maintain what they had—with an air of menace. Anyone with sense who saw these boys on the street would immediately know to cross it to avoid them. Some were missing arms, some legs.

"A white man brought his ass here, took our story and made a lot of money with it," the teenager continued. "He sent us a videotape, not one money. What white people sent *you?*"

"You want to make fools of us? You see pussy on our foreheads?" Another voice. "Fuck you. Fuck all of you! I have the mind to pluck your eyes out."

I wouldn't let them see my fear or disgust. Taylor's boys. It was "Papay" Taylor who first brought children into the Liberian war with his Small Boy Units, although eventually all the rebels used them. Tens of thousands fought, some of them as young as eight, carrying AK-47s they were barely strong enough to lift. They were a nightmare vision of childhood, these soldiers, desperate to please and too young to understand what they were doing, taken away from their families and kept high on alcohol and drugs until they became the most merciless killers of all. I heard all about them in the workshops I led in the countryside, and I never forgot the boy I'd seen covered in blood and washing his knife the day Daniel and I fled Monrovia.

Now I was to help them "reintegrate" and find something productive to do with the years ahead? It wasn't my choice, but we have a saying: "Can't help." I needed this work, so I couldn't help.

I worked with the ex-combatants for more than two years. They had nothing. Taylor had cut them loose when they were wounded and of no more use to him; their parents, if they could find them, didn't want them back. They lived in abandoned buildings and survived by begging. I began running workshops for them, tried to link them to social services that might help with daily needs like obtaining food or medicine, experimented with projects—like planting gardens with harvestable crops—that might suggest a viable postwar future.

Sometimes, there would be five straight days when the boys worked well together and made plans and I had hope we were getting somewhere. Then I'd get hit in the face with something murderous. *"You know how many women we raped? It was one of the best games for us. . . ."* A teenager sits back, watching for my reaction. *"The old ones were the best. They hadn't done it for so long it was like fucking a virgin."*

Or I'd get a call from someone in the office or community—my "sons" had showed up at the home of some government official screaming, "We fought for you and we want our pay!" and throwing stones—and my hopes would crash.

"My wish is that you'd do things that would help society understand what I know, that you're not evil," I'd say in desperation.

And someone would laugh. Speak proudly, "We *are* evil."

One week, some of Taylor's men offered a group of my boys money to attack an enemy. A riot broke out and I got called in. I was furious.

"These are the same people that used you and you're working for them again?" I shouted. "When you don't even have water or light at home? When someone offers you rice and you have to scramble over it like dogs?"

"Fuck you!" one of them shouted. "What do you know? They want to destroy Taylor, so we kill them, and fuck you!" He rushed to my side and raised his fist to strike me. I can't tell you why or how, but I didn't flinch, just looked in his eyes. Coldly. Daring him. He started laughing wildly.

"This woman!" he said. "She doesn't even shake! If she had carried a gun she would have been a killer! This woman is a general!"

The day the boys started calling me "General" was the day they began really talking to me, and I began getting to know them as something more than their frightening poses. The boy who'd bragged about the fun of raping middle-aged women had joined a rebel group at twelve because he thought it would make him a man. Now he was an amputee, and his mother had turned her back on him, saying she never gave birth to a one-leg child.

You could tell that Christian Johnson had been very tall, but he had lost both his legs. Sam Brown had been eight or nine when his family fled their village during the war; his mother had so many children she didn't notice that she'd left him behind. The fighters who moved in used him to fetch water, and when he was ten, he joined a Small Boys Unit. One day, he fell into an ambush and was shot in the arm. Infection set in, and the arm had to come off. Now he was fifteen and an alcoholic.

"Sam, that stuff's going to kill you," I'd chide him when he'd show up in the morning already drunk.

"I got one hand," he'd answer. "Tell me, Sis Leymah, what I got to live for."

Joseph Colley had only one leg. He knew where to find his mother but refused to go back to his village unless he could support himself. He dreamed of being a shoemaker but spent his days high on cocaine and marijuana. "I can't stop," he told me. "When I do, I remember things."

My work with the boys often stretched beyond office hours. One night, when I was going to dinner with Tunde, I heard a plaintive, "Sis Leymah!" and there was Joseph, looking destitute and wanting to talk. I sat on the sidewalk with him and the next thing I knew, an hour had passed and Tunde was coming out of the restaurant, very upset. I never let the boys come to my home, but I went to theirs. I met their girlfriends and wives. They were just as violent. One girl, Cleo, was heavily pregnant, but she would throw punches and kicks at her husband, and the words from her mouth were filthier than his. "You have to be like them," she told me.

Cleo had been a fighter, too—I hadn't realized until then that there had been female fighters among the rebels. Some of the girls who picked up guns did so because it was a way to protect themselves from rape. A number of the ex-combatants' girlfriends and wives had been abducted as young girls. Raped repeatedly. Violence was the only language they knew. And yet . . . at times they talked to their children with love the way I talked to mine. Like me, they hoped their kids would lead better lives. I could see my younger self in them—the broken dreams, the rage.

Did I help them? In the moment, yes. I got their babies food and diapers. When they got sick, I took them to the doctor. But I couldn't change who they were or even find the small amounts of money that might have helped them turn their lives around. About six hundred US dollars would have set Joseph up in a shoemaking business, but there was no one willing to fund that kind of effort.

I couldn't forgive the ex-combatants for all the evil they'd done. But I did come to feel pity and compassion for them, even though I wasn't always comfortable with those feelings. Everyone in Liberia hated these boys. In Monrovia, people spat at them when they begged. "Go ask Charles Taylor for money! Get your legs back and work for it!" When I admitted I was helping them, I heard, "Why? There's plenty children those boys killed their parents. Why don't you help them?"

There were times I wondered if I was crazy. But these young people didn't know why they'd raped, looted and killed—or even remember much of it, they'd been so high. They'd been exploited, used up and thrown away. The war had destroyed their childhoods the way it had destroyed mine. The ones I thought deserved our anger were men like Charles Taylor, Prince Johnson, Roosevelt Johnson and Alhaji Kromah, who'd started the war and perpetuated it, letting their selfish ambitions for power ruin the lives of an entire generation.

CHAPTER 9

A NEW HOME WITH GENEVA

IN MAY OF 1999, when I'd been at the Trauma Healing project for a year, BB rewarded my good work by putting me on a salary of one hundred US dollars a month, the first steady income I'd ever had. I used the money to rent a cheap two-bedroom apartment in Monrovia. My parents were furious that I was leaving Paynesville and told me I'd never take proper care of my kids. When I left, we weren't speaking.

The new place was supposed to be for the kids and me—it was always our arrangement that Tunde would keep his own place—but by the time we moved in, there were eight of us. One of the additions was my cousin Baby, daughter of the aunt and uncle Daniel and I had lived with on Old Road. My uncle drank and my aunt was constantly belittling Baby; she came to visit one weekend and never went home again. The others were my sister Geneva and her six-year-old daughter, Leemu.

After we said goodbye at the Monrovia docks during the terrible fighting of 1996, Geneva had spent two years in Nigeria waiting for her fiancé to finish his schooling in the US, so that she and Leemu could join him. Then she got a letter telling her not to come—he had married another woman. Heartbroken, she came home, first to stay with Ma, then with me. The rejection had crushed something in my timid sister. She went back to working in the records department at JFK Medical Center, though all she really wanted to do was retreat.

I couldn't afford to buy much for that little apartment, and we were so crowded that there were times I'd go to my bed, find it full, and end up sleeping on the floor. Everything my kids wore was secondhand. The lunch they took to school every single day was shortbread, a kind of biscuit, with gravy and Kool-Aid. But I was happy having my own space. And having Mammie, as the kids also called Geneva now, changed everything for us. My parents were wrong about my ability to care for my kids, but I was coming to realize that I needed to be more than a mother.

The work I did for the Trauma Healing program was thrilling to me. The challenges, conflict resolution, transformation, working to build peace—it meant learning something different every day, encountering new people, and talking to them about the issues that mattered to them. My old dream had been to be a pediatrician, and when I was with the child soldiers, I sometimes felt that I *was* a doctor; I was doing my best to heal these children, heal their minds. In the countryside, I did what I could to help the injured and heal the wounds to their souls.

Geneva loved my children. I could see it in her eyes as she cuddled and talked to them. When they were with her, they wanted for nothing. That spring, she and I made an arrangement, two single women forming a family unit and a relationship that in some ways was like a marriage. I would work and support us; she would take on most of the work of child-rearing, giving my kids and her own her boundless maternal love. Mammie had watched over me when I was young; now, Aunty Mammie would do the same for my children.

All of us depended on my sister for the next seven years. Tunde gave her the nickname "Manager." Without her, nothing else I did would have been possible.

WORK, SCHOOL, THE CHILDREN. Some nights, Fata would come in from Paynesville and we'd all gather in the living room for debates or talent "finds" where we'd dance and sing. Sometimes, Geneva ran "intellectual" night. Nuku, always her favorite, paired with Leemu in spelling competitions against Amber and Baby, and always won. If there was enough money, we'd go out afterward for ice cream.

School, the children, Tunde. I called him "Chief." I was a different woman with him than I'd been with Daniel. Sex had changed for me, because it was linked in my mind with violence. I felt cold. But Tunde and I were good, close friends. He read all the news he could; he knew about global issues and the world of NGOs, and in his quiet, gentle way, he always drew me out. I could talk to him endlessly without getting bored or feeling that I was boring him.

He had started working for the UN World Food Programme, and would pick me up at work, bring me home in the evening and we'd sit together, eat and talk. I respected him, and trusted him completely. He always encouraged me. We never fought. But in some ways, we were very different. I had dressed shabbily for years, but as I grew more confident, I also rediscovered that I was a pretty woman. When I went out, men paid attention, and no one could believe I was old enough to be the mother of four. Tunde paid no attention to how he dressed, and so I would shop for him, buy him cologne and clothes that would make him look even more handsome. Even on the weekends, he never drank or smoked and liked most to stay home and read. I craved going out, especially after a hard week.

Sometimes, I met a few of the boys who were in my social work classes for beer on Friday nights. One glass, two. My head was filled with images: Joseph Colley's sad eyes, Sam Brown dropping a dirty, crying infant on my desk. "I can't feed him, Sis Leymah. *You* take him!" Alcohol made everything easier to bear.

School, Tunde, church. My parents had been upset that I had so many children, but they loved the children and hated it when I moved them away. Eventually, they came to Monrovia to see us. "For the sake of these babies, we'll keep coming, because you people have no sense of responsibility!" my mother said, openly touching Pudu to see if she had lost weight. I didn't have time to get annoyed anymore. The kids began going back to Paynesville for weekend visits, and gradually my parents and I put away our quarrel.

In the spring of 1999, my mother complained that no one had been willing to chair the committee planning that year's Women's Day celebration. I still hadn't ventured forth publicly at St. Peter's, but with the help of Vaiba and three new friends, I took on the challenge. We raised thousands of US dollars. Afterward, I was elected president of the women's association. Every Saturday, there were meetings, fundraisers to plan. We had a lot of fun.

Tunde, church, Trauma Healing. One day, Sam Doe (no relation to the late president) came to our offices. He was a slender and intense young man with a close-cropped beard and wire-rimmed glasses, and a genuine local hero. Well educated, trained in economics and finance, Doe had changed his life after meeting a seven-year-old boy dying of starvation in the early days of the war. He'd founded the West Africa Network for Peacebuilding, or WANEP, whose mission was to promote peace by building links between grassroots organizations across national borders. WANEP, based in Ghana, emphasized using nonviolent strategies and encouraged women to join the effort to address problems of violence, war and human rights abuses.

That day, BB had given me a document to work on and when I went to ask him a question about it, Sam was with him. BB brushed me aside. "I'm busy! I'm talking to someone important!"

I snapped. "How do you expect me to do something when you won't even talk to me about it?" My tone was not polite.

"This is *Sam Doe*," BB said, gesturing.

"Hi," I said coldly and stomped away.

"That's why I like you!" BB called out. "You're a militant!"

My parents, Ma, family. One day at the Lutheran compound, I saw my father sitting with a nine-year-old boy who looked a lot like Nuku. He was crying. "Who is that?" I asked.

My father looked at me angrily. "He is your brother," he said flatly. "He came to me for money. I told him to go to his useless mother."

My brother. Out of nowhere, a memory surfaced. I was in twelfth grade, and my dad was taking me to school. We passed an elementary school and I saw a little boy at the fence waving at him. Just because my father had never brought home children conceived outside his marriage didn't mean they didn't exist. I learned now that there were five of them, by three different women. Was I shocked? Not that the kids existed, because it just wasn't that unusual for Liberian fathers to have other children, but I was amazed that he'd been so slick in hiding them.

I didn't judge him. Maybe because of the mistakes I've made, I don't feel the right to be critical of other people's decisions. But I felt disappointed that my dad wasn't providing for his children, and especially bad for this little boy, Diamond. He wasn't even living with his mother; she'd sent him to stay with a friend. He'd been given away by both his parents; no one had cared enough to make him a priority.

Over time, I got to know my father's other children, but I was closest to Diamond. I bought him shoes and clothes and took on his school fees. He began spending more and more time at my home. *"Enlarge the place of thy tent, and let them stretch forth the curtains of thine habitations,"* God said in Isaiah 54. Within two years, Diamond was living with me.

"Who are all these children?" an aunt asked my mother after the first time I invited all my half-siblings to meet my sisters.

I don't know what private conversation passed between my parents on this subject. My mother had such a hard life: difficult childhood, difficult teen years, marriage to someone she loved who chose to share his affection with others. But she also made it hard to get close to her. Because I was the one who exposed my father's secret, she was furious with me. "Sometimes the poison that kills you comes out of your own stomach," she told my aunt.

My apartment, home life, the office. I still remembered eating my sister-in-law's leftover yams in Ghana. My cabinets were always as full of food as I could afford to make them. I always had some cash in my pocket and I never turned down a job that paid. The day Amber graduated from kindergarten, I had a workshop scheduled. I didn't even think of trying to cancel it. I dropped her off at school, went to work, rushed back for the ceremony, then let my parents take her home. Later, we had a celebration and my triumph was being able to pay for it—not spending the time with my daughter.

Trauma Healing, the countryside. Sometimes, a group of us went into a village on Friday and stayed the weekend. Sometimes we were there a week. I was the trainer in charge of logistics—finding elders or chiefs or whoever fit our target criteria—and hiring local women to prepare food for us. As St. Peter's head of security, my father came along, though he often used the opportunity to make a temporary new female "friend." I avoided him.

I led the groups, and it was only over time that I started wondering why I was the only woman on our team and why the "leaders" who took our training sessions were all men. Often, once the workshop was done, I'd find myself in the kitchen area, sitting with the local women who were working for us. Mostly we'd just talk, laugh and joke. But questions would come up that made me think. Why were we sitting here, on the sidelines? And why, when I came to town to work on a project, was my boss asked about me, "Is that your cook?" Why were women, who bore the brunt of war, expected to remain quiet while men debated how to make peace?

On one trip, to a village in central Liberia, I met another little girl, this one maybe ten. She was as fair as I was, with red hair. A village child—mother dead in childbirth, no father, cared for by the community but never cherished. She didn't go to school, she walked through town barefoot, and her nickname was "Pig," because she was so dirty. She talked to me with the voice of an old woman. "Leymah, I wish I could have learned to write like you. Leymah, I wish I could read." I bought her trousers and a dress, gave her a bath and braided her hair.

"Take me with you!" she begged, but again I didn't trust in God to provide and left her behind. She was someone else I never could forget, because I also let her down. If I'd had more faith, I would have said yes to both those girls. Maybe they would still be with me. They might have done great things.

CHAPTER 10

HELPING WOMEN
FIND THEIR VOICES

In late 1999, WANEP was actively seeking to involve women in its work and I was invited to a conference in Ghana. My arrival in Accra was an emotional experience. I'd come to this city twice before, both times by sea, sick and poor. Now a jet brought me, and I took a car to a nice hotel. When I walked into the lobby, it all felt unreal. Was I really here? Was it really me?

I was one of the few individuals at the conference who didn't have a title or advanced academic degree, and in the beginning, I felt as I had when I began at the Trauma Healing office: I sat and listened, and except for introducing myself, didn't say a word. We were being trained to use a conflict prevention tool called "early warners." It was a way of teaching activists how to draw on local people's observations of odd events or behaviors to spot a problem brewing, then come up with strategies to defuse it. For example, the market women might notice the unusual presence of many men, strange men, on market day, a sign that fighters had come to town and a battle was about to erupt.

As I heard people talk, I began to see how much of the important work of peace-building was planning and strategizing. I wanted someone to help me understand not only *which* strategies might be used but *why*—the theory supporting that choice. I used most of the money my office had given me for per diem expenses to buy every pamphlet and book available. The complexity of the discussion was frightening—but also enormously compelling. Most of my work for the Trauma Healing project had focused on mending broken lives and communities, but wouldn't it make more sense to prevent the breaking in the first place? The more I learned about this work, the more convinced I became that it was something I wanted to do.

I could hardly wait to get home to tell Tunde and Geneva. But there was something else I realized I needed to do in Ghana. Hizkias Assefa wrote that there are four dimensions required for true reconciliation: you must be reconciled with God, with yourself, with your environment and finally with the person who offended you. I used his concept when I ran Trauma Healing workshops, illustrating the principle in my own way.

"You are in the Valley of Misery," I'd say, "a place of anger, depression and hurt. The person who hurt you—who raped you or killed your family—is also here. If you are still angry at that person, if you haven't been able to forgive, you are chained to him." Everyone could feel the emotional truth of that: When someone offends you and you haven't let go, every time you see him, you grow breathless or your heart skips a beat. If the trauma was really severe, you dream of revenge. "Above you is the Mountain of Peace and Prosperity, where we all want to go," I'd continue. "But when you try to climb that hill, the person you haven't forgiven weighs you down. It's a personal choice whether or not to let go. Nobody can tell you how long to mourn a death or rage over a rape. But you can't move forward until you break that chain."

It was true for me as well. The piece of my past that was holding me back was Daniel. I still had these thoughts: *I will go to school and become a great success. He will see!* The chain was still there. I left the hotel and took a taxi to Old Ma's house in Nangua. No one was home and no one in the neighborhood recognized me, except a few children playing in the dusty street. I looked around at the rundown houses with a kind of appreciation. I wouldn't be where I was now if I hadn't told myself I would never live that life again. One of Daniel's brothers-in-law was a pastor at a nearby church, and I found Daniel with him. He was shocked to see me.

"How are the kids? I heard from my sister that you had another baby. Was it mine?"

"Hell, no," I said.

"My sister said you sent a picture and the girl looks so much like our family . . ."

"No," I repeated. "She looks like Josephine." The conversation shifted then, to something meaningless. After a few minutes I was out of patience, and then I just felt very sad. "Do you know why I came here today?"

He shook his head.

"I came to let you go."

"Hmm," he answered. "I thought you let me go years ago."

"Not in my heart," I said. "I still carried a lot of anger, so I've come to say that I forgive you. I forgive you. I'm moving on."

There was a silence, then, "Thank you."

WHEN THE LEASE on my tiny apartment was up, my parents once again offered me the Old Road house for my extended family. My dad never apologized for any of the things he'd said. But Mama, who'd given me so much bitterness, kept cheering me on.

"Keep going. Keep going. God is going to help you."

And so the eight of us went home again.

Liberia wasn't in the midst of war, but what we had wasn't peace, either. The international community had accused Charles Taylor of actively supporting the RUF rebel leader Foday Sankoh in Sierra Leone, by trading Sankoh Liberian weapons in return for diamonds. We were pariahs, and we had no functioning economy, no jobs, no repair of all that had been destroyed, no support for families left destitute. In Lofa County, an anti-Taylor opposition group formed, calling itself Liberians United for Reconciliation and Democracy (LURD). In late 1999, fighting began to break out. LURD attacked Taylor-controlled towns and villages; government forces hit back.

No one could hold territory for long. Once again, civilians were caught in the middle, and Lofa became the country's largest refugee zone.

Since becoming president, Taylor had filled the ranks of the Liberia National Police and armed forces with many of his former fighters. As we continued Trauma Healing in the countryside, we heard more voices of protest and despair: "How can our minds be healed when we don't have jobs?" "How can we think about moving on when we can't even provide for our families?" And, "You're wasting your time here! The boys who victimized us during the war are now in the army! In the police force! You'd better keep coming back to heal us, because when you leave they just move in and do it to us all over again."

The THRP took on a new effort: running workshops for the country's security personnel—members of the police force, and immigration and customs officials. The hope was that we could help them reenvision their roles as protectors, not exploiters, of the community. I began traveling more and more, to every county in the nation. Sometimes it was a guilty relief to leave behind the houseful of needy young children. But other times, I grieved, looking at the disappointment on the kids' faces after I'd gone, returned, stayed two days and had to tell them I was off again. Nuku and Geneva were so close that people sometimes thought he was her son. Once, I came home and learned that everyone had been entertaining Pudu by singing her a silly song. When I tried, she pouted: I had the words all wrong.

"Mammie, I feel bad," I told Geneva.

"Leymah, what choice do you have? We're all relying on you."

There was no choice. If I didn't want my kids living in poverty, if I didn't want to rely on my parents or Tunde, there was no choice.

When the Trauma Healing staff ran workshops for the security forces, some of the participants were women. But we noticed that few of them spoke up when men were in the room. One day, we decided to run a session in Monrovia for women only. I was one of the facilitators. I started by following our standard agenda: get people to talk briefly about their personal issues, then move along to the theoretical discussion of how to defuse conflict, how it was important to forgive an offender, cut the destructive tie and move on.

"You don't think you're stuck?" I might ask villagers. "Look at your community. The grass hasn't been cut. You live in filth. Your children are miserable." After the workshop, some participants would come to tell me they had let go and taken action to cut grass or clean their homes. They felt better. I had the satisfaction of knowing that the drive to heal and to improve had been born in our conversation.

And yet there was a way in which the Trauma Healing program felt frustratingly incomplete. Sometimes workshop participants would cry as they told their stories and would want to keep talking. They'd insist, "I have something important to say," but there was no time allotted for this kind of sharing, so I had to cut them off.

This day, as I worked with the security women, the regular agenda wasn't working at all: the women kept interrupting, insisting on telling personal stories. I realized that it would be impossible to continue without first addressing what the women wanted and needed to say. I ended the session. "Let's meet here tonight when everyone has free time. We'll talk."

That evening, about forty women returned, and we arranged our chairs in a circle. The generator kept cutting out, so we decided to turn it off. Then we began. As each woman took her turn talking, she would hold a candle so everyone else could see her face. I expected to hear about the war. But as would happen again and again in the future, the stories the women needed to share that night started long before the fighting did. The first to speak told us about her husband, whose unending demand for sex had burdened her with too many children. The head of port security confessed that she'd never believed she had any value as a person. A mother of four talked about an abusive marriage that she'd entered in her teens. Each speaker wept with relief when she finished; each spoke the same words: "This is the first time I have ever told this story." The women talked for five straight hours, until 3 A.M.

When I did my Trauma Healing work, I never fell right asleep afterward, but would lie awake and think about how things had gone. That night, my brain was lighting up. I knew something extraordinary had happened. When I returned to the office the next day and told BB, he agreed that I had learned something important. From then on, each time I did trauma healing, whether for security women or for a group of pastors' wives, I set aside time and a private space for the women at night. It always had the same result.

"Let's talk about some of the things we've gone through," I'd say. I'd talk about Koffa, and about George, a neighbor who had lived across Old Road and who was killed because he was a Kpelle misidentified as a Krahn. I was learning to articulate all that I carried in my head and heart in a way that made an impact on listeners. I was learning to draw out those who needed to speak, but couldn't.

"I went to a place in Liberia where women watched their babies starve," I might say. "Many of them were raped. But I'm sure no one in this room had those kinds of experiences."

A strangled cry. "What? But I did. . . ."

"Okay, then." Gently: "Let's talk about how it was for you."

When I spoke to a group of women, I could control what happened. I became someone else, powerful and sure. Some nights were chilling; some were nothing but tears. I heard from women whose own conception had been the result of family rape. I heard about the death of children. And always, about the war.

"The soldiers came into the displaced persons camp. They said, 'Give us all the money you have!' I did. I gave them everything. Then they said, 'Take off your clothes!' I did what they told me. They all had sex with me. All but one. He was the last one and he said his penis was too good for me. And so instead, he used his knife."

Does it sound like a small thing that the women I met were able to talk openly? It was not small; it was groundbreaking. In Africa, few mothers talked even to their daughters about sex. Many women who were raped never told their family members; the stigma would make everyone look at them differently. Everyone was alone with her pain.

I thought about my own mother, who had seen a man killed because she gave him a bit of rice, who had been beaten by government soldiers, and fled with children on a boat whose destination she didn't even know. Who still carried the childhood secret she said she would never reveal. I didn't think she'd ever talked to anyone about any of it. There wasn't time; life had to go on and people were depending on her. *Women are the sponges,* I thought. We take it all in—the trauma of separated families, the death of loved ones. We listen to what our husbands and children tell us, we look at the destruction of our communities and belief systems, and soak up that pain, too. We hold it all because we need to be strong, and complaining—or even sharing—is a sign of weakness. But holding in that kind of misery was as crippling as holding on to rage. I had found a way for us to squeeze it out.

IN OCTOBER 2000, I went to another WANEP conference in Ghana, where we focused on nonviolence. One night, we watched the film *Gandhi*. There was something stirring about watching this great peace-maker's story in the presence of so many men and women who were also dedicating their lives to battling evil and injustice.

"There may be tyrants and murderers, and for a time, they may seem invincible," Gandhi said. "But in the end, they always fail. Think of it: always."

I'd had my doubts about nonviolence as a strategy, for I'd seen first-hand the power of guns. But increasingly, I was convinced he was right, for clearly the legacies of leaders who resorted to brute force were as brief as their reigns. Only decades after they rose to power, the world vil-ified Hitler and Stalin. In ten years, who would look up to Charles Tay-lor? *But we would always look up to Gandhi*, I thought. *We would always look up to Nelson Mandela, the Dalai Lama, Rosa Parks. Those were the kind of leaders Liberia needed now—people who advocated peace, but with vision and strength. The UN and ECOMOG peacekeepers could provide only temporary help. Above all, they wanted to get back to their own homes alive. We needed to help ourselves.*

Who was the Liberian Gandhi? BB, who could see in an instant who really wanted to help society and who was in it for the money or glory? Sam Doe, so passionate and intelligent? Tornolah Varpilah, who served on WANEP's board? These men were humble but fearless, committed and eloquent. They spoke truth to power. I wanted them save my country.

I wanted to be like them.

During the conference, a beautiful girl caught my attention. We were both in our late twenties, but she looked much more sophisticated, in a Western business suit and with her hair pulled back in tight ponytail. Thelma Ekiyor was from Nigeria; she was well educated, a lawyer who specialized in alternative dispute resolution, and she'd already published papers on the subject. Thelma was clearly a woman in charge of her own life. In discussions, she always knew the right thing to say. When a group of us went to the hotel bar for drinks, she stayed seated and asked Sam Doe to get hers—which he did. But we never spoke, and she didn't even seem to notice me. I decided she was a total snob.

Then, on the last evening, Sam herded a group of us into a car to go to a local nightclub. Thelma refused to go inside; as I later learned, that's not the kind of thing she enjoys. I was feeling shy and didn't want to go in, either, so I put on a baseball cap, which took care of things; the club refused to admit me. We were left sitting together in the car. Time passed; if she hadn't spoken first, we might have just sat there in silence until Sam and the others returned. I might have been the "militant" who had no trouble talking back to BB—in front of Sam, no less—but I always felt a lot more confidence with men than I did with women. I knew men found me beautiful and that when we talked, they weren't judging my brains.

But Thelma did speak. "Hi. Tell me about your work?" And for the next three hours, we never stopped talking. We have never stopped.

In many ways, we are opposites, Thelma and I. During the years I was with Daniel and having babies, she went to law school in England and held a fellowship at Stanford. Thelma's as quiet as I'm loud, and as studious and focused as I'm jumpy. She didn't marry and has no children. But we shared a passion for working with women. In the early 1990s, Thelma went to work in the Niger Delta, where ethnic minorities felt they were being exploited by foreign oil companies, and she saw the suffering of women there—saw that women's voices were not being heard.

Ten years after that first evening we talked, Thelma isn't just my friend; she's my sister, my twin, my shadow self, and someone who understands the political side of me in a way no one else does. I can tell her anything without feeling shy, and I know she will never judge me. We joke that we'll always be honest with each other: "If you kill someone, just tell me; I'll help you bury him and lie about it." Thelma pushes me intellectually—"You're using only 50 percent of what you have!" she scolded early on—and was among the first to see abilities in me that I hadn't yet learned how to tap into and use. We have our fights, but the love between us is something God himself ordained.

That night in Accra we talked about my challenges doing trauma healing in the Liberian countryside, particularly how no one took village women seriously, and how people treated me as my male colleagues' helper.

Thelma told me her secret. "I have this idea of starting a peace-building network like WANEP, but for women." It was an audacious, perfectly timed idea. Internationally, there was a growing recognition that women were being left out of peace and negotiating processes. In October 2000, the UN Security Council had passed Resolution 1325, which noted that "civilians, particularly women and children, account for the vast majority of those affected by armed conflict," and acknowledged the need to protect females from gender-based violence and "increase their role in decision-making with regard to conflict prevention and resolution." But the resolution's passage didn't mean that anything substantial had happened.

"Wow," I said. "I want to learn more about that."

Thelma told me she was going to take her idea to the WANEP board in hopes of getting funding. She promised to keep in touch.

I went home, my brain spinning. *Thelma was a thinker, a visionary, like BB and Sam. But she was a woman, like me.*

CHAPTER 11

THE WOMEN IN PEACE-BUILDING
NETWORK IS BORN!

THE SUMMER OF 2001, I graduated from Mother Patern with my associate of arts degree. There was a big ceremony; I bought Arthur and Nuku black suits, and after they dressed that morning, they announced to everyone of the Old Road community, "Mom graduates today!" There was a hill on the college grounds, and all the graduates were to march down it before heading together into the auditorium to get diplomas. Pudu, who was too young, stayed behind with Mammie, but I had Baby position all the others right beneath our path where we could see each other. Until today, the image etched on my memory is coming down that hill and seeing Arthur and Nuku in their suits and Amber in a red and white dress, waving to me, huge smiles on their faces.

We had a big party at the Old Road house that night, and dozens of people came: my parents, Tunde, Vaiba, church friends, community boys. I was touched to see the whole group of security women who had attended my training. Asatu Ben Keneth had brought them.

I'd noticed Asatu that first night, because she was clearly the Queen Bee—the other security women gathered around her and called her "Preso," for president. (At the time she was chief public information officer for the police force and president of the Liberia National Law Enforcement Association.) Asatu was a few years older than me and a

Muslim; she was assertive and strong, with an air of quiet power. She had a sociology degree and was married, with two children. Despite a slight physical disability in one leg, she'd made it through the police academy, which told me she was also intensely driven. She chose not to share a personal story during our session with the candle but sought me out later when I held a social event for the women.

"You are the sister of Geneva and Mala, aren't you?"

Asatu knew both my sisters from school, before the war. After the workshop, we kept in touch. As I went back into the field, I relied on Asatu to help me find women who worked in security to accompany me. She was intelligent, sweet, easy to talk to. By the time we learned that our mothers, too, knew each other, she and I had become friends.

At the graduation party, when it was time for me to speak, I first turned to my mother. "I thank you for holding my hand when I needed it most and taking care of the kids for me." Then I looked at my father coolly. "I thank *you* for your insults. If you hadn't insulted me the way you did, I might not have made the changes I was supposed to make." He looked embarrassed and I saw tears in his eyes.

Even more than my high school party a lifetime ago, this night made me feel that I had won: I had overcome studying with sick children, reading by candlelight, the stress and tension of having to balance work and school, the fear that I was not good enough to make it. Instead, I graduated cum laude.

Just after I got my degree, the THRP office hired me as a full-time staffer and doubled my salary to two hundred US dollars a month. And I heard from Thelma Ekiyor: WANEP had given her a grant to start her women's network, and I was invited to a launch conference in Accra.

How to describe the excitement of that first meeting of the Women in Peacebuilding Network, or WIPNET? There were women from Sierra Leone, Guinea, Nigeria, Senegal, Burkina Faso, Togo—almost all the sixteen West African nations. In her quietly brilliant way, Thelma had handwritten an organizer's training manual with exercises that would draw women out, engage them, teach them about conflict and conflict resolution, and even help them understand why they should be involved in addressing these issues at all. We began with a session in which everyone was to tell her own story, speaking honestly, woman to woman. It was exactly what I'd been doing in Liberia, and I told Thelma. Later, we joked that we were witches, reading each other's minds even before we met.

The sharing and unburdening, which we Liberian women would come to call "The Shedding of the Weight," began at 7 P.M. and ran until after 2 A.M. Everyone before me introduced herself as having a master of this or being executive director of that, but I no longer felt ashamed of the truth. "I am just plain Leymah, mother of four," I said. "I recently received my associate of arts degree. And I am very interested in women and peace-building." And then, in the receptive silence, I told the full story of how I'd come to this place, including something I'd never told anyone before—about the week I spent on the floor in the hospital corridor with Arthur. The words tumbled out; I couldn't stop. It was late and I talked so long that some of the other women fell asleep, and when they woke up I was still talking. Afterward, I was purged of shame. Like the women in the groups I'd led myself, I felt as if a great wound in me had healed.

The energy in those rooms! Just being in a gathering of so many women was empowering. The fun, the jokes, the happiness. You forgot that you didn't have food at home. We were full of excitement and plans. We needed more women to come on board, and the phrase we used to describe our recruitment was "take aside, deal with it, add and stir." We'd each go home, identify other women who might join us, work with them, and over the next five years blend them into the network.

No one else in Africa was doing this: focusing only on women and only on building peace. No one else was organizing activist women across borders. The potential power of this movement was immense. I remembered the wives and girlfriends of the ex-combatants, whose only way to assert themselves was through violence. And I kept thinking about a story in a Christian magazine that had haunted me ever since I had read it. It was about two groups of women in Sarajevo during the Bosnian war. One was Serb, the other Muslim. They were on different sides of the besieged city, and one had electricity, the other access to water. And the women with water carried buckets to those who had power, so they could use their washing machines to get the laundry done. During this time, they talked and discovered all that they shared: their husbands and sons were going out to fight and not coming back; their families were wounded and broken. They built a form of sisterhood that transcended the power of the guns.

WIPNET brought everything together for me: You can't cure trauma when violence is ongoing, so the primary effort must be working for peace. You can't negotiate a lasting peace without bringing women into the effort, but women can't become peacemakers without releasing the pain that keeps them from feeling their own strength. Emotional release isn't enough in itself to create change, but WIPNET channeled that new energy into political action. This was a way to do it all.

I threw myself into the organizing effort. While the others were sitting and drinking coffee, I'd seek Thelma out and ask, "How can I help you? Can I set up the room? What else can I do?" We spent nights together staying up late, stapling papers. "I really want to do this," I told her before the conference ended. "If there's any opportunity for training, I want you to call me."

Thelma told me later that she fell in love with me because I was honest, I was humble, and I was so willing to work hard. She took it upon herself to train me. From then on, each time she was invited to a conference or did a peace-building training, whether in Ghana, Nigeria, Senegal or Sierra Leone, she asked me to join her. Sometimes, she told me to do the training myself and gave an evaluation of my work afterward. That part was hard to handle—Thelma was my friend, but during those times there was a total transformation in her; it was like she was a forty-year-old teaching a teenager.

"You need focus," she scolded me. "You're all over the place." But Thelma also saw something in me that gave her confidence I could be a leader, and that began to change the way I defined myself: no longer as a social worker, but as a peace-builder. Not long after I got home from that WIPNET conference, I learned she had picked me to coordinate the organization's first chapter in Liberia.

Things moved quickly. First came an education in local politics. It hadn't been my world, but there already was a well-established women's movement in Liberia. The Mano River Union Women's Peace Network

(MARWOPNET) was working for an end to violence in the region where Liberia, Sierra Leone and Guinea come together. As far back as 1994, in Monrovia, the Liberian Women's Initiative (LWI) had led strikes and protests in a campaign to end the war and get women involved in the disarmament process. (My friend Asatu was active in LWI.)

Both groups were committed to focusing the world's attention on how the war was affecting women and children and the need for women to play a role in ending war and crafting peace. They did their work at some risk to their lives and were justifiably proud of it. But most of these groups' members were from educated, elite backgrounds. Charles Taylor, who invited some of them to participate in social events and official dinners, referred to them as "the eminent women of Liberia." They were also a bit insular and protective of their territory.

When Thelma came to Liberia, she chose to announce WIPNET's launch and my selection as coordinator at an LWI gathering at the home of one of its leaders, Etweda "Sugars" Cooper. The news didn't go over well.

"What? No!" The women were stony faced. "Who the hell is this Leymah?" I heard from one corner of the room. "She's never been part of the women's movement! She needs to be checked out and approved. This is a very exciting initiative and it should be run by someone who's already active!"

"I'm sorry, no," Thelma said. "This is who we've chosen, and we are not reversing the decision."

"How did she claim she's qualified? What did she say is her history?"

I stood aside, shaken. Tears were coming. I hadn't lobbied for this position; I wasn't trying to cut anyone out.

Suddenly I felt a hand on my arm. It was Sugars. Sugars wasn't just an LWI activist, she was essentially the godmother of the women's movement. In her fifties when we met and the mother of two sons, she'd been born into an elite family, educated in Switzerland, then turned away from what would have been a life of privilege to fight bravely for peace and women's rights. Sugars had been arrested several times for opposition activities. She was fiercely feminist, the most radical of the LWI women, passionately opposed to cruelty of all kinds and the enemy of anyone who took advantage of the weak. Now she pulled me aside.

"Dry your eyes and stop that shit!" she ordered. I did so, partly in shock. "If those women smell fear on you, they will use you for the rest of your life."

"I really don't know if I can do this," I said. "I've never done anything like it before."

"Don't say that. I know the men you work with, and you wouldn't be with them if you weren't strong." Sugars looked both intent and maternal, fierce eyes beneath a crown of graying braids. The women of LWI remained committed to the cause, but most were over fifty, and Sugars believed it was time for those who were younger, fresh with vibrancy and stamina, to step forward. Her sisters knew that once she took a position, she didn't budge. She had never socialized with Charles Taylor and later, even he would say that he respected her because she never gave in.

"I will support you," Sugars said. "You need advice, you come to me. You need anything, you come to me." She shook my arm. "Now, get back out there and be bold."

WIPNET was an impressive concept, but as an organization, we had very little money. When we finally rented space, all we could afford was an old apartment in a compound belonging to the Christian Health Association of Liberia, where WANEP also had an office. It was behind a gas station just off Tubman Boulevard, four rooms and a conference area, with furnishings donated by other institutions that were part of the WANEP network. My desk had a hole in it.

The position of coordinator didn't pay enough for my family to survive, so I would have to continue working at the THRP and hire an assistant to help me with day-to-day operations. Vaiba suggested Cerue Garlo, who had worked with the Lutheran World Federation and recently lost her job.

In February 2002, Cerue and I went back to Ghana for a new round of meetings. This session was a "training of trainers"; the WIPNET goal was to prepare us to teach others back home, so that as issues of war and peace arose, they could speak out. The hope was that in each West African country, a core of volunteers would bring twenty new women a year into the network; in five years, there would be a hundred and every region would have an activist prepared to come forward.

We used Thelma's training manual, with its exercises that didn't teach women but transformed them. All of us used that manual as we helped built WIPNET, and many, many women, including me, still draw on it years later.

In "Being a Woman" each participant completes the thought "For me, being a woman means . . ." She draws a picture of herself and describes herself to the group. The group always ends up laughing because most women focus only on the parts of themselves they don't like: skinny legs, pop eyes, nappy hair. But with a small hand mirror and piece of candy, you teach self-appreciation.

"Close your eyes and taste the candy. . . . Do you feel its sweetness running down into you? Open your eyes and look in the mirror, and see that look."

By the end of the exercise, every woman has found part of herself to love.

"Crown and Thorns" starts with another question: "As a woman, what is your crown? What are your thorns?" By the end of that powerful session, you see that they're one and the same. My thorns were my inability to care for four children properly, but my crown *was* those children, their love. Once you realize that, you don't look at your life in the same way anymore.

Just as a group sharing of pain let women understand all they had in common with their sisters, these exercises gave ordinary women a glimpse of their own power.

"Who are you as a woman?"

"I'm nobody . . . a mother. A *children-mother*."

"What are the things you do as a mother? Do you work to make money for your children?"

"Yessss . . ."

"Then you are also a provider."

A smile. "Yes. I am a provider."

"Do you work in your church?"

"Yes . . ."

"So you are also a leader. Do you help to solve problems in the church? In your community?"

"Yes, I do."

"Aaah. So you are a peacemaker."

"I am! I am a peacemaker!"

Again, the meeting swept us up in excitement. But the war was never far away. One afternoon, a group of us went out shopping in Accra. A car backfired—*pop-pop-pop!* In seconds, Cerue and I and several girls from Sierra Leone reflexively dropped flat to the ground. The Nigerians stood over us and laughed.

Then Cerue and I got genuinely frightening news. The anti-Taylor opposition forces of LURD were steadily gaining strength and after a shooting not far from Monrovia, President Taylor had declared a state of emergency; any group or individual who protested the order would be punished. The shadow was falling on Liberia again, and I was more than seven hundred miles from my children. I had to get home. Yet even in my panic, I felt my new sisterhood around me. Cerue and I were the only Liberian delegates at the conference and before we disbanded, the other women took up a collection to help us with whatever emergencies we might face.

Everything was tense. In the weeks after Taylor called the state of emergency, one of Monrovia's newspapers closed and its publisher and reporters were arrested and beaten. President Taylor's Special Operations Division and Anti-Terrorist Unit made a series of raids around Monrovia, hitting markets and internally displaced persons camps. Houses were looted; suspected dissidents were beaten or killed. There were reports that young men and boys were being forcibly recruited into the army, and people stopped sending their children to school for fear they'd be picked up and wouldn't return.

I needed to keep working, but if I did, Mammie would be left alone at home with the children. She couldn't run or even walk well; if anything terrible happened, they'd be helpless. I knew that once again, the best option was flight to Ghana. That would mean leaving the Trauma Healing project, walking away from WIPNET.

"I'll quit and we'll go," I told Geneva.

"No," she said. "We won't be able to live if no one is earning money. Besides, I know you—you can't just sit around doing nothing. Stay, at least for a while, and see what happens. I'll take care of the family."

I knew she was right. I asked for ten days off work. And on a Saturday, all of us, including Baby, Diamond, Fata and my mother boarded a bus for the three-day ride to Accra. We arrived at 1 A.M. A Liberian pastor lodged my mother and the kids in his two-bedroom apartment, while Geneva, Fata and I stayed in a cheap hotel. I found a house I could afford to rent—two bedrooms, a kitchen and front porch, within a small, fenced compound in a rough neighborhood. It was fifty US dollars a month, and after the bus tickets and travel expenses, I had almost nothing left for furniture. We bought mattresses, a few chairs, a refrigerator and gas cooker. We moved in on a Friday. Saturday night I slept with my children, and on Sunday I got back on the bus.

Once again, the journey: Accra, Abidjan in Côte d'Ivoire, Monrovia, Old Road. There was really only one thing that mattered about my kids' lives in Ghana: they would be safe. But Nuku had just turned nine, Amber was not quite eight, Arthur was six and Pudu only four, and we were apart and I was alone. I couldn't stand being in the house at night, and drinking was the only thing that made the pain go away. Sometimes it was beer, but increasingly I turned to hard liquor. If Tunde was there, he'd watch over me, help me if I got sick and get me home. If he wasn't, I'd go out with any friend who was around. If there was none, I'd go by myself to the Sports Commission stadium on Broad Street, where I'd gone in high school to watch National Basketball League games, and sit high in the bleachers in very short pants and sunglasses, drinking beer.

One night I sat through three games and when they were done, I was too drunk to stand. "I'm not as young as I used to be!" I gasped, unable to stop laughing and on the verge of tears. The year before, I'd finally gotten a cell phone, and I used it to call Ghana three times a day. Taylor's state of emergency didn't last long, so I was able to visit occasionally, too. But visiting my children wasn't living with them. For months, each time I came home to the house on Old Road and saw my front porch bare of kids clamoring to hug me and welcome me back, I went inside and cried. I never could bring myself to enter their empty bedrooms.

CHAPTER 12

"DON'T EVER STOP"

I traveled to an internally displaced persons camp, where, in a little outside shelter, fifty women gathered to share their experiences during the war. Listening to women unburden themselves of pain was always hard, but this day, there were so many stories of violence and shame and grief, so many sobs and wails, that I reached a point where I didn't think any of us could take it anymore.

"We can just stop," I said. "It's okay."

A very old woman rose up on her walking stick. "Don't let us stop!" she said. "The UN brings us food and shelter and clothes, but what you've brought is much more valuable. You've come to hear the stories from our bellies. Stories that no one else asks us about. Please, don't stop. Don't ever stop."

I CONTINUED WITH MY REGULAR WORK at the Trauma Healing office, but my heart wasn't in it. More and more, our standard agenda struck me as useless. We set up a program in one village simply because it had worked in another, then criticized the villagers for not participating. I listened sympathetically to men and women who had lost their homes and whose children were going hungry, but I couldn't offer them a new place to live or point them toward jobs that might provide money for groceries.

I'd spent two years counseling ex-combatants, but I'd had nothing concrete to give them, either, and several times a month I still saw Joseph Colley, drunk and standing aimlessly at the side of some store.

I threw my real energy into WIPNET. At night, I wrote proposals and worked on ideas for programs and training, using all my experiences to imagine how a women's peace-building network could work in Liberia and how it could be used to address our situation. What kind of training would help us reach the numbers we needed? Who were potential donors? Sometimes, I took my pillow and blanket to the WIPNET offices so I could work until late at night and just fall asleep there. And that spring, in the office, I had a dream.

I didn't know where I was. Everything was dark. I couldn't see a face, but I heard a voice, and it was talking to me—commanding me: "Gather the women to pray for peace!"

Gather the women to pray for peace! I could still hear echoes as I woke up, shaking. It was 5 A.M. What had just happened? What did it mean? It was like hearing the voice of God, yes, but . . . that wasn't possible. I drank too much. I fornicated! I was sleeping with a man who wasn't my husband, who in fact was still legally married to someone else. If God were going to speak to someone in Liberia, it wouldn't be to me!

When I got to the Lutheran compound that morning, I pulled Vaiba aside and shared my dream. She gasped. "We must find BB and tell him," she said. The three of us stood in the small entry room of the Trauma Healing office, and he listened to what I had to say. Sister Esther Musah, a female evangelist from the church, also heard. "We need to pray," she said.

In some ways, that dream, that moment, were the start of everything. We knelt down on the worn brown carpet and closed our eyes. "Dear God, thank you for sending us this vision," said Sister Esther. "Give us your blessing, Lord, and offer us Your protection and guidance in helping us to understand what it means."

My dream became the Christian Women's Peace Initiative. In April 2002, about twenty Lutheran women from local churches gathered to follow the message I'd been sent, praying each Tuesday at noon in the small upstairs chapel of the St. Peter's compound. Sometimes we fasted.

Soon, other church women heard what we were doing and began to join us. *"Jesus, help us. You are the true Prince of Peace, the only one who can grant us peace."*

It was a spiritual effort, intense but quiet, and by June I felt a restlessness set in. As LURD continued to gain strength in the north, Taylor clamped down harder in the city, and life grew unbearable again. There were roadblocks everywhere, trucks full of armed men roaming the streets, more stories of children being seized in broad daylight and forcibly recruited into the army.

Every morning and evening, the president traveled in a convoy with his bodyguards between his home in the affluent Congotown neighborhood and the huge, gaudy Executive Mansion that still stood on Capitol Hill. During that time, all traffic along the length of Tubman Boulevard stopped, and all those walking at the side of the road had to turn their backs or risk being shot as potential assassins.

To the growing numbers of women who gathered every Tuesday, prayers without action didn't feel like enough. A delegation from the World Council of Churches was due to come to Monrovia in July. The women of the Christian Women's Peace Initiative (CWI) decided that when they arrived, we would publicly declare the need to do something more tangible to bring peace.

Around the same time, I formally launched the Liberian chapter of WIPNET. As I look back, it's a little shocking to remember how limited our ambitions were. We dreamed of building a network of women activists working for peace and social justice; no one used a word like "movement." I'd asked local women's organizations to each send a representative to us to receive the kind of training I'd gotten in Accra: women-only sessions on nonviolence and how to use your own experience to understand gender roles; exercises to build self-confidence and teach communication, negotiation and mediation skills. The plan was that the women would then return to their own groups to teach others.

We wanted to reach out as widely as possible, but especially to those whose work was at the grassroots level. I admired what the Liberian Women's Initiative had done, but I thought their exclusiveness had really restricted what they were able to accomplish. Worse, the more established they became, the more insular they got, shutting out new voices. I wanted to avoid that mistake.

Our starting core—WIPNET's first "class"—included my colleague Vaiba, representing the Trauma Healing and Reconciliation Program; Asatu, from the Female Law Enforcement Association; Cerue and Cecelia Danuwali, from WIPNET itself; Janet Johnson, president of the Female Journalists Association; Mariama Brown, who ran the NGO Concerned Christian Community and worked with displaced persons; and thirteen others, including Grace Jarsor, a very poor and struggling young mother who belonged to a Monrovia Lutheran church and craved something more for her life. Grace represented the Christian Women's Peace Initiative. WANEP flew Thelma in from Accra, and she and I ran the training sessions. All of us stayed together at the Corina Hotel on Tubman, a low-slung mustard-colored building where local Peace Corps volunteers had lived until they fled the fighting.

Midway through our week, we went to St. Peter's to lend our support to the women of the CWI during their meeting with the World Council of Churches delegation. As CWI founder, I was scheduled to address the visiting bishops. I already had my own way to prepare for public speaking. I would read, gather information and make notes of what I wanted to say, but then I'd pray for inspiration in the moment: *God, what message do you want the people to hear?* This day, I stood at the front of a full church, men sitting with their hands clasped, women fanning themselves and their babies in the heat. Too many faces were lined with exhaustion and worry, and the words came to me.

"This is a completely terrible life to live," I said. "We are tired!"

"Yes!" women called back.

"We are *tired.* We feel it's now time to rise up and speak. But we don't want to do this alone. We want to invite the other Christian churches to come, and let's put our voices together . . .

"You are asking, 'Who are these women?' I will say, they are ordinary mothers, grandmothers, aunts, sisters. For us, this is just the beginning."

Applause. Cheers. I looked to where the WIPNET members all sat together, and saw Asatu raising her hand. She rose from her seat and came to stand before the congregation.

"Praise the Lord," she said.

"Amen!" several women called out.

"I have a surprise for this congregation," she went on. "I'm the only Muslim in the church."

"Hallelujah!" the women said. "Praise the Lord!"

"I was moved and impressed by the Christian Women's Initiative," Asatu said. "*God is up*. We're all serving the same God. This is not only for the Christian women. I want to promise you all today that I'm going to move it forward with the Muslim women. We will come up with something, too, and we will all work together to bring peace in Liberia."

It was a stunning moment—Asatu's hand reaching across a very old divide. Most of Liberia's Muslims are from the Mandingo tribe (and to a lesser extent, also Vai, Gbandi and Mende). Before the war, before President Doe's obsession with tribal identity split everyone apart, Christians and Muslims mostly got along. We were neighbors, friends; we intermarried, including in my family. But a lot of non-Muslim Liberians viewed the Mandingos as a group apart. Christian and Muslim women had never worked together, and certainly not for anything political. Asatu was proposing an alliance no one had imagined before.

A few days later, when the WIPNET training ended, others in the core group also stepped up to advocate doing more. These twenty-one women met to write their evaluation of the work we'd done and when I came to collect the papers, they stopped me.

"Leymah, we have something to say. The knowledge we gained here was too great for us to be content with only doing more training. We need to take action."

"Make me a proposal," I said.

That day marked the birth of the Peace Outreach Project. Its premise was that across Liberia, women saw negotiating and crafting peace treaties as "men's business." Few women could even say when the last official attempt to stop the war had been made, much less considered the possibility that they might play a role in the process. We would change that.

I was filled with excitement as we worked on the project. I still spent my workdays at the Trauma Healing office, but I was more frustrated than ever, not just with our work but also with the leaders I'd worshipped. It was astonishing how much people had learned to just accept. There was no fighting in the streets, so everyone went about their business pretending everything was okay.

It wasn't okay. Charles Taylor was doing nothing but enriching himself further and protecting his hold on power. Nothing that had been destroyed in the fighting was being rebuilt; we still lived in a city without lights or water. No one could speak out. Taylor had shut down the radio and television stations, except those he controlled. Even music was censored. I remember one singer who released a song that went something like this: "*What kind of life is this . . .*" It became popular, and then Taylor went on the radio to announce that he'd heard it. "You people like a new song. I can assure you that no one will be receiving salaries so you won't have money for batteries to listen to this music!" That Christmas, the finance minister didn't pay salaries to the many who held government jobs. The singer went into exile.

We lived in a closed, guarded box, and the most ordinary acts could bring down terrible punishment; there were evenings I'd come home from a basketball game and see a taxi driver who hadn't lowered his headlights properly at a checkpoint tied up at the side of the road while soldiers beat him with canes. Nobody seemed willing to do anything. At the compound, I would see Sam and BB and Tornolah conferring, and the result was always the same. Lamentations. Slogans. I found myself wanting to shake them. *Enough talking!* I thought.

Now, finally, we women were going to take action.

Three days a week for six months, the women of WIPNET went out to meet with the women of Monrovia; we went to the mosques on Friday at noon after prayers, to the markets on Saturday morning, to two churches every Sunday. We always went in pairs; if we set up a table at the market, we always had a two-woman team. (Sometimes, we temporarily paired women who weren't getting along, so that was their punishment.) We gave all our sisters the same message: Liberian women, awake for peace!

"Hello, sister, I'm Leymah Gbowee from WIPNET and I'd like to tell you about a campaign we've just started. This war has been going on a long, long time and all of us have been suffering. People have tried to end it, and there have been some big meetings, but we think the answer lies with women. We need to step forward and get involved."

"I don't know, my sister. How can we do that? Why would we?"

"Why is this your business? You are the one who has been raped by the fighters! Your husband is the one who has been killed. It is your child being forced into the army."

"Yes . . ." A slow, nodding comprehension. "We've just been sitting here and people take our children! I will join with you."

It wasn't always easy. Women who have suffered for nearly as long as they can remember come to a point where they look down, not ahead. But as we kept working, women began to look up and listen. No one had spoken to them this way before.

We handed out flyers: WE ARE TIRED! WE ARE TIRED OF OUR CHILDREN BEING KILLED! WE ARE TIRED OF BEING RAPED! WOMEN, WAKE UP—YOU HAVE A VOICE IN THE PEACE PROCESS! We knew many of the women we'd reach couldn't read, so we hired a boy to do colorful drawings that explained our mission. One drawing showed an image of a woman standing before a group of fighters and talking to them. Hour after hour, we patiently answered questions, and each week we could feel more of an awakening.

Women hung our flyers on the poles of their market stalls and passed out extras to their customers. The activists went back to their organizations to report on progress, and each time we went out into the community, more women joined the effort.

We worked in a world inhabited by women and we used women's networks to communicate. When the market women bought fruits and vegetables from women in rural areas, they passed along our message, and when they sold their goods in the city, they shared it with the women who were their customers. We worked quietly; no news organizations noticed what we were doing or reported on our efforts, and we liked it that way. We were laying a foundation, though for what, we didn't yet know.

While the outreach campaign ran, the Christian women continued meeting to pray and Asatu continued to organize her Muslim sisters. But bringing the two groups together was turning out to be difficult. The new rebel group, LURD, was predominantly Muslim, and there were muttered comments that Muslims were the ones responsible for prolonging the war. Some of the Christian women felt that praying with Muslims would "dilute" their faith. They pointed to the Bible, 2 Corinthians: *"Do not be bound together with unbelievers; for what partnership have righteousness and lawlessness, or what fellowship has light with darkness?"*

And so we ran a new workshop, and together the Christian and Muslim women did the exercise "Being a Woman."

"Write your titles on this sheet of paper," I told the assembled group when we were together in one room. "Lawyer, doctor, mother, market woman. Put them in this box." I held up a small carton. "See? I am locking them away. We are not lawyers, activists or wives here. We are not Christians or Muslims, we are not Kpelle, Loma, Krahn or Mandingo. We are not indigenous or elite. We are only women."

We did "Crown and Thorns." In large letters I wrote the word NON-SENSE on a chalkboard, then crossed out NON. "Everything we will say in here makes sense. So don't be afraid to talk. Say what is true for you." We did "The Shedding of the Weight." As always, there was no predicting what would emerge. There was one woman who came—we called her "Ma B"—who we'd been warned had a history of stepping out on her husband, especially with young men. As she talked, she began to cry. On her wedding night, she said, her husband had approached her, then lost his erection. It had happened again and again; through their twenty-year marriage, they had never had sex. Everyone in her village condemned her for seeing other men, she said, but no one knew why she did.

This is the first time I have ever told this story. The safety to speak that we created during this exercise resonated, because it had traditional roots. In the Sande, women had a secret space where men were not allowed. Yet using shared personal revelation to organize was completely new, and over time, it became one of the reasons our movement grew strong. Over the years, in "Shedding of the Weight" sessions, I watched two good friends learn of each other's sexual violation and a mother discover that her daughter had been raped by the neighbor who had promised to guard her. I saw an activist confront memories of genital mutilation that had her screaming and digging her legs into the ground. Afterward, we *knew* each other, not just as comrades but as sisters.

We at the core of WIPNET also came up with a slogan to show how important it was to stand together: "Does the bullet know Christian from Muslim? Does the bullet pick and choose?" By the end of the workshop, the women came to an agreement that the Christian and Muslim women would each have their own leadership, but they would work together. At first, they thought to turn their new activism toward combating the rising rates of HIV infection in Liberia. But the war was spreading and getting closer every day. It was clear there was one overriding issue to focus on: the need for peace.

In December 2002, we ended the Peace Outreach Project, announced the Christian-Muslim alliance and shocked Monrovia with a march down Tubman Boulevard to city hall—two hundred women, Christians in their *lappas* alternating with Muslims wearing head scarves. As we walked, we sang: a hymn, a Muslim song, a hymn again. Crowds turned to stare. This time we'd notified the press and they were waiting. And I read a vision for peace written by Grace:

"We envision peace. A peaceful coexistence that fosters equality, collective ownership and full participation of particularly women in all decision-making processes for conflict prevention, promotion of human security and socioeconomic development."

I remember the crowd listening intently and hundreds of heads nodding. I had no idea where we were going next in our alliance, our quest. But I did know this: I had lived in fear for a long time. When the fighting stopped, the fear faded; when the war reignited, as it always did, the fear returned with greater force. I'd seen friends, whole families, wiped out, and never lost the awareness that I could be next. I'd been depressed for a long time, too, isolated in my own world. When I had to send my children away, I felt the worst kind of loneliness.

But now, as the women of WIPNET gathered together, my fear, depression and loneliness were finally, totally, wiped away. Others who felt the way I did stood beside me; I wasn't alone anymore. And I knew in my heart that everything I had been through, every pain, had led me to this point: leading women to fight for peace was what I was meant to do with my life.

By this time, Liberia had been ravaged by thirteen years of war. We could not have imagined there was anything more terrible than what we'd known—but there was, and it was about to fall upon us. In early 2003, yet another rebel group, the Movement for Democracy in Liberia (MODEL) split off from LURD and began capturing towns and villages in the southeast. A new wave of violence swept through that part of the countryside—killing, looting, rape. Tens of thousands of men and women, with children on their backs and everything they owned in bundles on their heads, poured down rural roads into the brutal poverty of the internally displaced persons camps near the capital or the city itself. In some areas, entire counties emptied, and gunmen looted the deserted towns.

Monrovia was exploding with shacks, refugees, filth, crime, desperation. I was glad that Mammie and the children were gone. A family living near the house on Old Road had a little girl Pudu's age; before my daughter left, they sometimes played together. Now the girl, Lucia, was practically an orphan. Her mother was simply gone. Her father disappeared for hours, then reeled home drunk at 2 A.M. Lucia, only four, would wander around alone, then show up at my door looking for food, a bed.

Life here was dangerous as well. Taylor's antiterrorist unit had set up a base at the airfield just down the road. Sometimes, a childhood friend and I would sit on the porch to eat dinner and as soon as we picked up our spoons, shooting would start. When we ran inside, the fighters moved in and stole our food. Other times, the boys, in their bandanas and oversized jeans, just passed through the cluster of homes, cradling their guns while they looked us up and down and leered. *"One of these days we'll be back to fuck you."*

In Ghana, I'd managed to get my family into a larger house in a better neighborhood. The kids were in good schools; Geneva worked for a seamstress with a small backyard shop down the road. They were doing well. I still visited when I could and called constantly. And yet . . . I could feel the separation widening between us. I needed Geneva to tell me that

Nuku was becoming good at art and that Amber studied hard and that Pudu had lost her first tooth. She had a mother's knowledge of the small, daily events that made up their lives, the funny things they said, what it was they feared when a bad dream woke them.

One night, Arthur fell and cut his head and needed stitches. Geneva called me from the hospital. I could hear my son screaming, but I couldn't hold him.

BB Colley had resigned as the head of my program to go back to school, and I thought my new boss lacked his vision. I still depended on the THRP for a paycheck, but as the spring passed, I got more outspoken about my unhappiness there: the lack of innovation, the way our budget was spent. My boss decided I was frustrated because I wasn't getting into the field enough and started sending me outside Monrovia again.

Immediately, my teams and I were in danger. One week, when we traveled to a village in River Gee County in the southeast, a big government military truck arrived at the same time we did. Chaos erupted— young girls and boys took off running, while men with guns chased and grabbed them, and threw them into the back of the truck. They would be tomorrow's anti-rebel fighters. All we could do was watch, frozen, then get the hell out, feeling lucky not to have been killed for witnessing the scene.

Not long after that, I went out again with a driver and three helpers to mediate a problem in the same area. Whenever we had jobs outside Monrovia, we carried cash to pay the villagers who cooked or did other jobs for us. Usually, there was something left over and we brought the money home in a traveling bag. This day, without stopping to think why, I did what I'd done during the early days of the war when my mother sent me out to look for food: I wrapped the bills and wore them between my legs.

On the way back to Monrovia, we encountered three men who worked for the Adventist Development and Relief Agency. They'd been in the field, too, and told us they were going to get something to eat before heading home. At the border of Nimba and Grand Gedeh Counties, we came to a roadblock manned by Taylor's soldiers. Trucks like ours, that belonged to nonprofits, were supposed to get waved through, and we'd never had a problem before. But this day, they stopped us.

"Come outside the truck!" one of them shouted. "Put everything down!" Music was blaring. The men were smoking weed and their eyes were red.

"Everything out!" We had put our bags in the back of our pickup and covered them with plastic. We tried to hurry to untie everything, then open the bags, remove items one by one and spread them out on a large table.

My heart was pounding. *Thank God I didn't put the money in the car,* was all I could think. We would be safe, unless . . . I was the only woman there; rape was always a possibility. Finally, they waved us on.

At seven that night, when I was home, I heard a news bulletin: an Adventist car had been found burned near the border of Nimba and Grand Gedeh Counties; the staff was missing. A few days later, the bodies of the men we'd met were found. We later learned they'd had money in the car. The last checkpoint they'd passed was the one where we'd been searched. The soldiers there reported that "rebels had attacked."

I had come that close to never seeing my children again. How much more clearly could God have said to me, "This job isn't worth it—leave and do what you really want"? Within a week, I resigned from the Trauma Healing office. Occasional consulting work with other social service agencies brought in a little cash, and Tunde provided for the children. I would get by. My work with WIPNET was what mattered now.

CHAPTER 13

STANDING UP TO CHARLES TAYLOR

AND SITTING DOWN FOR PEACE

PRESIDENTIAL ELECTIONS were scheduled to take place in Liberia in 2003, but with Taylor under attack from LURD and MODEL, it seemed unlikely they would. International pressure for a truce increased, especially from the United States. Members of eighteen political parties met with the Interreligious Council of Liberia and signed a resolution calling on the government and LURD to meet and declare a cease-fire. With the support of the International Contact Group on Liberia and ECOWAS, the Interreligious Council was also trying to find a place where peace talks would be held—Accra or Dakar, Senegal.

Taylor wouldn't hear of it. The rebels were terrorists and he wouldn't negotiate with terrorists. We were a sovereign nation and he wouldn't tolerate international troops on our soil. He headed a democratically elected government and wouldn't leave office. His refusals gave the LURD leadership their own excuse for not negotiating. They would accept nothing less than Taylor's ouster. Meanwhile, the suffering grew. By now, 360,000 people had been driven from their homes and were living in the foul tents of twelve camps in five counties, and scattered across five foreign countries. And the fighting went on, growing closer and closer to the capital.

April 1, 2003, was my first day without a paying job. I was home alone worrying about raising money for WIPNET. My malaria had flared up and I felt feverish and awful. Asatu phoned. Fighting had broken out near the Po River, less than ten miles from Monrovia. "We need to come together," she said urgently. "Can we all meet tomorrow?"

Word went out and when we arrived at the WIPNET office the next day, everyone was there, distraught and emotional: Asatu, Cerue, Vaiba, Grace, Janet, Mariama. Sugars was in a meeting in another room, but we pulled her in to join us. Ideas poured out. "We need to step up! Let's get on the streets and pressurize the government! Who's got markers? Posters?"

There were too many of us for the small space and we spilled into a vacant apartment across the hall. Mariama had just returned from the United States, where she said that exiled Liberians had cornered her, demanding, "What are the women doing?"

"We need to think about this!" she said. "All eyes are on us, because the men have failed!"

"Let's make a public statement," Asatu suggested.

We wrote one, condemning violence committed by all sides and making a single demand: "The women of Liberia want peace now!" We affixed all our names. How were we to get the message out when Taylor controlled the airwaves? Asatu knew the editor of the *Enquirer*, a local paper. Janet operated Radio Veritas, which was under the control of the Catholic church. The next morning, our statement was an *Enquirer* cover story. And in a crumbling nation where few had phones and everyone listened to the radio, much of Monrovia heard our statement, along with an invitation to future WIPNET meetings.

Suddenly, we were the center of attention. Reporters wanted to talk, now, and Grace and a few others went out into different communities passing out flyers. Mariama provided transportation for women in the displaced persons camps who wanted to talk to the press. On April 5, almost one hundred women arrived in Monrovia. None of us had imagined things might happen this quickly, and we had no real plans; everything was being invented day by day. We held meetings every night. On April 9, there was a battle between government and rebel forces at a displaced persons camp just outside the city. That night, the WIPNET office was so packed the room couldn't hold everyone. Some of the women there lived in the community that had been attacked, and were still wearing torn, mud-covered clothes.

Again, we decided to make a public statement. We scheduled a gathering at city hall for April 11. The president had banned street marches. "Nobody, n-o-b-o-d-y will get into the street to embarrass my administration!" he warned. We were determined to assemble anyway. We sent out word through Janet's radio show: "If you want peace, make it your duty to come to the Monrovia city hall at 8 A.M. Wear white." We also sent three separate invitations to Charles Taylor. "We have a statement to present to you," we wrote him.

The morning of the eleventh, the steps of city hall were a sea of white. There were hundreds of women there, maybe as many as a thousand. Some of the city's religious leaders turned out as well. Taylor supporters and soldiers mixed through the crowd, and local media was everywhere. Emotion ran high as women stood to testify what the war had done to their lives, and I got a little afraid that WIPNET would lose control of the gathering. As the Liberian proverb says, "Sudden rain brings the sheep and goat under the same shed." There were women here who'd lost children and were filled with rage, women who were political radicals interested only in ousting Taylor, and women who were just drunk.

Our demands were nonpartisan, simple and clear: the government and rebels had to declare an immediate and unconditional cease-fire; the government and rebels had to talk; and we wanted an intervention force deployed and sent to Liberia.

"In the past, we were silent," I told the crowd. "But after being killed, raped, dehumanized and infected with diseases, and watching our children and families destroyed, war has taught us that the future lies in saying *no* to violence and *yes* to peace! We will not relent until peace prevails!"

The women erupted. "Peace! Peace!"

The president never arrived, and perhaps that day it was a good thing—in his presence, our shouts might have escalated to boos, and there was no telling what his guards would have done. We later learned that they'd been told to flog us if we marched in the streets.

We gave Taylor three days to respond to our demands. If there was no answer in that time, we told the women, we were going to stage a sit-down. Taylor didn't respond, and we moved ahead.

The move was a deliberate provocation. Taylor had said no one would embarrass him, so we would do just that—in an action so dramatic and public it would make the demands of Liberia's women impossible to ignore.

In a short amount of time, we planned things meticulously: WIPNET meetings ran round the clock and when I finally lay down to sleep, slogans ran through my head. The site we chose was the field near the fish market where I used to play soccer and kickball. It was large enough to hold a crowd and right on Tubman Boulevard, a place that almost every Monrovian went by at least once a day. Charles Taylor passed it twice, as he traveled to and from Capitol Hill. We had to make sure the protest focused on peace, not politics, so we'd only allow the nonpartisan posters and placards that we made ourselves. We'd only permit nonviolent protest. Everyone was to wear white, to signify peace: white T-shirts with the WIPNET logo, white hair ties.

Liberian women love to dress up, but we'd come to the field completely bare of makeup and jewelry, in the kind of "sackcloth and ashes" described in the Book of Esther, where the heroic queen stands up to save her people from extermination. And to make sure our message stayed on target, we would have only one spokesperson, one public face. As coordinator of WIPNET, it would be me.

Was what we were about to do dangerous? Opposing Charles Taylor always was extremely dangerous. His Special Security Service and the Anti-Terrorist Unit, run by his son Chuckie, took opponents to a military base prison in the center of the country, where they were tortured and killed. There were stories of prison cells behind the Executive Mansion, where girls were raped. But to me, there was no choice. When I dreamed at night, it was of struggling to climb a rugged hill or swerving through endless blockades on the highway. When I looked back on my life, I saw my lost childhood. Every night, I walked past my kids' empty bedrooms. With the new round of fighting, all of us would be brought close to death again.

There was something else that was hard for me to put into words. The women of Liberia had been taken to our physical, psychological and spiritual limits. But over the last few months, we had discovered a new source of power and strength: each other. We'd been pushed to the wall and had only two options: give up or join up to fight back. Giving up wasn't an option. Peace was the only way we could survive. We would fight to bring it.

From the Old Road house, it was a short walk to the field near the fish market. On the morning of April 14, I woke before dawn and made my way in the dark. I was the first one there. As the sky got lighter, I looked around anxiously. For the protest to succeed, we needed at least a few hundred women. Finally, one group arrived. Then another. The sun rose. And then I heard the sound of diesel engines and up the road toward me came a line of buses. Mixed in were trucks—trucks full of women. There were a hundred on the field . . . three hundred . . . five hundred . . . a thousand.

I started to cry and to pray. The women kept coming. Fifteen hundred . . . We asked where they were from and learned that some government agencies had taken the day off. NGOs with women's programs had required their staffs to join us. University students and female professors were there. More than two thousand women were on the field now. Market women. Displaced women from the camps. Some of them had been walking for hours and wore clothing so old it barely looked white. One woman had used a curtain for a hair tie because she didn't have anything else.

WIPNET workers handed out T-shirts and placards and gathered the women to sit for peace. After a while, we got word that Charles Taylor had left his home and would be driving by. It was the hour when anyone on the road was expected to turn away or risk being shot. No one actively made the decision, but the women rose, walked to the roadside and faced the president's convoy holding a huge banner: THE WOMEN OF LIBERIA WANT PEACE! NOW!

Taylor slowed but didn't stop. I knew that he'd seen us—all of us. We sat again. By noon it was ninety degrees; by four it was over a hundred.

We ran out of water and I had to fetch more from home. We sang. People passing by stared. At the end of the afternoon, Taylor's convoy went by again. We were still out there with our signs. We had started something too big to stop. We would see this through to the end.

The three days we had given Taylor to respond came and went. When we heard nothing, we gathered outside Parliament. The president didn't acknowledge us and we returned to the field. We met at dawn and always started the day with prayers.

The Lord is my shepherd; I shall not want . . .

In the name of Allah, the Beneficent, the Merciful
Praise be to Allah, Lord of the Worlds . . .

When another three days had passed, we notified the press that Taylor's time was up, and returned to Parliament, filling the parking lot so no one could get in or out. It was pouring that day, and we stood in the rain, not moving, as our clothes clung to us and our signs ran and tore. Local media were filming and photographing, and the Speaker of Parliament came outside, embarrassed by the spectacle. He told the security guards to move some cars so we could stand under a shelter. We refused to move.

"Who's the leader of this group?" he asked. I stepped forward. "Why are you using these women for your personal interests?"

I was enraged. "If anyone is using anyone, it is *you!* You are all using the people of Liberia for your own selfish gains!"

Once again, we publicly declared that Taylor had three days to meet with us. "We will continue to sit in the sun and in the rain until we hear from the president!" As we returned to the field, women from the street joined us.

Once again, we sat. The movement we called the "Mass Action for Peace" would later appear to be a spontaneous uprising. It was prompted by emotion—by women's exhaustion and desperation—but there was nothing spontaneous about it; managing a huge daily public protest was a complicated task and we planned every move we made. The women from CWI and Muslim Women for Peace were responsible for the day-to-day activities on the field. If they said it was time to sing, we sang. We also formed committees to handle different jobs, such as finding buses to bring women to the protest from the internally displaced persons camps. Every night a core of us, the WIPNET 21, met at the office and spent hours going over what had happened that day. Later still, when that meeting was done, a smaller number stayed behind, Vaiba, Asatu, Sugars, talking even more.

We all had our roles. I was the strategist and coordinator of our actions; I talked to the media and got everyone fired up about continuing to fight. Vaiba liked to stay in the background and never expressed an opinion until the small group of us were alone, but she had a keen eye for which of our strategies had worked and which hadn't, and didn't hesitate to tell us. Cerue was brilliant at handling finances. Grace, so quiet and shabby when she first joined us, had started dressing better and speaking up more. Passion for the work shone in her face. She had planning skills and a fearlessness that no one had ever tapped. If you gave her letters to deliver, she would get them where they had to go, even if she had to walk there. If you needed to assemble a crowd of women, she would find them—she would talk to anyone.

I will lift up mine eyes unto the hills, from whence cometh my help
My help cometh from the Lord, which made heaven and earth . . .

In the name of Allah, the Beneficent, the Merciful . . .
Guide us on a straight path,
The path of those whom Thou has favored;
Not of those who earn Thine anger nor of those who go astray.

Dawn to dusk, twelve hours. We passed the time in different ways. Sometimes women would dance. Sometimes they would preach. The slogan of our action was a simple one: "We want peace, no more war." The women on the field turned the chant into a song:

We want peace, no more war.

Our children are dying—we want peace.

We are tired suffering—we want peace.

We are tired running—we want peace.

About a week after our trip to Parliament, the Speaker came to where I sat on the field. "I have a message," he said. "Come to the Executive Mansion on April twenty-third. President Taylor will see you."

We held an excited, edgy organizers' meeting. This was a rare opportunity, and we had to make the most of it. Taylor had given us a date but no time, so we decided to get to Capitol Hill early. We would assemble our group in front of the university and cross Tubman together, to the Mansion. It was hard to guess what would happen then.

What did the president want from us? What would he say? Sugars, Asatu and several others insisted that only one of us should speak, so our message was clear. Again, it would be me.

A crowd of women had already gathered when I arrived at the University at 6 A.M. on the twenty-third and it quickly built to over two thousand. We crossed the street to the Mansion, passed through its gilt-edged iron gates, and a feeling of anxiety, even panic, swept over us. We were going to meet the monster. Women were desperate to use the bathroom; some were breathing hard and feeling faint. Volunteer nurses we'd brought with us moved through the group taking blood pressure and calling out for cold water.

Finally, we were taken inside and assembled on the main stairs. Taylor's staff offered us chairs, but we said we'd sit on the floor. "When the bombs fall, we don't run carrying chairs. We are sharing everything our sisters are going through."

A podium had been placed at the top of the stairs. I walked up the steps and stood in front of it. Behind me, Charles Taylor sat on an upholstered couch, in a dull olive military-style suit. He wore dark glasses, but I could feel him observing me. I realized I had come too far to hate this man. It was almost as if I just needed to *see* him, see the human being who had caused so much death and pain. I needed to say something to him that would convey that anguish.

My prepared text said only that we women wanted an unconditional cease-fire, a dialogue between the government and the rebels, and the intervention of an international force. But as I said these words, I felt that God wanted me to add more—something real. The women before me were holding hands, praying: *"Give her strength. We rebuke any evil force that would make her weak."*

The podium was placed so that I spoke facing away from Taylor. I turned sideways so he could see my face and directed my next words to Grace Minor, president of the senate. She was the only female government official in the room, and I wanted to speak to her as a woman. "We ask the honorable pro tem of the senate, being a woman, and being in line with our cause, to kindly present this statement to His Excellency, Dr. Charles Taylor," I said, my voice strong. "With this message: that the women of Liberia, including the IDPs [internally displaced persons], we are tired of war. We are tired of running. We are tired of begging for bulgur wheat. We are tired of our children being raped. We are now taking this stand, to secure the future of our children. Because we believe, as custodians of society, tomorrow our children will ask us, 'Mama, what was your role during the crisis?'"

The president listened, expressionless. He replied smoothly that he was sick that day but had decided to meet with us anyway. "No group of people could make me get out of bed but the women of Liberia, who I consider to be my mothers." Then he challenged us. He said he was willing to engage in peace talks, but if our movement was truly fair we should demand the same of the rebels.

Afterward, when the president and the media had left, Grace Minor approached me. "The president insists that he wants to contribute to your effort."

We'd expected this moment to come. At the organizers' meeting, those who knew Taylor from the past, like Sugars, said that he always gave money: buying loyalty or a feeling of obligation was a favorite tactic. Some of the women had argued we would have to take it, because culturally, you couldn't visit a chief and refuse his gift.

"I'm not interested."

"Please . . ."

"Let's just hold it," whispered my colleague Cerue, who was in charge of finances. Grace handed us five thousand US dollars in brand new bills. We surely needed the cash—it was costing us close to five hundred US dollars each day to provide transportation for the women coming to the protest from miles away, and to buy water for the women on the field. But this was tainted money. We kept it, but for the moment, we simply put it aside.

Thank you, Lord, for this day. Guide our hands in our work.

Dawn to dusk in the heat. It's one thing to go about your business on a very hot day and another to sit, unmoving, while the sun bakes you. It was a kind of torture. I turned as black as I've ever been, and many of the women broke out in terrible rashes. But there was something compelling in the pain, too: your body was being beaten, but you were doing it for a reason and your mind settled into a focused stillness. *Oh Lord, I give my time to you. You will not let my sitting here be in vain . . .* From dawn to dusk in the rain. Liberia is one of the wettest countries on earth and the water comes down at you with the strength of a fireman's hose. We sat wretched as the flood sank into the field's sandy dirt.

The people of Monrovia passed by each day and saw us, sweating, drenched. As if ashamed of their own inaction, some offered to build us shelter. We always said no. "When a battle breaks out," we explained, "there's no time to grab an umbrella."

The core of the group continued to meet at the WIPNET office to plot and plan. Sugars was our advisor, the veteran who knew what had worked for LWI and what should be done differently. There was no idea that we didn't run by her first.

"Sitting is good, but we also need to mix strategies," she told us.

"Why don't we picket?" Asatu suggested, and Sugars helped train women who had never done such a thing before. Soon we were sending teams of women to stand on Broad Street, on Benson, with their placards. WE WANT PEACE, NO MORE WAR!

Sometimes the people passing by ignored us, but often someone would walk up and offer a little money, saying, "Thank you, mothers."

At the end of April, we learned that LURD's leaders had agreed to meet with Taylor in peace talks; the unresolved issue was where the talks would be held. A delegation from the Liberian Council of Churches announced a plan to meet with LURD in Sierra Leone. They would try to find a site for the talks. We scraped together money to send our people—Asatu, because she was a Muslim; Grace, who was from an ethnic tribe allied with the LURD leadership; and Sugars, who knew one of the leaders because his cousin had been a member of LWI.

The three of them stayed in Freetown, and Grace went out to a refugee camp for displaced Liberians to mobilize volunteers to picket at the meeting. The women there greeted her with joy.

"We heard that the peace women were coming! We want to see them!"

"I am one of them," Grace said proudly.

When the LURD leaders arrived to meet representatives from the Liberian Council of Churches, they walked through rows of women in white carrying placards: THE WOMEN OF LIBERIA WANT PEACE. Grace, Asatu and Sugars were able to arrange a private meeting with them.

"You are our children!" Grace rebuked the young men. "We've born you! We are *tired!* We want you to go to Ghana for peace talks! People are dying and you must listen to us!"

To her surprise, Asatu recognized an old schoolmate. "What are you doing here?" he demanded of her. "Don't say anything to me."

Asatu never backed down. "Are you not happy to see me? Your mothers, your sisters have come this far to talk to you! If you don't go to peace talks, don't you know people will die in Monrovia? And don't you think you will be guilty for their deaths?"

Sugars just played to their egos. *You're such important men! . . . Everyone depends on you to save Liberia.* By the time the meeting ended, the LURD leaders had agreed to participate in peace talks.

"Our mothers came all the way from Liberia to talk to us," the men told Asatu, Grace and Sugars. "Well, mothers, because of you, we will go."

And still we sat on the field.

We want peace, no more war.
Our children are dying—we want peace.
We are tired suffering—we want peace.
We are tired running—we want peace.

Sometimes a group of us left Monrovia to sit in solidarity with the women in the more distant internally displaced persons camps. "We must come together as women, only as women, the one thing we share that can never divide us," we told them. "When a rich woman bathes, what does she see? Breasts. A vagina. When a poor woman bathes, what does she see? The same. When the soldiers come to rape, what do they look for? When children die, it is always the mothers who grieve."

Before long, fifteen separate groups of women in nine different counties were dressing in white and sitting with placards demanding peace.

If you were looking from the outside, our unity was effortless. But almost everything we did required endless work. The women's movement politics were exhausting. In Liberia, as in the US and other countries, it's a sad truth that we often spend more time fighting each other than anyone else. Sugars was a member of WIPNET's inner circle, but our relationship with the other older movement women was hard from the day Thelma chose me, an unknown, to run our chapter. No one else from LWI or MARWOPNET came to our actions, though they were always invited. The class tensions were pronounced. They were the educated elite; we were the indigenous poor. To my mind, Sugars threw away her social standing once and for all when she allied with us. I think the older movement women saw us as immature young girls who wouldn't last in the struggle; our members were suspicious of them, fearing they might use us for their own purposes or later try to take the credit for our work.

In May, we held a peace festival on the field to try to raise money. There were cultural performances on a stage we set up, singing, food for sale. A local archbishop spoke. We invited all the older women's groups, while warning everyone who came that that we were still actively protesting, so they should be prepared to sit in the sand.

But the older women brought chairs—not just that, they placed their chairs in the front row. There was serious anger, especially from the women who'd come from the displaced persons camps. Several got up and stormed over to me.

"Take away those chairs or we will leave!"

I had to confront the older women and lead to them to the back of the audience, near the food stands. They took their chairs with them. It was the last time they came to one of our events. Meanwhile, when we of WIPNET held a post-event evaluation, several women suggested that my failure to banish the older to women from the peace festival showed that I was a "paid agent."

Internal struggles were no easier. We'd meet, argue, finally make a decision about doing something, and then if it didn't go well, everyone would suffer a sudden case of amnesia.

"What happened? Who decided we should do that? *I* never approved!"

There were constant personality clashes to resolve. Women came to the nightly organizers' meeting with endless complaints and accusations: "So-and-so disrespected me today!" "So-and-so is a spy for Taylor!" "Of course you'll stand up for her! You have your favorites!" It was my job to work everything out, and many days I got sick of it all. There are times it's so satisfying to be a leader and others when you just want to sit back and let someone else handle the problems.

For me, the worst confrontations were those that got personal. Because Tunde still wasn't divorced, there were whispers that I pretended to be working for good, but I was evil and immoral. It was hard to ignore them. Sometimes, I met Sugars at her office where we could talk privately. I could say anything I wanted, knowing she wouldn't repeat what she heard.

"Maybe I should resign," I said after one of these attacks on my character.

"Wear these kinds of stories like a loose garment," she advised. But still, they bothered me, and truthfully, some of the choices I made then still do. How can you claim to be a Christian and live a life the Bible calls sinful? I understand why I became involved with both Daniel and

Tunde; I don't blame myself. But I do believe that my involvement with men who were still married was a personal failing.

I also ran into problems over something that I naively supposed my sisters would see as a great help to us. CNN never paid us real attention, but other media, such as the BBC's *Focus on Africa*, had regular coverage of our protest. I was its public face, so I was the one they called. I still went to the field every day at 6 A.M., and if something important was scheduled, like a fast, I stayed. But other times, I left at ten for the office, meetings, radio and newspaper interviews. As the weeks passed, I was the one whose name and voice became known. And I was attacked for promoting myself, for working to be a "star."

"This has always been all about you!" one of the other women screamed at me after we disagreed one night. "You *love* the attention! You were nobody before this!"

Someone else: "We do all the work, and your life is easy!"

"That's such bullshit!" I shouted. I jumped up, on the verge of getting physical. I was so angry—*these ungrateful women!*—but also hurt. I lived and breathed this movement; I had no other life anymore. I barely slept, my phone rang constantly and I was always on the move. I wasn't able to visit Ghana anymore; I couldn't even call the way I used to—most of the time, when I found a free minute it was during the day and the kids were at school, so I never heard their voices. Even on Sunday, when I went to church, I saw other WIPNET women and talked about the movement.

This anger, the accusation that I unfairly became famous as a result of our protest, would come back at me again later, in even more painful ways. This day, we got past it. We had no choice: the war continued, we had plans to make. We had to keep moving forward.

Sometimes it felt as if everything was happening so fast, there was no time to sit back and feel any pleasure. Look at what we've done! Sometimes all I could feel was dread. What if we failed? What if I was leading all these women into something terrible? The more we pushed ahead, the more the pressure grew. I never liked to drink alone, so I would organize a gathering of women at my house, and we would drink together. More work, more pressure, more alcohol.

Every day on the field.

In the name of Allah, the Beneficent, the Merciful . . .

~ ~ ~

I will say of the Lord, He is my refuge and my fortress . . .

What does it take to make those who fight listen to reason? What haven't we tried? One day, when Asatu was talking to a journalist, she joked, "Maybe it will just get to the point where we deny men sex!" Everyone laughed, but it was something to think about: as a woman, you have the power to deny a man something he wants until the other men stop what they are doing.

We announced on the radio that because men were involved in the fighting and women weren't, we were encouraging women to withhold sex as a way to persuade their partners to end the war. The message was that while the fighting continued, no one was innocent—not doing anything to stop it made you guilty.

The women protesting in rural communities were more organized in their sex strike than those of us in Monrovia. They already had set aside a separate space where they sat each day and the men couldn't come. They made their refusal religious, saying they wouldn't have sex until we saw God's face for peace. Bringing God into it made their men fearful of opposing them. In the capital, some of the women gave in. Some came back to the field with bruises, saying that their husbands hit them when they said no. The strike lasted, on and off, for a few months. It had little or no practical effect, but it was extremely valuable in getting us media attention. Until today, nearly ten years later, whenever I talk about the Mass Action, "What about the sex strike?" is the first question everyone asks.

Lucia, the motherless girl in the Old Road neighborhood was now five years old, and still had no one. She was another child tossed aside by the war, another of its victims. I was an absent mother to my own children, but the village girls I'd turned my back on still haunted me.

"Why don't you let me raise her?" I finally asked her father. He had no problems with that. While the movement absorbed my days, I asked a family friend to watch over Lucia, and eventually moved her to Ghana and Geneva's care. The little girl, whom I called "Malou," was now my fifth child.

Tunde was so kind, so encouraging, so good at hiding his emotions. He was never anything less than supportive of what I did. But I didn't respond to him the way I once had, and my distraction was taking its toll. His own job was demanding but it ended at five. When he came over seeking my company, the house was full of women and there was no space for him. The intimate, endless talking that had bound us was now what I did with my sisters. The energy that I'd normally have given to a relationship, I gave to the movement. If Tunde and I went out, I'd want to get home early. When we got in bed together, I had no energy for making love. We were still "together," but I learned that he'd had a brief affair. The sad thing is that I was too busy to care.

> We are tired suffering—we want peace.
> We are tired running—we want peace.

Every day we were on that field. *Every day*. We refused to go away. Refused to let our suffering remain invisible. If people didn't take us seriously at first, it was our persistence that wore them down. Some of the women who took buses to reach the field each day told us that when drivers realized where they were going, they refused to take money for the ride. The women were proud of this recognition, and wanted to have something that even more publicly marked them as part of the peace effort.

We created WIPNET identity cards, and the women wore them proudly. They were especially important to women coming from the displaced persons camps. Each day, they were able to leave behind the poverty and limbo of their lives to do something that mattered. Wearing

WIPNET T-shirts, with ID cards hanging around their necks, they were transformed from being no one to women of importance, acknowledged by everyone who saw them as they trudged down the road.

Monrovia's bishops and imams stood at the edges of the fish market field supporting us. The men in our lives, our families, offered their help. Tunde and Cerue's husband used their cars to pick up women without transportation. Asatu's husband reminded her when she had to be at meetings. My mother came for a time from Ghana and helped us hand out water. People warned my father, "Talk to your daughter—she's putting your family at risk!" but he shook his head.

"God sent that girl," he said firmly. "You will see something good come of it."

The Mass Action got most of its funding from churches, but often ordinary men and women, even soldiers and government workers, stopped at the field and offered us food or money. "Thank you, mothers," they said. "Our future depends on you." We received secret donations from those in the top reaches of business and government. Two men I still can't name—one a businessman, the other a prominent figure who had split from an alliance with Taylor—donated a lot. And Grace Minor, president of the senate, gave a great deal of her own money and at enormous personal risk. Once, she even attended one of our candlelight vigils, hidden behind a veil.

Thelma encouraged me to write grant proposals on my own, rather than under the auspices of WIPNET. I did, and we began getting money from serious donors, like the Global Fund for Women, American Jewish World Service and the African Women's Development Fund.

Our movement changed how the world saw us and it also changed who we were. That was not only true of women like Vaiba and Grace. A woman we called "Ma Annie" had come to the sessions I ran for pastors' wives. She joined the Mass Action, and you could see her slowly emerging as a leader. Early one morning, another one of the protesters came to my house. She'd been beaten. It was raining and she was covered in mud and blood. Her husband had thrown her out. They'd just finished building a house and he wanted to live there with a younger woman. She had access to another house, but needed ten thousand Liberian dollars—about two hundred US dollars—to buy straw matting to make it habitable. I took her to my bank and gave her the money. In a week, she came back and said, "My story would have been different if I didn't have a place to stay. Knowing I'm not alone in this life is why I continue to come back to the field."

Dawn to dusk . . . Some afternoons, women gave testimony about how they became involved in peace work. Small groups did "The Shedding of the Weight" exercise and everyone cried. One morning, in the pouring rain, we stood barefoot outside the United Nations compound in Mamba Point, where the International Contact Group on Liberia—a diplomatic coalition of representatives from the UN, ECOWAS, the African Union, World Bank and seven nations—was holding a meeting. As soon as the guards rolled back the gates and we saw a few diplomats getting into their limousines, the fearless Grace along with Olive Thomas, a young journalist, ran across the road. They thrust position papers into the hands of the Swedish ambassador.

"I have something for you!"

"Sure," the man said. Soon, he was calling the other ambassadors to see these women standing in the rain. They stared and asked a few questions.

"It's this group of women who are protesting the war," said a UN Development Program official.

The ambassadors drove off, but they went with a copy of our statement.

One morning, the son of a woman who lived near me on Old Road, a senior in high school, was abducted by soldiers, along with four other young men. Students in school uniforms taken at eight in the morning! But determination and anger had begun to replace hopelessness. Someone saw it happen, took the license plate of the pickup truck and knew which police station the boys would taken to before they were sent off to be pressed into fighting. My neighbors walked to that station and *demanded* their sons.

"We have seen the women at the fish market," they told me. "We are learning from them."

We hadn't brought peace to Liberia, but our work was emboldening the nation. God's hands were under our effort and I saw daily how right it had been to begin the work by mobilizing at the bottom. You can tell people of the need to struggle, but when the powerless start to see that they really can make a difference, nothing can quench the fire.

CHAPTER 14

WHEN PEACE TALKS ARE JUST TALK,

TAKE ACTION

IT WAS AFTERNOON on the field when one of the older, more spiritual women, had a vision. "Something important is about to happen. Let us pray."

Within the hour, we heard the news: ECOWAS and a UN-backed contact group had scheduled peace talks between Taylor and the rebels, to start June 4 in Ghana. Everyone broke into song. The Christian women sang Muslim songs. The Muslims sang hymns.

The talks would be mediated by General Abdulsalami Abubakar, a former president of Nigeria, and were scheduled to last around two weeks. Members of MARWOPNET were invited to observe (and later to participate) to represent Liberian women. No one came to us, but we were determined to be a presence anyway. With small contributions from the community, and part of the $5,000 we reluctantly took from Charles Taylor, seven of us, including Sugars, Vaiba and me, went to Ghana.

We got there two weeks early, and Vaiba, Cecelia and several other delegates joined me at my already overcrowded house. The children were thrilled to know I would be staying a while, but the truth was I hardly saw them. Each day, I left by 5 A.M. and didn't return until after 10 P.M. Even on weekends, I had meetings. Tens of thousands of Liberians were still at the Buduburam refugee camp, where I'd lived early in the war, and we wanted to convince women there to join us in protest at the conference center where the talks would be held.

It was harder than we'd thought. Women who called themselves pro-peace but really were looking to support Taylor had been there canvassing already, and people didn't trust us. Some women's groups in the camp accused us of trying to take advantage of them; some mocked us as "Congo People"—elites. Even Sugars got discouraged. But by the time the conference began, we had over five hundred women with us: camp dwellers, refugees living in Accra, WIPNET members from northern Ghana.

The war in Liberia had mostly been a footnote to the rest of the world, but as the fighting and its aftermath crossed borders into Sierra Leone, Côte d'Ivoire and Guinea, the international community began to see it as the epicenter of a problem with the potential to destroy the entire region. The Ghana peace talks, which opened in Accra, then moved to Akosombo, fifty miles away, then went back to Accra, felt to many like West Africa's last chance.

The presidents of South Africa, Nigeria, Ivory Coast and Sierra Leone, along with a US delegation, arrived at the three-star Lake Volta Hotel in Akosombo, where they were joined by representatives of LURD. Charles Taylor flew in, sounding cooperative. He had already granted amnesty to prisoners arrested while fighting his government and announced that he wouldn't leave Ghana without a peace deal. He even said he might be willing to leave office. "If President Taylor removes himself, fellow Liberians, would that bring peace? If so, I will remove myself."

Then, a shock wave. Three months earlier, in March, a UN–Sierra Leone war crimes tribunal had secretly indicted Taylor on charges of "bearing the great responsibility" for the ten years of murders, mutilations and rapes that had been committed by the Foday Sankoh–led RUF rebels. Taylor was the first sitting head of state since Bosnia's Slobodan Milosevic and the first African leader to face such charges. Now, to the great frustration of those in Akosombo, who could not fathom the choice of timing, the court unsealed its indictment and asked Ghana to honor a warrant for Taylor's arrest. Ghanaian officials later said that by the time they got the word it was too late—President Taylor left his delegation behind to negotiate for him, hurried onto a plane, and fled back to Liberia.

As the news broke, panic hit Monrovia. People rushed from work to find their kids and barricade themselves at home, while Taylor's "boys" roared through the streets in jeeps. If the president was arrested, they vowed, "We will kill everyone and burn everything. Liberia will cease to exist."

The talks were postponed. In two days, LURD forces reached the outskirts of Monrovia—only six miles from the city's heart. Seven displaced persons camps around the capital with more than a hundred thousand residents were now under rebel control, and in torrents of rain, people fled in every direction. The entire countryside seemed to pour into Monrovia.

In Ghana, General Abubakar pleaded with the fighters to stop. Talks were scheduled to resume on June 8, the day representatives from the newest rebel group, MODEL, were to arrive. Another postponement was announced, till the tenth, to enable the MODEL group to assemble a full negotiating team.

Throughout, we women sat, a hundred of us at first, then two hundred, then three hundred, in white, bearing signs, chanting, "WE WANT PEACE."

"We are their conscience," I told a reporter. "We are calling on them to do the right thing. And the right thing now is to give the Liberian women and their children the peace they so desperately crave."

The talks began but went nowhere. The men of LURD and MODEL insisted that Taylor, "an indicted war criminal," had to go. Taylor's representatives said it was "ridiculous" to expect the president to abdicate.

Day after day, we sat with our signs as the delegates and observers, nearly all of them men, filed past. One morning, General Abubakar, stately in his traditional Nigerian robe and hat, the *agbada* and *fila,* stopped to talk.

"I saw a group of women protesting for peace in Liberia when I was there with the International Contact Group," he said. He seemed genuinely interested. "Are you the same women?"

"Yes," I said.

He nodded and smiled. "Keep up the good work."

A few days later, the general approached us again. "I respect what you are doing. I believe you should be with MARWOPNET at the negotiating table." He said he had made three spaces available for us.

I said thank you, but refused him. Strategically, I thought making such a move would have defeated our purpose. The women of the Mass Action had come to sit outside the peace negotiations, not participate in them. And we needed to show solidarity with our sisters. Perhaps the members of MARWOPNET were elites, but they still represented the interests of all Liberian women as observers of the talks, just as we represented our country's women in protest. If we had stepped in to share their role, it would have suggested that we didn't trust them and that we were competing, which would have widened the divide between us. "We'll stay outside," I said.

By the time I left the room, someone had told the MARWOPNET women participating in the peace conference what I'd said. We met and they thanked me.

"Our arguing has to stop," I said. "We must show that we're together. We will protest, while you sit at the table, but you feed us information on what you hear during the negotiations that's unfavorable to the interests of the women of Liberia. We'll collaborate on a daily press release saying 'this is what the women think.'" They agreed, we agreed, and for the first time, we had unity. Whenever a warlord at the peace talks stood in the way of negotiations—for instance, saying no to a proposed timetable for elections—we knew about it, and used our placards to let the world know as well.

Day after day, there was no progress in the peace talks. Sugars knew many of the men involved in negotiating, but none of them talked to me, unless it was to ask, "Would you like to have a drink?"

"I don't drink with killers," I said.

On June 16, the peace talks moved back to Accra and the meeting rooms of the M Plaza Hotel. On the seventeenth, the two rebel groups and Taylor signed a cease-fire agreement that included establishing a transitional government without Charles Taylor. The UN announced it would lend support and troops. There was dancing in the streets of

Monrovia, and for one afternoon, we WIPNET women felt happy. I even posed for pictures with the warlords.

What's more painful than allowing yourself to hope? Almost right away, Taylor went back on his promise to leave office, the cease-fire fell apart, and LURD launched three separate attacks against Monrovia so horrific they came to be known as World Wars I, II and III. There was a frenzy of killing and raping, of fighting in the streets. Days of bombardment left more blocks burned, pavement strewn with rubble, trash, piles of broken furniture. Every house, every store, was looted and smashed. People ran on carpets of shell casings and carried their wounded by wheelbarrow or on their backs, desperately trying to reach the makeshift clinics operated by international volunteers. Not a single public hospital was open anywhere in the country.

"We will never desert the city!" cried Taylor. "We will fight street to street, house to house!"

The roads to Sierra Leone and Guinea, and from Monrovia westward, were closed. The UN Security Council held meetings to discuss the possible deployment of a multinational force; Secretary General Kofi Annan asked the United States to intervene.

And in Accra . . . *nothing*. We sat outside the negotiating room with our signs, running a parallel "Liberian Women's Forum," where women could discuss the proceedings. One afternoon, I briefly met Ellen Johnson Sirleaf, who in more recent years had investigated the Rwandan genocide for the Organization of African Unity and served as a chairperson of the Open Society Initiative for West Africa. She had become a staunch opponent of Taylor. She asked me about the work we did, and about Amber, who had come with me that day. The next day, she called me over and handed me an autographed copy of *Women, War, and Peace,* a study of women in conflict and peace-building that she'd coauthored for the United Nations Development Fund for Women (UNIFEM).

In the evenings, the warlords would come out to the hotel patio to have drinks. Sugars and I would sit at a table close by and try to overhear their discussions. Usually they were just about sports or girls or retold war stories. But sometimes people we knew sat with them and reported that they argued about how to use the peace talks for personal gain.

That's what the war was about for them. Power. Money. One warlord, for instance, said he wouldn't stop fighting unless he was guaranteed a lucrative job afterward. We made up new placards: KILLER OF OUR CHILDREN, YOU WILL NEVER GET THE JOB YOU WANT!

The jockeying for power and wealth continued each day: what would peace mean, what would a restructured government look like, who would govern which counties and control which resources. One LURD leader told Sugars it didn't really matter what happened—they'd kill everyone in Monrovia, then go back with their own women and replenish the population.

Though the talks were going nowhere, we saw definite changes among the rebel participants. Here at the M Plaza and at the four-star La Palme Royal Beach Hotel, where they slept, the mood was relaxed and even festive. The warlords were on vacation, with the international community paying for it all. They traveled in police motorcades and appeared each morning, well rested and satisfied. Stripped of their guns and the protection of their red-eyed young soldiers, it was easy to see them for what they were: small-time hoods, criminals, bullies, con men, nobodies who never wanted the war to end because without it, they would never have access to this kind of life.

And still we sat protesting in Accra, anxiously close to running out of money. In Monrovia, despite the fighting, the women still sat in the fish market field. But their prayers were becoming bitter, changed from praising God to calling on Him for retribution. Isaiah 49:25: *"This is what the Lord says: Yes, captives will be taken from warriors, and plunder retrieved from the fierce; I will contend with those who contend with you . . . I will make your oppressors eat their own flesh; they will be drunk on their own blood, as with wine. . . .*

In July, fighting broke out on Bushrod Island. The rebels captured the bridge that separated the central city, controlled by the government, from the port warehouses holding supplies of food. Famine spread. My father survived at the Lutheran compound and Ma got by because Tunde's UN job gave him access to food, but others were living on leaves and sea snails until finally their bodies gave out. The cemeteries were unreachable, so families slipped their dead into the swamps. The beach was a long stretch of public toilet. There was no clean water, and an epidemic of cholera began.

As many as eight thousand people seeking shelter moved into the ruins of the once-grand Masonic temple on Benson Street. Sixty thousand huddled in the rain in what was still called, because no one had thought to rename it, the Samuel K. Doe Sports Stadium; Taylor had publicly offered it as a place of refuge. Terrified families entered parts of Monrovia from one direction while others fled the other way. The entire country was on the run, but there was nowhere left to go.

In Accra, we took anguished calls from home every day. *"Nobody can go outside. We are on the floor, hiding from bullets. Everyone is hungry."*

"Mother," one of Sugars's sons told her, *"today, I helped dig a mass grave."*

"Leymah! Oh God!" Cerue screamed one afternoon when I called her from Thelma's office. Her voice rose to an almost hysterical pitch, as if she no longer knew where she was and what she was saying. "They're shooting! They're bombing! Boom! Boom! Boom!" I stood in Thelma's office in Accra, safe and sound, while the sound of Cerue's imitation of gunfire filled the room.

All I could do was cry. My eyes were bloodshot from crying so much. Our money was nearly gone, and no one would fund us. There was no resolution to the negotiations in sight. The descriptions of the stalemate were always the same: the talks are stalled; the talks are at an impasse.

Meanwhile, the men of LURD and MODEL woke up every morning in their ocean-view hotel rooms, went downstairs to breakfast, and then to sessions that appeared to be completely, outrageously useless. In the off-hours, you could observe these self-satisfied negotiators lounging around the hotel pool in crisp new shirts, having drinks.

One morning, something in me just broke. I was done. I went to the hotel to greet the women who arrived for the daily protest, but I didn't wear white, and I didn't stay. It was too much. I had been beaten.

July 21 was a Monday, the start of a new week. That morning, before going over to the hotel, I decided to go to the WANEP office to check email and watch the news. No one was there yet. I clicked on the Yahoo! News website. Another nightmare. Just that morning, shells had hit part of the US embassy's diplomatic compound in Monrovia where ten thousand people had taken shelter from the fighting. Dozens were killed—women, little children. An enraged crowd laid a pile of bodies at the embassy gates, a tangle of white T-shirts, bright *lappas* and blood.

"Why don't you help us?" they screamed at the American guards. "We are going to die for nothing!"

I sat there feeling sick to my soul. How could I have been so stupid as to think a handful of women could stop a war? *You fooled me, God.*

There was a video on the site: Two little boys had been brushing their teeth outdoors when the missiles hit, and all that was left of them was their slippers. The camera shifted to an old woman holding a baby who had been born the night before. The baby's mother had come outside to hang up diapers. She had been standing next to the boys and she, too, was dead.

I looked at the baby; I thought about the dead children—their slippers were the same size that Arthur would be wearing now—and my despair was so deep that crying couldn't begin to ease it.

"What is the essence of this?" I'd shouted at Sugars a few days before. "What are we accomplishing? People are dying every day! We were supposed to stop the killing!"

"What else do we do?" she had said, grabbing my arms and shaking me. "Leymah! Leymah! Listen to me! Do we just give up? Do we just allow them to win?"

What else should I do? Allow them *to win?* Across nearly a decade, I heard the voice of the woman with one breast from Sierra Leone. Suddenly, I felt a rage greater than any I'd ever known. If I'd had an AK-47 right then, I would have returned to the conference room and slaughtered everyone inside.

We kept some white T-shirts in the WANEP library. I pulled one on and went back to the hotel. Sugars met me.

"We got a little money last night," she said wearily. "You weren't here, so I sent a bus to the camp to bring in about thirty women."

"Thirty isn't enough for what we need to do today," I said. I don't know what was in my voice, but she looked at me strangely. "Send for more," I said. "We're going inside."

The world shrank for me into this one moment. I knew what I had to do. The negotiating hall was full that day, with representatives from LURD, MODEL and Taylor, as well as Liberian political parties and civil society groups. It was time for their lunch break. I led our women into the hallway, then dropped down, in front of the glass door that was the main entrance to the meeting room. "We are sitting right here." More women came, then more until there were two hundred of us, and the hall grew hot and crowded with a sea of white T-shirts and black-lettered signs: BUTCHERS AND MURDERERS OF THE LIBERIAN PEOPLE—STOP!

"Sit at this door and loop arms," I instructed them. "No one will come out of this place until a peace agreement is signed." I tapped on the glass and when the door opened, I handed a note to a man inside. "Please give this to General Abubakar."

I saw the general read the piece of paper: *We are holding these delegates, especially the Liberians, hostage. They will feel the pain of what our people are feeling at home.*

Suddenly, his voice sounded on the public address system. "Distinguished ladies and gentlemen, the peace hall has been seized by General Leymah and her troops!"

Immediately security guards rushed into the hall. "Who is the leader of this group?" one called out.

"Here am I," I said, rising to my feet.

"You are obstructing justice and we are going to have to arrest you." Behind me, the door to the negotiating room opened and men's faces peered out. *Obstructing justice?* Had he really said that to me? *Justice?*

I was so angry, I was out of my mind. "I will make it very easy for you to arrest me. I'm going to strip naked." I took off my hair tie. Beside me, Sugars rose to her feet and began to do the same. I pulled off my *lappa*, exposing the tights I wore underneath.

"No, no!" shouted the husband of one of our protesters, a Liberian banker who had come to the talks that day.

I didn't have a plan when I started taking off my clothes. My thoughts were a jumble—*Okay, if you think you'll humiliate me with an arrest, watch me humiliate myself more than you could have dreamed.* I was beside myself, desperate. Every institution that I'd been taught was there to protect the people had proved evil and corrupt; everything I valued had collapsed. These negotiations had been my last hope, but they were crashing, too. But in threatening to strip, I had summoned up a traditional power. In Africa, it's a terrible curse to see a married or elderly woman deliberately bare herself. If a mother is really, really upset with a child, she might take out her breast and slap it, and he's cursed. For this group of men to see a woman naked would be almost like a death sentence. Men are born through women's vaginas, and it's as if by exposing ourselves, we say, "We now take back the life we gave you." Fear passed through the hall.

"Madame, no!" It was General Abubakar. "Leymah, do not do this."

Sugars and I stopped, and I stood there weeping in rage and frustration. "I will listen to you, but these people, these people . . . They have come here . . . when they came, they were all pale. Now they are wearing fine Ghanaian milled textiles. And they are passing around, telling us, 'We will kill your people!' They won't come out! We are going to keep them in that room, without water, without food, so they at least feel what the ordinary people in Liberia are feeling!"

"Madame, please, lead your women out of here."

"No!"

"Don't you know what they are doing?" one of the women with me began to wail. "My family in Liberia is starving! They may be dying! I may never see them again!"

More voices. "They should not eat! Let *them* know that it pains to go without food, too."

"We will not allow them to come out until they give us peace!" I shouted.

There was a commotion behind the general. One of the warlords pushed forward to step over the women blocking his way. They pushed him back and he lifted his leg as if he would kick them.

General Abubakar's voice was steely as he turned to the warlord. "I *dare* you!"

There was a moment of silence. "If you were a real man," said the general, "you wouldn't be killing your people. But because you are not a real man, that is why these women will treat you like boys. I dare you to leave this hall until we have negotiated a peace with these women." The man retreated.

While the protesters remained in the hall to keep the negotiators locked in, Sugars and I and a few others followed General Abubakar to his room at the hotel. For a while, I just sat and cried.

"You have all the right in the world to be so upset," he told me. "If I was in this situation, I would feel the same way."

Over the next hour, we came to an agreement, and returned to the hall where the women still sat. We called the press who were covering the talks, the Ghanaian television crew, the international stringers.

"Here is what we want," I told them. "The peace talk has to move on. All of them will attend sessions regularly. They have to pass by us and don't ever insult us, because we are not crazy. . . .

"What we've done today is send out a signal to the world that we, the Liberian women in Ghana, at this conference, we are fed up with the war, and we are doing this to tell the world we are tired of the killing of our people. We can do it again—*and we will do it again!*"

The Liberian war didn't end on the July day we blocked the hall in Accra. On August 4, West African peacekeeping troops arrived in Liberia to crowds that lined the streets, weeping and cheering. On the seventh, Nigerian peacekeeping troops intercepted ten tons of AK-47s and rocket-propelled grenades bound for Taylor, at the Monrovia airport. If the weapons had gotten through, the president might well have continued to fight.

But what we did marked the beginning of the end. The atmosphere at the peace talks changed from circuslike to somber. The talks proceeded without further delay. On August 11, Charles Taylor resigned the presidency and agreed to go into exile in Nigeria. The peace talks were suspended the morning he left. The leaders of the Mass Action gathered at my house to watch the departure on TV. We were quiet and afraid. Perhaps the president had planned something terrible; fighting would break out, death would spread. But he simply spoke to his supporters at the Executive Mansion and prepared to go.

"God willing," he said, "I will be back."

"In your dreams!" we shouted.

As Taylor's plane lifted off and nothing happened in Monrovia, it was a huge weight lifting. On August 14, the rebels ended their siege of Monrovia and American troops landed to support the African peacekeepers. On the fifteenth, the first international aid ship docked at the port. Women crying and singing gospel songs rushed over the bridge, which was covered in bullet casings, and began a desperate search for food.

Three days later, leaders of LURD and MODEL and representatives of forces loyal to Taylor signed the Accra Comprehensive Peace Agreement, agreeing to establish a transitional Liberian government headed by Gyude Bryant, a businessman with no allegiance to any side.

Ironically, I wasn't even there when it happened. All of us had expected that the negotiating would last another week, so I'd gone with Sugars to a meeting of West African women leaders in Côte d'Ivoire. President Bryant called me at 2 A.M. "Something great happened," he said, "and we can say it happened because of you all."

I knelt on my hotel room carpet and prayed.

When we returned to Liberia, a crowd of women came to meet us at the airport. They wore their WIPNET T-shirts and were singing. *"We want peace—no more war!"* Sugars and I looked at each other and laughed. Everyone at the airport nodded at us, touched us, smiled at us as we passed through security.

"These were the peace women! These were the women who did great work. Thank you, mothers. Thank you."

PART THREE

CHAPTER 15

IS THE WAR REALLY OVER?

A T THE FIELD, we held hours of celebration: songs, prayers, tears. For weeks, whenever any of us walked the streets wearing white WIPNET T-shirts, people stopped to shake our hands and offer thanks. Sometimes, crowds of children followed us, joyously chanting, "We want peace—no more war."

Yet a sense of terror lingered. Was it really over? The fighters had signed more than a dozen treaties during the war, so it was hard to believe that this latest one would hold. The months after I returned from Accra were almost as nerve wracking as any had been before. Rumors flew. These people were approaching, those people were running, an attack would start any minute. . . . Since no one knew details or even what to look for, one whisper was all it took for us to fall into a state of panic.

A war of fourteen years doesn't just go away. In the moments we were calm enough to look around, we had to confront the magnitude of what had happened to Liberia. Two hundred and fifty thousand people were dead, a quarter of them children. One in three were displaced, with 350,000 living in internally displaced persons camps and the rest anywhere they could find shelter. One million people, mostly women and children, were at risk of malnutrition, diarrhea, measles and cholera because of contamination in the wells. More than 75 percent of the country's physical infrastructure, our roads, hospitals and schools, had been destroyed.

The psychic damage was almost unimaginable. A whole generation of young men had no idea who they were without a gun in their hands. Several generations of women were widowed, had been raped, seen their daughters and mothers raped, and their children kill and be killed. Neighbors had turned against neighbors; young people had lost hope, and old people, everything they'd painstakingly earned. To a person, we were traumatized. We had survived the war, but now we had to remember how to live. Peace isn't a moment—it's a very long process.

Interim president Gyude Bryant took office in October 2003, but I knew I couldn't bring Geneva and the children back to such devastation. And in any case, there would be no resting after the triumph in Accra. The women who'd stayed in the field through the terrible last days of the war said they had prayed and believed it wasn't yet time to end our protest there. Not everyone in WIPNET agreed—the Mass Action had demanded such sacrifice that some women just wanted to get back to their work, their lives, but I supported the decision to keep going.

We had to ensure that what we'd done had a lasting impact. We'd shown women's awesome power, but to me, our actions were the foundation of a movement, not its end product. It was time now to build on what we'd done, so in the future women's concerns wouldn't be pushed aside and we'd be full partners in running our communities. Maybe those in power imagined that once we got the peace we wanted, we'd stop making demands and return to our old places. We had to show them that they were very wrong.

We'd already started to extend our reach in Accra, when a group of us along with representatives from MARWOPNET and UNIFEM signed a declaration emphasizing the importance of involving women in every aspect of the peace process. Back in Monrovia, we joined with LWI to run a three-day conference that helped break down the thick, bureaucratic language of the peace agreement into information an ordinary woman could understand. *This is what the agreement promises. This is how and when you should see certain things happen in your community. This is what to do and where to go if you don't.* Later that same month, we worked with UNICEF on a campaign to encourage kids, especially former fighters, to go back to school. Our March in Monrovia drew a huge crowd.

But when it came to the "official" peacekeepers, like those with the UN mission in Liberia (UNMIL), we might as well have been talking to the air. It was hard to swallow their arrogance. UNMIL was supposed to help with tasks like humanitarian assistance and refugee return, but the agency never consulted with anyone from civil society how best to do these things. The result was entirely avoidable disasters.

Early that fall, for instance, droves of women from Bong County poured into Monrovia in a panic saying there'd been an attack the night before. The UN had a policy not to give supplies to former fighters. In this case, they'd made a food delivery to civilians, but because they never consulted the locals, they didn't know armed men were in the area. Of course the fighters came in and took everything.

Another problem was UNMIL's approach to persuading former fighters—there were maybe forty thousand of them—to turn in their weapons and rejoin society. (The official name for this process is "DDR," or disarmament, demobilization and reintegration.) We visited the UNMIL office on Tubman Boulevard to offer our help. "You should involve people with local knowledge of who and what's involved," I said. No one was interested. "Don't worry!" we were told. "We're bringing in experts with a great deal of experience from Kosovo."

The plan essentially was to offer money for guns; the kickoff, scheduled for December 7, was supposed to be a small, symbolic exchange staged for the media at Camp Scheffelin, an army base outside Monrovia. But none of the "experts" let the fighters know that December 7 was just for show. Instead, UN helicopters buzzed villages, dropping leaflets describing the upcoming event into communities where almost no one could read or write.

On the seventh, twelve of us, including Sugars and me, went to Chocolate City, a Monrovia suburb, to escort two dozen former fighters to Camp Scheffelin. While we waited with them, we watched a little boy, maybe twelve years old, carrying a gun, come to a table staffed by one of UNMIL's experts.

"Which group did you fight with?" he was asked.

"I fought with LURD."

"And where did you fight?"

"Grand Gedeh."

Sugars and I looked at each other and shook our heads. Grand Gedeh County is in eastern Liberia; LURD had been active in the north. The UNMIL expert nodded and waved the boy on to the next step in the disarmament process. Later we approached him ourselves.

"What did you really do in the war?" we asked. "We know you didn't fight for LURD." The boy looked away, but finally answered. "Well . . . I never fought. My brother gave me his pistol, so I could get money for it."

What happened next would have been funny if it hadn't been so frightening. The dropped leaflets, with their pictures of cash, attracted more than three thousand heavily armed former fighters, most of them Taylor's troops. There wasn't enough food, water or money to go around, and after the men had stood on line for hours in the hot sun, they started drinking and smoking weed. Suddenly, that familiar, terrible sound: *pop-pop-pop!* The line broke down, bullets were flying, people were running, and the Chocolate City boys took back the weapons they'd put down and got us out of there fast. That night was total chaos—rioting, looting. The UN staff fled, leaving locals to clean up the mess.

WIPNET, with LWI, the Christian Community and several NGOs held a press conference pointing out why so much had gone wrong. Three days later, UNMIL shut down the DDR program. As discussions began of how to try again, Sugars and I approached two of Taylor's former generals and offered our help. "We know how to work with these boys," we told them.

Ultimately, UNMIL offered to pay for twenty WIPNET workers, but we recruited over fifty volunteers. Over the next few weeks, we aired radio announcements in the local vernacular explaining simply how the DDR process worked. Grace led a team of women to River Gee County, where they mobilized local women. We did the same thing throughout the country.

From then on, the process went smoothly, if not perfectly. Far fewer girls and women turned in guns than we knew possessed them. I sometimes wondered about fierce girls like Cleo, whom I'd met during my trauma healing days. I knew some of them had had their weapons taken by male commanders who wanted to claim the DDR money for themselves. Others didn't show themselves because they feared being stigmatized. The majority of Liberia's female fighters evaporated, as if they'd never existed.

A 2004 UNIFEM report on DDR in Liberia praised the women of WIPNET for our assistance, noting that we'd performed "many essential tasks that would normally be the responsibility of armed military personnel." It was good to be recognized but frustrating that our work was unexpected enough to deserve special mention.

Organizations like the UN do a lot of good, but there are certain basic realities they never seem to grasp. One is that every war is different, even those with surface similarities, because the reasons and the ways countries fight have everything to do with their histories and the way their societies are organized. If conflicts aren't identical, resolution can never be one-size-fits-all. Maybe the most important truth that eludes these organizations is that it's insulting when outsiders come in and *tell* a traumatized people what it will take for them to heal.

You cannot go to another country and make a plan for it. The cultural context is so different from what you know that you will not understand much of what you see. I would never come to the US and claim to understand what's going on, even in African American culture. People who have lived through a terrible conflict may be hungry and desperate, *but they're not stupid.* They often have very good ideas about how peace can evolve, and they need to be asked.

That includes women. Most especially women. When it comes to preventing conflict or building peace, there's a way in which women *are* the experts. Think of how intimately women know their homes. If the lights are out, we can walk through rooms without bumping into anything. If a stranger has been there, we sense it. That's how well we know our communities. We know who belongs, and who is a potentially threatening stranger. We know the history. We know the people. We knew how to talk to an ex-combatant and get his cooperation, because we know where he comes from. To outsiders like the UN, these soldiers were a problem to be managed. But they were our children.

During the disarmament campaign, near Tubmanburg, a LURD stronghold northwest of Monrovia, I met a young woman, of maybe twenty-six. She'd married an older man and was pregnant with their fourth child when the war reached their community. As they ran away, he was killed in front of her. His family refused to recognize her as his wife, and she ended up in a displaced persons camp. She was so thin, her clothes hung off her; she carried one child and held the hand of another, and you could sense her exhaustion. Her eyes were empty. I asked her what she hoped to do with her life. She replied that she wanted to buy dry goods to sell, a business that might support her family. It was a small dream, but in the context of her life, next to impossible. I scraped together five hundred US dollars and gave the money to her. Last year, I met another like her, equally young and desperate. She told me how her husband had beaten her. She had scars on her face, and she, too, had four children. I gave her money also. There are hundreds of thousands of needy Liberians, but I felt particularly drawn to these two. Compelled. When I met them, there was a second when something came over me, a whirling sensation that made me think I might black out. I felt as if I was looking at myself.

I stayed in the house on Old Road, moving from field to WIPNET to Tunde. After his affair, we'd reconciled. He said he'd made a mistake, that he loved me. In my way, I loved him, too. No matter what happened between Tunde and me, the bonds of friendship remained. I could still talk to him about anything. I think we both hoped we would find a way back to the old spark. Just after Christmas in 2004, an earthquake in the Indian Ocean caused a series of tsunamis to slam into the coasts of eleven countries. The World Food Programme sent Tunde to devastated Banda Aceh, in Indonesia. We talked every day, and he flew home whenever he could.

Every day I called Accra, and every other month or so I managed to get there to see Geneva and the kids. The visits all had a rhythm. I'd make my way from the airport, turn down the road to the house and see Mammie waiting at a particular spot by the gate, a big smile on her face.

"Welcome! Come and tell me everything!" We'd talk into the night. At 5 A.M. I'd wake to her call: "Nuuukuuu! Puuuduuu! Arthurrr! Leeemuuu! Let us pray!" After I took the kids to school, we'd spend hours more at the kitchen table.

By evening, the kids, who were always a little shy at first, would be moving toward me, and I'd end up sleeping with all of them in my bed. But the times also had their struggles. My mother thought that when I visited all I did was criticize—*Why is Arthur not wearing slippers?*—without ever saying thank you for all the work she and Geneva did for me. Maybe she was right; maybe my lack of gratitude was a way to hold on to a role that wasn't really mine anymore. My mother managed my family's finances; Geneva did the parenting. In some ways, I wasn't even part of the family. The kids would be so happy when I got home, but the novelty would wear off fast. If they came to me instead of Mammie for help with homework, she took it personally. "Oh today, you know you have a mother!" Outside of cooking breakfast on Sunday morning, there was nothing for me to do.

WITH MORE THAN fifteen thousand UNMIL forces in Liberia, the peace held and the country struggled on: DDR, resettlement of internally displaced people, plans for economic development, what to do with a population 76 percent of whom lived below the poverty line. There was a lot that was hard for me to watch. The UN was spending many millions of dollars in Liberia, but most of it was on staffing resources—and their workers were always the ones eating the best food and driving the best cars. If they had just given some of that money to the local people, it would have made a real difference.

Some of the pain people were in was psychic, but a good deal was connected to basic reality. A man might say, "I spent all my life working to take care of my family and build my house. During the war, my son was killed and the house was burned down." What is he trying to tell you? "I'm sixty. The son who I hoped would take care of me is gone. The house that I thought would afford me shelter is gone. I know cannot get the child back. But can you get me a house?"

Most of the institutions that come in to offer help after disaster don't have the resources to provide concrete help like that. Donor communities invest billions funding peace talks and disarmament. Then they stop. The most important part of postwar help is missing: providing basic social services to people. Not having those resources might have been a reason men went to war in the first place; they crossed the border and joined an armed group because they didn't have jobs. In Liberia right now, there are hundreds of thousands of unemployed young people, and they're ready-made mercenaries for wars in West Africa. You'd think the international community would be sensible enough to know they should work to change this. But they aren't.

A postwar truth and reconciliation commission (TRC) was formed and I was named a commissioner-designate, though it turned out to be a less impressive honor than it sounded. A TRC had worked in South Africa, but ours was artificially imposed, a requirement of the peace agreement. The process ended up politicized, there were objections to my being there, and I was glad to resign early on. Other, more exciting projects demanded my attention.

The Western media hadn't taken note of what WIPNET had accomplished, but in the world of conflict resolution, peace-building and the global women's movement, we were big news. In the same way the job as WIPNET coordinator had taken me from one level to another almost overnight, I made another instant jump. I was called to present papers at regional and subregional meetings. Each year, WIPNET held a conference bringing together West Africa's top activists to brainstorm and share strategy. The international groups that had given money to the Mass Action sent out publications with news of what their grantees were doing, further spreading the word. I spoke on a *Voice for Women* radio program funded by Oxfam Great Britain. Thelma started a publication called *Herstories*, and I did my best to always have something in there. She, as always, pushed me to go even further, to reach beyond the borders of Liberia. "Broaden what you know," she said. "Be more regional in your focus. Read more."

Meanwhile, there was almost no consultation on the future of Liberia that didn't include a voice from WIPNET—often mine. In 2004, I made my first trip out of Africa, to USAID conferences in New York, where I gave presentations on the women's role in DDR to representatives from nations contributing to the Liberian recovery. Though I grew up on American TV, the reality of the country was different, jarring. The unexpectedly sharp edge of freezing air (someone lent me a coat; nothing I owned was even vaguely appropriate). White people everywhere. And on the subway, I saw a young black woman with a three-year-old, begging. She was surrounded by dilapidated bags and obviously homeless. For the first time, I understood what my father had said when I was a child and he came back from a business trip to Atlanta: "It's not what you think."

I was so short of money that I stayed in the Bronx with the daughter of someone who'd been part of the Mass Action; that way I could save the per diem the UN gave me for expenses. The girl missed Liberian food terribly, so one day I walked to a local Asian market, bought fish and crab and cooked a big pot for her, along with *fufu* (boiled cassava) and rice. She said she loved the way the house smelled.

In the mornings I got on the subway, rattling away from her redbrick neighborhood to the clean, open plaza of the UN, its many flags whipping in the winter wind. Canyons of glass and steel. Men in suits everywhere.

I wasn't prepared for the enthusiasm my talk about WIPNET's DDR work received. People sought me out during the breaks. "We've never heard of this kind of hands-on engagement! . . . Can you join our team? We're writing a paper."

The next thing I knew, I was being invited to join an interagency working group that planned to meet in Switzerland. Then I *was* in Switzerland. The world was opening to me. We had accomplished something great in Liberia, and there were other countries that wanted to hear about it. Best of all, I believed I had something important to say.

"Yes, women's rights are big right now," Tunde said when he called from Indonesia. "You could find very good job here."

A good job *here*. Tunde and I were at a place where I think both of us were having trouble imagining what the future held for us. We kept making a different plan. For a while, it was that the kids and I would move to Indonesia to live with him. We'd build Geneva a house in Liberia and give her money to start a shop where she could sell clothing—an old dream of hers. When I told Geneva the idea, she wept. "Don't take those kids away from me! They're my life!"

The next plan was that all of us would move to Indonesia. Geneva would stay home and I would get a job with a UN agency, something worthy but more settled and less demanding than WIPNET. It would be perfect.

I wanted to want this. Tunde was my friend. By now, he was the only father the kids could remember. Making a home with him would bring them comfort and stability. But if I had been honest with Tunde, and with myself, I would have admitted that my heart wasn't in it. Yes, I'd make good money at the UN, but I'd be part of a system, one of the staff. I would leave no legacy; there'd be no chance to break out and do something startling. When I was old, what would I tell my kids? That I got practical and let my passion die? I also couldn't see myself outside Africa. So many professionals had gone. Some of us needed to stay.

There was one more thing. After all this time, Tunde still was legally married to his wife. If he had come to me then and told me that he'd finally gotten the divorce we'd talked about many times, I would have put my other doubts aside, married him, and moved to be with him. But he didn't. And so instead I listened to him talk and simply nodded. "Of course," I said. "It sounds good. When the time comes, we'll figure out how to make it work."

IN SWITZERLAND, I had encountered a Nigerian in charge of UN programs in Liberia who seemed to think that no one in my country knew anything. As he spoke, he gave reasons why members of civil society couldn't add a thing to the process of DDR. I couldn't stand it and just took the mike.

"Excuse me," I said. "I'm here to tell you how it *can* work." It was the first time I really stepped on the toes of someone who held international power, the first time I asserted myself in such a way, to speak what I knew to be the truth. It felt good. There was no way we Liberians could talk about taking charge of our country if we shied away from correcting those who came in and acted as if they knew everything.

But many times when I was at international meetings, I felt far less confident. All around me were highly intelligent people who held master's degrees and represented powerful institutions. They not only talked about what was being done in the world, but *why*—the theories behind the actions. I could only talk about what I'd experienced myself, and it was obvious I wasn't well read. At one conference in South Africa, I was asked to compare the Rwandan genocide to what had happened in Liberia. I knew very little about Rwanda and stumbled through the answer. I realized that if I was serious about a career working for peace, I had to be able to speak with more knowledge and authority.

"Read more," Thelma had said. I began amassing books on conflict resolution theory: *The Journey Toward Reconciliation* and *The Little Book of Conflict Transformation*, both by Jean Paul Lederach; *The Peace Book* by Louise Diamond. Whenever I could get Internet access—in Liberia, that often wasn't easy—I spent hours tracking conflicts, not just in Africa, but around the globe, paying special attention to issues of women and peace. In the future when I was asked about something, I would know the answer.

If you go to one conference, you meet people who invite you to another. If you do well at one meeting, you get invited to more. Whenever I traveled, I used the fee or per diem it paid to buy gifts for the kids, especially clothes—*new* clothes. As long as I could afford it, they would never have to wear secondhand again. I always got a special gift for Geneva: perfume, underwear, a gold ring. We laughed about it. She'd say, "It's like you're the husband and I'm the wife."

There was a sweetness to that, but sadness, too. When she was young, Geneva was the prettiest of the five of us. But now she was so heavy she was ashamed to even go out. Sometimes I'd beg her, "Manager, do your hair! Yes . . . I'll give you money! One hundred dollars, American dollars, if you'll just put on some nice clothes and come out with me!"

She always said no. But in the house, at the kitchen table, she'd grab on to every detail I offered about what I'd done. "What club did you go to? Who did you dance with? How many bottles of beer did you drink?" If I gave a speech, she'd demand that I describe the scene. "What were you wearing? Did people applaud? Did they stand?"

When I told Fata, she sighed. "She doesn't have a life," Fata said. "She lives through you."

During some of my travels to the WANEP office, I'd heard about Eastern Mennonite University (EMU), an American college with a well-known program in peace-building and conflict resolution. It was a Christian school that emphasized community and service; it had a long-standing relationship with WANEP and a history of recruiting Africans to study there. I was invited to attend a monthlong summer program, but during the war and Mass Action, that was impossible. Now there was time, and in May 2004, I left for Harrisonburg, Virginia.

Those four weeks were another transformative time for me. I studied with Hizkias Assefa, whose concepts had helped me let go of my anger toward Daniel (and whom I met again through WANEP), and Howard Zehr, who taught me the concept of "restorative justice." This was a response to criminal behavior that shied away from punishment and retribution in favor of repairing the harm done through a joint effort between victim and offender. The offender took steps to repair the harm done; the victim was restored and then forgave, and then both became contributing members of society. It felt very right to me. In village tradition, if you killed someone, you had to compensate for his absence. If you were a farmer harvesting one crop a year, you did the work of the man you killed, and brought in two. Restorative justice was that tradition applied on a larger scale, something we could see as ours and not artificially imposed by Westerners. And we needed it, needed that return to tradition. A culture of impunity flourished throughout Africa. People, officials, governments did evil but were never held accountable. More than we needed to punish them, we needed to undo the damage they had done.

On a more personal level, the idea of restorative justice gave me a deep sense of recognition and relief. So my response to child soldiers like Joseph Colley and Sam Brown, my desire to bring them back into society rather than casting them out, hadn't been crazy! I also felt supported in my feelings of impatience with trauma healing. It was a good process, just not enough. Purging oneself of pain was only the first step. If a community was to be made whole after war, especially civil war, perpetrators and victims had to come together.

When I left EMU, I knew there was more here for me. Somehow I would find a way to come back.

CHAPTER 16

TIME TO MOVE ON

In 2005, my sister Fata, who had been going to school and volunteering in the office of the African Women's Development Fund, developed a medical problem. The family thought she would get better care in the United States and we went to work getting her a visa. There was another reason for her to leave the country as well. Ma was important in the Sande, but no one else in our family had followed her into the secret society, and in recent months, there'd been growing pressure from my mother's side of the family that one of us do so. Having another Sande would bring the family power and prestige. Fata was in her twenties, old enough to make a decision for herself, but this kind of tradition isn't about personal choice. My mother is a modern woman, but she never could stand up to Ma. No outsider can say precisely what initiation into the Sande entails, because it's secret—but we did know that female genital mutilation was part of it. And so we sent Fata away, and she was glad to go. A cousin in Philadelphia had just had a baby and wanted someone to help her. Fata got the medical care she needed, and she never came back.

The summer of 2005 marked the end of the two years that the Accra peace treaty had afforded Liberia's transitional government, and it was time for elections. Twenty-two candidates crowded the ballot, with five having at least some chance of winning. One was Ellen Johnson Sirleaf. I was thrilled at the idea of a woman candidate, but still ambivalent about this particular one. I thought Ellen hadn't sufficiently addressed her own involvement with Taylor in the early days of the war, which meant electing her might threaten the peace. I had never forgiven her for her comment, "Level the Mansion, we will rebuild it!" I still remembered being in the compound with Doe's soldiers shouting, "We know you support Sirleaf!" That day was one of my most bitter memories of the war.

But I still felt strongly about the need for Liberian women to vote, so that our voices would be heard and the voting wouldn't be what we call "the same old six and seven" (the same old thing). Women didn't have the right to vote in Liberia until 1947, and even then you had to own property to cast a ballot. Indigenous women, market women, poor women had never gone to the polls in large numbers. In 1997, many who tried to vote didn't know they had to register beforehand and were turned away.

From the information my WIPNET sisters and I received, women still weren't registering—mostly because they didn't see the point. From their perspective, *no* government or political party represented their interests or did them much good. I went to speak with officials at the United Nations Development Program, which was overseeing the election to ensure its fairness. At the agency's invitation, I spoke at a meeting organized by a group of NGOs that would be involved in election oversight. I explained the problem, saying that what we needed was a voter registration campaign specifically targeting women. Sometimes you see what to do so clearly, but the official response you get is the same old six and seven. No one listened to me. Then, five days before the registration process closed, I got a call from a UNDP official. *"Come in! Hurry! We need to talk!"*

We need to do something, the official told me, as though he'd made a great discovery. Women are not registering to vote!

I just sat there looking at him. *Did you not hear me speak at your own conference?* Then I went back to the WIPNET office and assembled the tiny staff: Cecelia, Cerue, Lindora Diawara, who'd started as an office assistant and become my own assistant. (As it happened, Lindora was also the niece of Charles Taylor's wife, Jewel.) "We need women. Now." As soon as we reached out, volunteers stepped forward. Within a day we'd

We played endlessly with friends in the space and freedom of the Old Road community. My sister Josephine holds our niece "Baby," I'm in the blue shirt and vest, and my sister Fata is the little girl standing in front.

In our home, helping my mother prepare the Sunday morning meal was a mandate.

During the war, battles between government and rebel soldiers raged in the very center of Monrovia, leaving buildings destroyed and the streets covered in bullet casings. (Photo by Carolyn Cole/ *Los Angeles Times*)

After we fled to the Buduburam Refugee Camp in the early days of the war, I fried doughnuts to sell. This is one of the only images I have of my sister Geneva (behind me), who hated the camera.

I was so proud to graduate from college with my children there to watch. Amber and Nuku are in the back row; Arthur and Pudu are in the front.

Day after day, the women of the Liberian Mass Action for Peace sat in protest and would not retreat. (Photo by Pewee Flomoku)

The women's demand for peace spread until it included fifteen separate groups in nine counties. Hundreds joined in as we launched the action in rural Bong County, where my father was born.

On May 18, 2009, I received the John F. Kennedy Profile in Courage Award on behalf of the women peace activists of Liberia. "Close your eyes," I told the audience, "and dream of a world where babies no longer die by the roadside, where women are no longer brutally raped with impunity." (Photo by Lisa Poole/AP Photo)

In 2010, when I held a series of workshops to build bridges between women's groups in Congo, I met many brave, determined women. What we accomplished in Liberia is possible everywhere. (Photo by Alissa Everett) mapped out ten communities to target and sent ten teams of twenty women to work them. Each had a leader and a cell phone loaded with minutes. I stayed in the office to coordinate.

In a Monrovia market crowded with at least five hundred women selling their goods, our volunteers met a man who'd been part of the earlier registration effort. In five days, he'd registered ten women. (The women we met told us he'd spent his days sleeping.) The WIPNET volunteers spread out and went to work.

"Hello, Ma. Have you registered to vote yet?"

"No . . ."

"Well, why is that?"

"I can't leave my market stall! I have no one to stand and watch it."

"If there's war again, there won't be any market. Two of us will watch your stall—you register."

"Good morning, my sister. Have you registered to vote?"

"Ohhh, I can't. I don't have anyone to take my baby."

"I'll carry your baby on my back and we'll go together."

Everyone knew us: we were the "peace women." By the time registration closed, we had documented bringing in 7,477 women. Varbah Gayflor, who'd been serving as the minister of gender in the transitional government, and whom I counted as a friend, was running her own effort in rural areas. When we began, only 15 percent of registered voters were women. When we were done, it was 51 percent.

In August, more than 75 percent of Liberia's registered voters turned out to vote—thankfully, without violence. It took a week to count the ballots; Ellen and George Weah, a football star, would face each other in a runoff. Weah was a local boy, a slum child who'd become Liberia's greatest footballer, a FIFA World Player of the Year. The country's young men worshipped him. He'd gotten more votes than Ellen in the first round and was widely expected to win the second.

Friends from the community and church began approaching me and asking me to support Ellen. Finally, I agreed, for a few reasons. One of those who spoke to me on her behalf was Joseph Boakai, who would serve as her vice president. Joseph had not only funded the Mass Action, he publicly and respectfully advocated for us in a way very few others did. Another was Varbah Gayflor. I asked her for a pledge that a Sirleaf government would respect women's rights.

"Leymah," Varbah said, "if it gets to the point where the rights we've been fighting for are threatened, I will join you in the street."

Maybe the strongest persuasion came from my son Nuku. Shortly before the election, I was on my way to a conference in Cape Town and spent a few days in Accra. As usual, Geneva and the older kids wanted to talk a bit about Liberian politics. I was telling them about what had happened during the first round of voting and how Weah was expected to win.

"So people will choose a *footballer* to lead the country?" Nuku asked. "A school drop-out?"

From the time they were young, I had told my children that what mattered most was education. With my own struggles to get a degree, I had shown them. The conversation made me realize that this election wasn't about my personal feelings for Ellen Sirleaf, but about the values I'd taught my kids.

"No, that won't happen," I told Nuku. "He will not be our president."

WIPNET couldn't take sides publicly in the election, but we all had our private conversations with prospective voters. We emphasized the need to elect a candidate who'd represent women's interests.

International observers monitored voting on November 8, and UN military helicopters filled the skies. Ellen Sirleaf won 59 percent of the vote to Weah's 41 percent, and made history as she became Africa's first modern-day female head of state. When she took office, she thanked her sisters, "women of all walks of life whose votes significantly contributed to my victory."

A small irony is that the sole activist group she mentioned by name in her speech wasn't WIPNET or the Mass Action, but MARWOPNET, which just the year before had been given the UN Prize in the Field of Human Rights for its work bringing peace to Liberia. I have friends who were outraged by this, but I wasn't. The work I did for peace—that we all did—was never about winning prizes or finding glory. We did it because our country was in trouble and we needed to stand up, and because God ordained that we should be the ones to do so.

The war was over. We had elected a president. We elected a woman!
But after Ellen's election, the focus and discipline that had held together
our movement started to weaken. The WIPNET staff was losing control
over the protest at the field. People gave press interviews without going
through the office. Money was donated and disappeared. It was time to
end the sit-in. We held an emotional ceremony at the field marking the
end of the Mass Action. I thanked everyone, including the protesters'
husbands, partners and families, for their support. President Sirleaf was
there, and after I spoke, she approached me.

"Well said," she told me. She took my hand. "I'd like to have lunch
with you."

I told the president I'd call her, but I didn't. I didn't see a future for
myself in her government, or any government for that matter. I couldn't
envision a specific future for myself at all right then. I talked to my staff
and the WANEP office about what would come next, but I felt restless
and edgy. Nothing in my current work triggered the adrenaline rush I
craved, the feeling that I was being forced to grow and push past my own
limits each day. I wasn't taking action as much as looking back, and I
didn't want to rest on what had been done or become the chief of a small
neighborhood. I believed I had a future in the field of peace-building,
but to make the most of it, I had to learn more. I didn't think I could do
that in Liberia.

I told no one, but I had made a decision. In December, WIPNET held
its annual conference at Monrovia's city hall. I spoke about how I'd discovered WIPNET, about all the organization had accomplished and all it
meant to me. Over the years, I said, WIPNET hadn't just brought women
into peace-building, it had enhanced our wholeness in life. "We have
grown from twenty to over five thousand members. We are known as one
of the key contributors to the peace in Liberia. Not many can understand
how a humble beginning can produce such a magnificent institution."

Then I added news that no one expected to hear. I was leaving. This
day's event would be my last as WIPNET coordinator. When I finished
the speech, I recommended that Lindora, who I thought had shown real
strength as an administrator, take over as coordinator of WIPNET
Liberia, with Grace as her assistant.

The room fell silent. I could feel the shock. I'd chosen to be dramatic, because I am dramatic, though I realized later that this choice backfired badly. Resentment over how abruptly I left WIPNET and the fact that I'd consulted and told no one beforehand caused a lot of bitterness. My relationship with Cerue, who might have expected to succeed me, was never the same.

But at the time, I felt only relief. Shortly before my last day in the WIPNET office, I oversaw the start of one final project. Village women who wanted to participate in political life faced a key challenge: the men around them tended to suffer from terrible amnesia about what they did during the war. The women needed a space where they could assemble and set up a committee to work with local decision makers. We asked various communities to each give us a plot of land where we could build a "peace hut" to fill that need. The Evangelical Lutheran Church had given us $20,000, and construction on the first few structures was just getting under way.

So much of what I'd hoped for in the darkest days of the war had come to pass. And within just a few months, Charles Taylor would finally be in jail. In late March, President Sirleaf asked that the former president be extradited from Nigeria, where he'd been living in exile, to face a UN war crimes tribunal. On March 27, Taylor disappeared from his villa and two days later was spotted in a jeep with diplomatic tags, trying to cross into Cameroon. He was taken into custody and flown to Monrovia, where UN security officials arrested him.

In handcuffs, Taylor flew on to Sierra Leone to face charges of crimes against humanity for his part in supporting that country's civil war. (Later, because of security concerns, his trial was moved to The Hague.) To me, the moment was bittersweet. Taylor committed his greatest crimes in his own country, and we should have been the ones to try and punish him. But his arrest was another chapter ending. It was time for me to move on.

MY FRIEND THELMA was now working as a senior manager for a project at the Center for Conflict Resolution in South Africa. She and I still spoke constantly, not only sharing the details of our lives but debating political strategies and plans. For a long time, a joint dream had been transforming WIPNET into an organization that stood on its own. It had been necessary and good for us to work under the auspices of a larger organization when we began, but now it felt like a constraint. We'd grown at a rate faster than anyone had expected, and that our "parent" group couldn't match, particularly in Liberia. Every time we had a program, it sold out. Every time we sent out a grant proposal, we got funding. Yet because of the way we were set up, this money had to come to us through our WANEP "parent," which made us a women's network controlled financially by men. Feminist organizations that funded us didn't like that, and WANEP's program director in turn complained that "these women are very arrogant. We asked them how much money they are giving you and they wouldn't answer." We felt like we had to apologize for our success.

But if we became independent . . . I could run the organization, while Thelma could take her preferred role as the brains in the background. We'd still be a part of a greater network, but we'd be the ones in charge. We could do great things for the women of Africa.

In February 2006, I was in New York at a meeting of the UN Commission on the Status of Women. Thelma was there, too, as was Ecoma Alaga, a Nigerian who'd come to WANEP in 2003 as an intern and taken over Thelma's old position. On a very cold afternoon, we sat in my tiny hotel room and talked about our fantasy more seriously. We'd become autonomous, and make a couple of organizational changes. We'd add a program aimed at reforming security forces, like armies, police, and immigration and customs officials. Whenever wars ended, such forces invariably were reorganized, but women were never involved. That mattered, because what happens to women during conflict reflects how they're treated during peacetime, and vice versa. If in peace you have a military for whom abuse is common and normal, what happens when that military goes to war? The abuse rises to an unimaginable level. We would focus as much on preventing conflict as we had on dealing with its aftermath, so we'd be doing more than just putting out fires. We would track and document our strategies and actions more systematically than we had before, so we'd be clear on what worked and what didn't and also create a template for other activists to use.

We also decided to expand our focus from the West Africa region to the whole continent, where so many women suffered because of corrupt regimes and terrible civil wars. The new WIPNET would be the nexus where women from the east and west, north and south came together to discuss our common problems and merge our talents—West Africans who excelled at mobilizing, South Africans who brilliantly used the written word. We would reinvigorate languishing women's movements in countries like Uganda. And we would find a way to bring in young women, so our strength would continue across the generations.

It was a powerful vision. As it took shape, we held hands and prayed for guidance. "Lord, tell us Your wishes. Is this the direction You want us to take?"

We all felt the answer was "Yes," and that night, when I opened my Bible to my special verse, Isaiah 54:4, my eyes landed on the words "*Do not be afraid. You will not suffer shame. Do not fear disgrace, you will not be humiliated.*"

BACK HOME, we took the first baby steps to set up the new organization. We began contacting possible donors and partners, and then, with six hundred US dollars from Tunde, we rented a tiny, one-room office in Accra. (There was no way for us to operate in Liberia; donors made it clear that we needed to be based in a country easily reached by air and with a functioning banking system.) We also sent a letter to the WANEP board telling them that we were going off on our own.

We never questioned our right to do this; from the start, WIPNET had been Thelma's baby. She brought the idea to WANEP and assembled the first training group, and the peace-building manual she relied on when she taught us—the book full of exercises now being used throughout the conflict resolution movement—was something she'd worked on for years.

We were stunned when WANEP announced that WIPNET was theirs, ordered us to stop what we were doing, and even took us to Commercial Court in Accra over our use of the name. We had nothing with which to fight back, no documentation of Thelma's original approach or evidence that the program had been hers. Later, I understood this reaction as fear: the child was overpowering the parents. Sam Doe, who'd left the organization to get a PhD, spoke in our defense, and my old hero Tornolah Varpilah (who would become Liberia's deputy minister of health) eventually acknowledged that "we encouraged these women to do their work, but we ourselves didn't understand the concept of empowerment. When you empower another, you have to give up some power of your own." But we lost. To found the organization we envisioned, we had to change its name to WIPSEN: the Women in Peace and Security Network.

As we struggled to get WIPSEN off the ground, I moved my extended family to a larger, four-bedroom house in Accra that had a garage and yard—and four dogs that we inherited from the previous tenant. (The kids loved that.) My mother returned to Liberia. And Tunde and I changed our plans for the future. He was suffering from some health problems and said he was tired of the bureaucracy of the relief agency world. I'd been talking for a long time about my wish to go back to school; he said he'd invest in my education and help me do it. With a graduate degree, I'd earn a much higher salary. He could then quit his job and move to Accra; we'd get married and live off my salary and the fees he'd earn by taking consulting jobs.

I can admit now that deep down, I knew this scenario could not come true. I had a strong sense of where I was going with WIPSEN. I could feel a rebirth of the passion and focus I'd felt in the early days of organizing, and I felt that I had a lot to prove. I knew that the organization would eventually consume my life.

And yet I said nothing. I held on to the image of a shared future. I desperately wanted to go back to school. Whatever I did, a degree would give me legitimacy, and legitimacy meant more options for the future.

When I was accepted as a master's degree candidate in conflict transformation studies at Eastern Mennonite University (EMU) in Harrisonburg, Virginia, Geneva was thrilled. The day I waited to see if my travel visa would come through, she called every five minutes. She reminded me that she'd missed my graduation from Mother Patern because she was home taking care of Pudu.

"But not this one! This one I will travel to the United States to attend!"

April 12 was her fortieth birthday, and we had a wonderful time when I came to visit.

"Manager, drink a cold beer with me!" I insisted as I lay sprawled on her bed. "You haven't had sex in a long time, at least have a beer!"

She burst out laughing. The kids crowded at the door. "Can we come in?"

"Out!" I yelled. "Sister talk! Out!"

I gathered a group of friends for a big celebration. We got Geneva the denim miniskirt she'd asked for and for once, she had her long hair done and put on makeup. She looked gorgeous. When she came out of her room, my friends started screaming, "Woooo!"

Mammie smiled her beautiful smile. "I've started to live—because life begins at forty."

CHAPTER 17

AN UNTHINKABLE LOSS

My preparations for going to the US were in order. The reports I got from Ghana suggested everything was stable. Arthur had gone mad for football. Geneva talked about losing weight, because every time she walked down the road, her heart bothered her. One of the house dogs had a litter, and the kids fell in love with a yellow puppy they named Nashat.

One night, I woke in terror. In my dream, a voice I'd heard somewhere before was speaking. *The death news. The death news. Who's going to tell it?*

All I could think of was Ma and even though it was the middle of the night, I called Geneva in Accra. As it turned out, Ma *was* sick, but she recovered.

"I miss you," Geneva said. "Come home to me."

June, Accra. I was visiting Mammie and the kids. Sugars was in town and had come by. We drank beer and talked and afterward, I drove her to her hotel. When I got back, my sister and Leemu were in the living room.

"Okay, Manager," I said, "I'm off to bed."

"It's so early," she said, pouting. "Sit with me. Let's talk."

"I told you I'm not your husband," I said. "I need my beauty nap."

She laughed. "All right. See you in the morning then."

Time passed. I was half asleep when Leemu rushed into my room. "You have to come! My mom can't breathe!"

Geneva was on her bed, gasping. "I can't! . . ."

"Come! Come!" A friend who was staying with us helped me carry her outside and into the car.

"I can't breathe!" Geneva said again. She was terrified. "Please, God, don't let me die!" Suddenly she doubled over and began to throw up.

I raced to the nearest hospital, and we found a wheelchair and struggled to get her inside.

The nurses on duty just stared at us. "The doctors are all on strike," they told us. "We can't help you."

My sister seemed to faint and slumped to the floor.

"Manager!" I shouted, hardly knowing what I was saying. "Manager, if this is your last day on earth, please, God, don't die on this floor!"

Mammie's eyes fluttered. We got her back in the wheelchair. And then she looked at me with an expression of such . . . sadness. Such love. Her look said, "I'm so sorry." Her face was peaceful but very pale.

In desperation, I pushed her back to the car. "We'll go somewhere else! We'll find a doctor."

"Just let me rest," she whispered. She lay down in the back seat, clinging to my friend's lappa.

"Is she okay?" I asked.

"Yes," said my friend. "She's holding me so tightly . . . "

I slowed down and a strange calm came over me. When we got to the next hospital, I found a nurse. "I think my sister is dead. Can you confirm it for me?" She held a stethoscope to Mammie's chest, and then she nodded.

Every doctor in the country was on strike and every mortuary in Accra was full. We spent three hours driving around the city before we found one that would accept Geneva's body. By then it was dawn and I had to go home and tell the children. Leemu and Nuku wept inconsolably. Amber had a crazy smile on her face. Pudu insisted that a man had already come to her bedside to tell her that Aunty Mammie had died. For two days, she roamed the house without sleeping.

I called Sweden, France and, worst of all, Monrovia.
The death news: I had to tell it.

We brought Geneva back to Liberia and held her funeral at St. Peter's. We could only afford to bring Leemu and Nuku, who was so close to her she considered him her son. All the kids wrote a tribute that we read in the church, their memories of daily life with Aunty Mammie, her cooking, love for Bollywood movies, her orders that they all politely "listen to Pudu's never-ending boring story." Recognition made everyone there laugh. "We will see you on Judgment Day," the children concluded. *"We love you!"*

I didn't go to Mammie's grave after the funeral; I couldn't bear it. Until today, I've never been.

Pudu woke me in the night and said she was hungry; she wanted cereal. Geneva would have known exactly what to do: the kind of cereal, the amount, which bowl, how much milk. I had no idea. I took everything out and put it on the table. All the kids had come out and were looking at me.

"She used to fix it for me," Pudu said.

I can't do this, I thought. But I poured the cereal into the bowl and added milk. Handed it to Pudu. None of us cried or said her name.

It was all the little things that Geneva had known and I didn't that frightened me. Having to guess who drank milk and who liked juice. Who sat where at the table.

"You don't know anything about us!" my children said.

As kids, Nuku and Amber had run from bullets, gone hungry, lived through the filth and stink of the *Bulk Challenge*, fled with me from Daniel. Arthur and Pudu had left me to live with Geneva before they were old enough for school. Leemu had never known her father. Malou had been abandoned by both her parents. For all of them, Geneva was the one constant, the stable center of their lives.

I talked to my old friend Jill Hinrichs, the American social worker and grief counselor I'd met in the early Trauma Healing days. "If you were in this country, people would tell you to put all those kids in therapy," she said.

That wasn't a possibility, so I did the other things she suggested: I talked to the kids about Mammie, hugged and kissed them endlessly, reassured them as much as I could. But I couldn't change our situation. I needed to make a living to support my family. A graduate degree would help me do that. The school term would start in a few weeks, and I needed to go. I knew my kids were suffering, but I thought if we absorbed all the pain at once—the pain of Geneva's death, of separation—later on we would reap the benefits. I did not want to uproot them. I hoped I could find a way to keep them in our rented Accra house. But my mother said she would not come back, and the friends in Ghana whom I'd hoped could be caretakers, turned out to be completely untrustworthy. When I went to Monrovia for Geneva's funeral, I left them in charge of the house, and a month's worth of food vanished in a week, along with a lot of cash and some new underwear and perfume I'd bought for Geneva.

The only solution, it seemed, was an old one: Paynesville. My parents told me that coming back to their roots and to family would help the kids. But they didn't want to go. All of them were silent when I told them they were moving, too distraught to protest. It was agonizing, and all I could offer was the dog. You don't usually find Africans traveling with animals, but they adored Nashat, and they had lost so much. I spent five hundred dollars US that I really didn't have to bring him with us on the plane.

I resettled everyone at my parents' house and then flew to Virginia. All I could think of was getting back home as fast as possible. I completed a two-year program in nine months, and the time I was away nearly broke all of us.

AT GRADUATE SCHOOL, I could feel my mind expand, my comprehension deepen. I realized I now could put a formal name, "strategic peace building," to what I'd done instinctively in Liberia. Classes like "advocacy versus activism" helped me understand some of what hadn't worked. The Mass Action infighting, for instance. When a group is in the spotlight, others working for the same cause don't get as much attention as they deserve, then everyone rushes at the media—"Me, me, me!"—and the togetherness that fueled the action collapses.

I did consultancies and spoke at conferences whenever I had the chance, to help pay the bills. Some of this work was surreal. I went to Egypt, because then–First Lady Suzanne Mubarak held a conference focused on starting an Arab women's peace network. The disparities of power made it a waste of time. If someone from Saudi Arabia spoke, the Yemeni women were supposed to listen respectfully, but not vice versa. We heard that Palestinian women didn't trust those from other countries in the region, so they weren't there. I was told not to even mention the word "Israel." By day two, most of us who'd flown in as consultants were going to the local market and drinking beer or smoking hashish. I was paid $10,000 and because I was a special guest of the government, two bodyguards with submachine guns stood outside my hotel door.

Many of the other students at EMU had lived through conflict, and there was a relief in being among them. During my WIPNET days, I often felt that my role as leader required me to hold back my own feelings. One week, in 2004, I'd learned that the young nephew of a friend had been shot in the face in some kind of accident; then my dad lost someone he'd known since childhood, was grieving hard, and with my mother in Ghana, it was up to me to prepare him to go to the village for the funeral.

When I went back to work, Cerue stared at me. "You look horrible."

I knew I looked like shit, but I smiled. "I'll get over it."

How do you complain about your problems when all around you there are women who are suffering even more? You don't. You don't say a word.

In Harrisonburg, a small old city in the Shenandoah Valley, far from Liberia and its sorrows and people who expected something from me, I didn't have to be strong. Every now and then—for instance, when I saw a mother with her children—I would burst into tears. No one at EMU thought that was strange. I met an old man who'd lost his entire family in the Rwandan genocide. An Afghani who'd never known a time when his country was not at war, and who drank too much. He had never celebrated his birthday, and I made him a surprise party with a cake. Some of the other students called me "Big Mama" or "Mother of Peace."

Being away from my own children never stopped hurting. They were not doing well; they were grief stricken and furious at having been pulled from an indulged, comfortable existence to the deprivations of Liberia and a house where no one ever asked "How do you feel?" but just expected them to wash up after themselves and carry on. They couldn't stand being without water, electricity and TV. School was terrible—the other kids talked back to the teachers and undercut each other. And there was nothing I could do. I used all my cash to buy calling cards. When I heard that Nashat was sick, I spent hours on my knees praying. *Please God, watch over that dog!* He died. Food in Liberia remained scarce. One day, Leemu gave me a vivid, graphic description of the meal she was eating: plain yam with palm oil and a little salt. When I thought of my children's hunger, I couldn't eat.

CHAPTER 18

BUILDING A NEW
WOMEN'S NETWORK

SOMETIMES, the biggest changes in your life begin in moments you barely notice while they're taking place. In September 2006, just after Geneva died and just as graduate school started, I traveled to New York to address the UN. It was the fifth anniversary of the passage of Resolution 1325, which called for bringing more women into UN peace and security efforts, and for warring countries to take special measures to protect women and girls from gender-based violence. There wasn't anything new to say: the resolution still hadn't been widely implemented. (Today, after another five years, the story's the same. Every time there's a conflict, the resolution is dusted off and everyone shouts, "We need to do something!" Then nothing happens.)

While I was there, I got a call from a woman named Abigail Disney, a longtime feminist and philanthropist. After President Sirleaf's election, she had gone to Liberia with a delegation from the Women and Public Policy Program at Harvard's Kennedy School of Government to offer sisterly help and support. While she was there, she heard about the Mass Action. Now she and Gini Reticker, an independent filmmaker, were hoping to make a documentary about it. Sewanee Hunt, another philanthropist whom I knew, had suggested she contact me.

"Can we talk?" Disney asked.

"I'm leaving tomorrow," I said curtly.

"We'll come to your hotel."

"All right, all right." I agreed only because my mother always advised me, "Never refuse a call but what is in it." I was tired and I didn't see what I had to say to these white girls.

The next day, the three of us met in the lobby of my hotel, a small, plain place within walking distance of the UN. Gini and Abigail, who introduced herself as Abby, were older than me, simply dressed, and carrying notepads.

"Tell us about your work in Liberia," Abby said.

Oh Lord. I went through the story and they listened, jumping in every now and then with a "Who was that?" or "Wait, which happened first?" There was a lot they hadn't heard.

After two hours, I said I had to go, and I wasn't very friendly.

Well, I thought when I got back to my room, *I'll never hear from them again.* I was sure nothing would come of this film idea. *Disney?* Were they planning to make a cartoon?

Within a week, though, I got another call. The project was progressing. Gini and Abby were planning a trip to Liberia in December; would I be there?

It was my holiday, so of course I went home. Things were terrible. Leemu was having angry outbursts, screaming at my parents. Nuku, who had always been so chatty, was withdrawn and silent. I could see the stress on my parents—not just the burden of the children in their house, but their own loss. My mother never got over the death of her firstborn. She blamed the war: if not for it, her child would still have been home, with her.

Tunde was back, too. His contract in Indonesia hadn't been renewed, his health wasn't strong, and once again he wanted to talk about our future. When I brought up my commitment to WIPSEN, he got upset. Yes, he'd given me $600 to rent the office, but he'd paid far more in tuition. What was the point of spending so much money for a degree if all I was going to do was struggle? I had no answer for him.

In the midst of my stay, Gini and Abby arrived, and I went with them to a meeting at the offices of WIPNET. It was tense. Lindora tried to tell Gini about some of the organization's current projects; Gini only wanted to talk about the Mass Action, and Lindora got insulted. A few days later, she called me.

"How much are those women paying you?"

At the end of the week, I got another call, asking me to come back to the WIPNET offices. Except for Sugars, Vaiba, Asatu and Grace, everyone who'd been part of the Mass Action was there. We formed a circle—and one by one, the women I'd considered allies and friends attacked me: I was undermining them, I was still trying to run things, I had stolen money, I had taken credit for everything WIPNET had done while "not doing shit," and all I'd ever wanted was power.

Does this fighting sound petty? It was not. Some time later, I met the American feminist Gloria Steinem, who talked to me about the "pull her down" syndrome, a way in which too often women denigrate other women. This infighting happens in any society or group that has been impoverished or disenfranchised for a long time. You see one person doing well, think she's getting it all and want only to take it away. I understand it, but it is very destructive. That day, I broke down and cried. If what I'd wanted was power, I'd had plenty of chances to take it. When the interim president, Gyude Bryant, was first putting together his government, he'd asked me to work with him. When George Weah first decided to run for president, he'd asked me to run as his vice president. Both times, I'd said no. I did the work I did because I wanted a stable Liberia for my kids, not because I was after power and glory. And money? There were no secret bank accounts in my life—I barely had enough to live on.

"I taught you," I choked out to the women in the circle. "When you came to WIPNET, I held your hands. And now I regret having laid eyes on every one of you."

Back in Virginia, living through the long winter months, I got a cold that never went away and then a throat infection. I went to class and did my work. But inside, I felt panic, sadness and cold, swirling blackness.

Thelma and I were being sued by former friends at WANEP over our desire to move in a new direction. I was terrified that our new organization might fail. When Thelma, Ecoma and I had held hands and prayed, we'd formed a pact. God had heard, and you don't go to Him with something and then give up. Tunde wanting something from me I wasn't prepared to give. The anguish that emanated from my kids when we spoke merged with my own over being away from them, and the loss of Geneva. Mammie had been like a mother to me while I was growing up. When I was a teenager and she got a big bed, I used to snuggle up next to her. As a woman, she was my truest, best friend. I would never be able to confide in anyone as freely as I did in her. And in dying, she had taken all her memories of my children, all the moments I'd missed and depended on her to describe and give back to me later: Pudu's baby speech, Arthur's football games, Nuku's struggles with math. There was so much I'd never know. All of it was gone now.

The words and accusations thrown in that circle of confrontation at WIPNET over the Christmas break continued to eat into me. I could live with being criticized by generals, UN officials, even the men of WANEP. But these women had been my family—the family I'd often put first, before my children. I gave them everything I had and being with them was what made me happy. If there were a way to split open my heart and see what was in there, it would show that to me these women were my sisters.

I worked, phoned home, tried to raise money for WIPSEN, fielded complaints from the kids. And I drank. More and more and more still. So much of what had happened in my life had been unplanned. My years with Daniel. My leadership of the Mass Action. I never expected to be living without my kids or imagined that Geneva would die. When I drank I didn't forget, but I could relax a little. When you have a history of ulcers, abusing alcohol is taking your life in your hands. One night the pain in my stomach was so bad, I ended up in the ER.

"If you want to get better, you're going to have to stop drinking," the doctor told me.

The scare stopped me. For a little while.

WHEN ABBY AND GINI BEGAN work on their documentary, I traveled to New York for interviews and taping sessions. There was a lot I didn't want to talk about, such as my private life, and a surprising amount I couldn't remember. Everything had happened so fast. There was never time to sit back and think.

Now I was rushing to finish the school year, and during one session I was so exhausted I literally started falling asleep. The next thing I knew, I heard Abby's voice: "Leymah, open your eyes!"

I was too busy to think much about the documentary slowly taking shape. As part of my schoolwork, I was doing a final paper reviewing the ECOWAS gender policy, as well as developing a training manual on how to get women involved in the electoral process in West Africa. But during the filming, a friendship quickly grew between Abby and me. I could not have found someone from a more different background than mine—this white woman, raised in wealth and privilege, with a family name everyone in America knew. But as women, we were very much alike. Abby completely threw herself into projects that she believed in; she was driven but could see the humor in difficult situations and liked to laugh about it. She was blunt, too—not everyone would come out and call my generous butt "that wagon you drag behind you."

For all our financial disparity, I never felt she saw me as anything but an equal. On one of my first trips to New York to be interviewed, she invited me to stay at her apartment. It was a homey place, with a welcoming spirit that actually reminded me of Liberia, where no one's a stranger for more than a night. I was surprised to see that Abby had four children; truthfully, my image of wealthy white women was that they had one child, if any, and gave all their attention to their dogs. The morning after I arrived, I was in my bedroom and Abby knocked on the door.

"Why are you hiding in here? Don't you want breakfast? Don't be shy . . . Whatever you see is for you."

Later, the whole family and I sat around eating waffles. Joking. Playing. I was a bit shocked that Abby did her own dishes.

Abby knew a lot about the situation in Liberia—after her outreach to President Sirleaf, she'd donated money to help rebuild schools there—

and had launched and run her own foundation in New York, so she understood the struggle I faced getting funding for WIPSEN. She said she couldn't give me money while we were working together, but she threw a dinner party for me and introduced me to local philanthropists and heads of foundations. She hit the streets of New York with me, knocking on doors and speaking in support of WIPSEN. By the time I left, I had $50,000 in funding. Abby also introduced me to Gloria Steinem and Marie Wilson, a former president of the Ms Foundation for Women and founder of The White House Project, which works to advance women in politics, business and media.

During one of my roughest patches that year, when the rent was due, exams were about to start, and my parents were calling to say that the money I'd sent for the kids had run out, I got very sick. Abby phoned about something—I don't remember what anymore—and I confessed that I wasn't feeling well. I must have sounded terrible, because within a day, there was a guy at my door with an enormous bouquet of very colorful flowers and a get-well note from her. I just broke down and cried. I was so far from home and struggling, and it was good to know that someone cared.

On April 30, 2007, I finished my coursework at EMU. In my program, you had the choice of writing a thesis or going to work on a practical project. I already knew I would work on WIPSEN's development. One week later, I returned to Accra, helped run our first conference and plunged into a campaign

Two women from Sierra Leone whom I knew from the WIPNET days came to the conference and told us they were once again afraid for their country. Their own first postwar elections were coming up and women's organizations were observing that indicators of violence were high. Each of the political parties had a specific color: the ruling party was red, and the main opposition was green. Anyone who wore red in a community favoring the opposition might get beaten. Some deaths had been reported. The specifics of Sierra Leone's civil war had been horrific—child soldiers, civilians massacred and displaced, gang rape. Rebels had amputated the hands of children. Everyone lived in dread of a new outbreak of fighting, but no one knew quite what to do.

We did. It was the first time we'd taken our strategies across a national border, and it worked brilliantly. We brought in twenty-two Liberian women with experience in our movement to work with their Sierra Leonean sisters. We talked to women from all the political parties, as well as rural women, and planned a women's campaign for violence-free elections. Everywhere we went, we let political leaders and the community know: We are watching you. Avert violence. Work for peace.

We divided the country into four regions and scheduled activities to raise awareness in different communities. The day these activities were held, a "peace train" came to town. Actually, it was a big bus filled with women, including Sugars, Vaiba and a few of the other old-timers. The day we marched through the streets of the capital, Freetown, people ran out to see what was happening. We went to the headquarters of the various political parties, and the women issued their statements. The Liberian women danced and held up placards and banners that said PEACE IN SIERRA LEONE! Sometimes, when we gave radio interviews, the host would joke, "Beware, the Liberian women have come to inspire Sierra Leone to elect a woman president!"

The people of Sierra Leone went to the polls, and there was no violence. Afterward, the president-elect, Ernest Bai Koroma, gave us a certificate crediting some of that success to us.

Even as the Sierra Leone campaign went on, I went back and forth to Monrovia to see the kids and Tunde. I now had my master's degree. The long struggle was over. But now, strangely, the achievement that had been his idea seemed to cause problems between Tunde and me. When I visited him in Monrovia, he talked uncomfortably about how educated I was. "I guess you're too high class for me now," he said.

I sent an email to everyone I knew telling them that whenever they saw him, they should offer thanks on my behalf—I only had a master's because he had made it possible.

It wasn't her style, but even Thelma came to talk to him. "There's no need for you to be intimidated. Leymah loves you."

We talked about the future, and suddenly it was Tunde who was holding back. "How can I move to Accra? What would I do there? I don't have a job."

Tunde, who showed me my value when I thought I was worthless. Tunde, who became my friend when I was used to abuse, who never tried to put himself above me. The mother who'd been forced to give him away was a poor woman who went out late at night to pick up bottles to sell. A helpless woman. I think that for Tunde, "love" is saving a helpless woman. When I grew strong and no longer needed a savior, something went out of the relationship for him.

Our end was a familiar kind of story. There was a young woman who lived near the Paynesville house—single, poor, a number of children. I knew her. Her stepfather was distantly related to my dad. She came to Geneva's funeral and called me "sister." I had given some of the kids' clothes to her and money to her brother, who came by with stories of need. Then she'd done me a favor and I kept mentioning to Tunde that I meant to thank her.

"Yes, it would be good to meet her," he said. And "Yes, introduce me because I don't know her." And "What does she look like? I don't know who she is."

I got a mysterious phone call one day from someone who said that Tunde was involved with this woman. He denied and denied, and when he finally broke down and confessed, I started packing my suitcase. *I don't know who she is.* It wasn't that there'd been someone else as much as it was all those lies.

Later, Tunde wrote the kids a long letter, apologizing and blaming himself for the fact that we weren't together. He promised to stay in their lives, but that didn't really last. We never completely lost our friendship—we still talk. We can always talk. But the breakup hurt, a pain edged with anger and regret. We held on too long when both of us should have realized it was time to go our separate ways. It was ten years of my life.

Right before I began the WIPSEN Sierra Leone campaign, I ran into my friend Vaiba at the airport. She introduced the man who was with her as her nephew, James; now based in Accra, he'd left Liberia as a child and grown up in London. James was in his forties, tall, attractive, an information technology and services consultant. He gave me his business card, and I called him to talk about putting together a website for WIPSEN. I didn't ask for favors, but he did a prototype for free. When I offered a "Thank you, nephew!" he said, "Don't call me that," and asked to buy me lunch. Then drinks. Then dinner. Then I had backed away. I hadn't been single or free.

But there was no Tunde now. I arranged to move into a small house that Ecoma, my WIPSEN cofounder, had rented, but the kids hadn't yet come from Liberia, and I was brutally lonely. With all I can do, I'm not good at being by myself. Not long ago, I found one of Thelma's leadership training manuals that we used during the early years. As an exercise in self-knowledge, you wrote down your greatest fears. Mine were having unsuccessful children and growing old alone. James called again. He had a calmness that drew me. We connected physically. I told myself I needed the distraction. Later, my kids joked that "Aunty Vaiba loved you so much she made sure you really became family."

By August 2007, WIPSEN was thriving and I was determined to bring back my children to live with me like a real family. On the plane from Monrovia to Accra, Malou, who, like Pudu, was nine, began to cry.

"Why are you crying?" Nuku, now fourteen, demanded.

"I miss Grandma. She looked so sad when we left."

Nuku started laughing. "No light! No water! No gas for the generator! What else do you miss?"

I broke in. "Do any of the rest of you miss Grandma?"

"No," said thirteen-year-old Amber flatly. "We've been around too much and we're always losing things. It's hard to miss anyone."

I felt like someone had hit me in the heart. I was angry at life, and at myself. Look what I had done. Yet if I'd had to do it again, I'm not sure what I could have changed. I know my children were angry at me. Later, when I asked if any of them wanted to grow up to be a peace-builder, Amber's response was, "No. I want to stay home with my children."

But if I ask, "Could I have done this differently?" my answer is always no. I still don't see what other options I had. I know many women who saw and went through a lot, with their children. Many of them didn't make it. Either they succumbed to the misery of war violence or domestic violence and died, or they abandoned their children and ran. We stuck it out and survived.

We still had one more loss waiting for us: the departure of Geneva's daughter, Leemu. Though we never learned why, not long before Geneva died, she had given her email password to Josephine, in France. After her death, Josephine called me to say there was something I needed to know: Geneva had been writing to Leemu's father, the fiancé who had broken her heart so badly, now a doctor in the United States. Geneva's hope was that Leemu might join him in Ohio, that there she would have opportunities and the chance for a life Geneva couldn't afford to give her. I decided that if this was what my sister had wanted, I would make it happen. My parents were furious, but I contacted Leemu's father.

He came to Accra, and he and his wife spent a week with us, so I could learn what kind of people they were; so they could see that Leemu was loved and lacked for nothing. She decided she wanted to go with them. The morning she left, we were all crying, and after a year of such sadness it was almost a surprise that any of us had tears left to shed.

During this time, my drinking got worse. It was the sadness, the pressure, the frustration.

You wake up in the morning and rush right to work because ensuring women's place in Africa's future is so important. We must have a say in all the processes that lead to peace; we must be accepted as equal partners in nation building. But the work is always a struggle. For me, the pleasure of moving from the local to the international stage was a chance to accomplish more, yet it still took exhausting effort to make anything happen. A war ends, and the international powers insist that an army be reformed, but when it comes to gender equality, nothing changes. Case in point: Liberia, where if a female soldier got pregnant out of wedlock, she had to get married or be discharged. But if she was impregnated by another soldier who refused to marry her, there were no consequences for him. Case in point: Ghana, where a woman who joined the army was required to stay unmarried for three years, and one who worked for immigration and wanted to wed had to ask her boss for permission first. And Sierra Leone, where women regularly were sexually harassed, even raped, on duty.

In civil society, women were still not voting or running for office. Young girls were dropping out of high school to have sex and babies, because they saw no other options. One of WIPSEN's programs was to work with the women of the Zongo community in Ghana—predominantly Muslim and desperately poor. Their practice was marrying off their girls as soon as they reached sixth grade. We wanted to work with the girls, but you can't make a child excited about completing school unless you can make her mother understand that a girl's education doesn't have to end at twelve. That requires finding prominent Muslim women who have made it to work with you, too. And addressing these families' poverty, because a mother will tell you that the dowry a marriage brings is all that keeps the family going.

You have to find money to do all this. Dozens of international laws and pieces of policy call for women's inclusion in the work of running the world, but everybody wants it to simply happen, not to have to spend money laying the groundwork to *make* it happen. Women's work gets the funding dregs. What most organizations go through in a month, you make last a year. The energies you might spend in the field you instead use to persuade people to give you small sums.

The cry for your help is constant. Elections are coming, violence is erupting, rape is epidemic, meetings are scheduled, an appearance is urgently requested . . . *We hear you work in this area, can you please come to our conference? Can you make a speech? Can you work with our girls? Can you please, please write a report?*

It is so hard to say no. After you do this work for a while, you meet enough people that nothing feels distant anymore. When something happens in Zimbabwe, I think of my friends Betty and Jenny and their children. How are they faring? If the problem is in Uganda, I worry about Ruth. In Sierra Leone, Barbara and her small adopted nephew; in Afghanistan, my classmate from EMU; in Kenya, Dorine and Norya. . . . Every conflict has a face, many faces. Every problem touches your heart.

So you say yes. You leave your children—again—and go. Come home. And then the next day it all starts again. You wake up at five in the morning, sometimes four, thinking about what has to be done, and by the time you give up trying to sleep and get out of bed, you're already behind on the email coming in from other parts of the world, and you need to skim five newspapers online to keep up with what's happening, and the cell phone is buzzing.

Don't ever stop, that old woman had said to me during the war. You encounter a lot of women like that who otherwise wouldn't have had the opportunity to speak out. When I wanted to give up, I heard her voice. Every disappointment, every time the donors didn't approve a grant, every time I thought, *The hell with it, I'll find a well-paying job and take it easy,* I heard it. *Don't stop.*

There was no way to slow down. At the end of the day, I'd have a glass of wine and tell myself that was it. But the second glass tasted better, and after it, there always was another and another. James was very careful about how he behaved in front of the children, and I saw the disapproval in his face. I shrugged it off, but he enlisted the kids.

"Mom!" one of them would chide at some point. "What are you doing? That's . . . too much."

In April, for Amber's fourteenth birthday, we had a crowd over to celebrate. And I drank—I know this, because the kids watched and counted and told me—fourteen glasses of wine. They were staring at me, looking disgusted. I didn't care.

"This party's over, so I'm going out with my friends," I announced late in the evening. When I woke up the next day, I was sick, my head was pounding, and I'd lost a good gold ankle chain and bracelet. I never figured out how or where.

"Mom," Arthur said. "You have to stop this."

Not yet. Not yet.

I had a meeting and passed a bar on my way home. I meant to have one gin and tonic. I don't remember how many I drank, but the pain from my ulcer pushed me to a pharmacy and after I took a painkiller, I passed out for a while in the front seat of the car with the engine on and the air conditioner going. I made it home and begged James to take me to the doctor. "The pain's so bad . . . I think I'm dying. . . ."

Then I saw the kids gathered around us, their terrified, helpless faces. After all their losses, this would be the final one. No. Not possible.

It might sound too easy, but that was the end for me. I still don't sleep easily and I still wake up too early, but I don't drink anymore.

CHAPTER 19

PRAY THE DEVIL BACK TO HELL

IN THE SPRING OF 2008, I went to Abby's apartment to see a rough version of the documentary that was being called *Pray the Devil Back to Hell*. It's unnerving to witness your own struggle played back to you, and the contrast—the violence and deprivation on-screen, the comfort in which I now sat—made it surreal. In a way, it was the first time I could see the story *as* a story: the difficulty of our effort, its context and importance. While the Mass Action unfolded and the war raged around us, we didn't have time to think or reflect; we just reacted and tried to keep moving forward.

Beyond the interviews with me, Vaiba, Asatu, Sugars and Janet Johnson-Bryant—the journalist who broadcast WIPNET's messages over the radio—Abby and Gini had included battle scenes that were very painful to watch: children wailing, women fleeing, on their faces the expressions of desolation and hopelessness I remembered very well. There was footage I'd never seen of me, of us.

It had been nearly impossible to find. Abby and Gini had talked to a number of the photojournalists who covered the Liberian war. Between them, they'd recorded scores of images of carnage, terror and the brutal exuberance of soldiers as they cradled guns or held up enemy skulls. But no one had filmed the women of the Mass Action. *"Why would we?"* the photographers asked Abby and Gini. *"They just looked pathetic."* But it turned out that the official videographer for the Executive Mansion had footage of the day I'd presented our demands to President Taylor. News cameras had captured the confrontation at the peace talks in Accra. And there we were.

At my first glimpse of the once-familiar sight of women in white bearing placards, my eyes filled with tears. We looked different than I remembered. *So dark from the sun! So thin!* We had all gone through so much, yet resolve radiated from us, especially the rural women. Ordinary people had been *that* hungry for peace. When I watched myself in the hotel hallway in Accra, I broke down. Look at how low we'd been driven! I had been ready to strip naked, in public! When the film ended with our triumph—Taylor gone, the war over, the election of Ellen Sirleaf—everyone in the room applauded.

Fata, who had driven in from Pennsylvania to join us, understood the implications of the film better than I did, and reached over to take my hand.

"Leymah," she said, "this is going to be huge."

She was right. *Pray the Devil Back to Hell* had its premiere on April 24, 2008, at the Tribeca Film Festival in New York. The final version was more polished and less violent than the one I'd seen, but if watching myself on the screen in Abby's comfortable living room had been a little surreal, this time I felt like I was in a dream. Dressed in a traditional head tie and African suit of vivid black and green, I entered the theater on an actual red carpet. Around me clustered American celebrities: Robert De Niro, Jane Fonda, Rosie O'Donnell, Edie Falco. We won the Best Documentary Feature award, and almost as soon as we got home, the phones began ringing.

One of the early callers was Sugars. "Get your ass over here and show us your movie!"

Gini and Abby and I flew to Monrovia almost right away, and we held a screening for women who'd sat on the field. It was a very emotional night. For them, as for me, this wasn't an abstract story; it was their lives, and whenever there was a shot of a wounded child or crowds fleeing, their belongings piled on their heads, you could hear everyone inhaling sharply with the memory.

One scene—a clip of President Taylor proclaiming that "if God didn't want me to be here, I wouldn't be here"—had everyone roaring. Because, at the end of the day, apparently God *didn't* want him to be there! In these moments, Gini and Abby couldn't understand why everyone was laughing. It wasn't easy to explain.

Someone once said to me that slave culture affected Liberians in a strange way; he said that the more slaves were beaten, the more they sang as a way to resist, but when something evil happens to Liberians, we laugh. I sometimes think that was the way all of us survived those terrible years. I remember one day in July of 1990, when we were at Josephine's and there was a missile blast. We were running all over the place, and when we got to a bit of safety, someone pointed to Josephine's boyfriend's uncle, who wore a Muslim praying gown. "Did you see that guy run? Is he even wearing underwear?" Everyone broke out laughing.

The first time I went on the road with the researchers from Manchester during my Trauma Healing days, we ended one afternoon drinking palm wine together. Of course the conversation turned to the war.

Our driver, whose name was Moses, told us about a time when he and half a dozen other men had been arrested. They'd been locked in a room, stripped and hung by their wrists from the ceiling. Each morning, a soldier would come in and sing a nursery rhyme while moving his pointing finger from man to man: "Eenie, meenie, minie moe, catch a rabbit by the toe . . ." At the end of the rhyme, whoever he was pointing at would have his penis cut off. The process went on day after day after day until Moses was the last man left. And then, inexplicably, they let him go.

"Every time they started that rhyme, I would *shrivel*," Moses said, grinning. "By the end, I was practically a woman!"

We all howled and choked. A Swedish boy who was working with the Manchester researchers looked at us in horror. "You people are *sick!*" he shouted and ran off. We almost killed ourselves laughing.

You laugh instead of cry. You laugh because you survived and in an hour, something else might threaten your life. What else can you do?

Interestingly to me, when we were watching the film, the people from America laughed at the scenes where we talked about withholding sex from our husbands as a way to get them to fight for peace, too. In Liberia, nobody thought that was funny.

Soon, calls were coming in from around the world. Film critics loved *Pray*, calling it "gripping," "inspiring," "exhilarating," "enough to make even the most cynical believe." Abby had her own publicity efforts, too, which included free screenings for organizations and churches that wanted to use the film as an advocacy and organizing tool, to encourage discussion of nonviolent alternatives to conflict. Sometimes Abby went and spoke; often, I did. Sometimes Vaiba was the one who went; occasionally, it was Asatu.

We showed *Pray* in Srebrenica, Bosnia, on International Women's Day, and to indigenous women in Peru. There were screenings for women's groups in Georgia, Germany, Afghanistan, Iraq; showings in Korea, the Netherlands, Brazil, South Africa, Rwanda, Mexico, Argentina, the United Arab Emirates, Kenya, Cambodia, Poland, Russia.

The reaction was remarkably similar: no matter how different the country and the society, women recognized themselves and started talking about how they could unite to solve their own problems. In Sudan, they spent two hours discussing the film and eventually decided to create a position statement demanding peace in Darfur and get one million women to sign it. In Ramallah, in the West Bank, youth in the audience got so charged up, I thought they were going to mob the women—as if they were failures because they hadn't done what we had. In Israel, the women acknowledged, yes, we *should* do something like this, but we are too comfortable.

We showed the film in high schools, libraries, at academic conferences and churches of every denomination in several hundred US cities, where young people told us that our story had given them the desire to do something important with their lives.

The film showed our struggle, and the world enlarged it by responding. Ordinary people in Liberia had been *that* hungry for peace, and ordinary people everywhere were *that* hungry for a story in which the powerless take control of their lives and the good side wins. For hope.

It seemed so ironic that very few people knew about the Mass Action while it was taking place, but now the whole world did. Increasingly, the world also knew me. When I agreed to let Abby and Gini film me, fame was the last thing on my mind, but here it was. Talk-show hosts wanted to know my story. I would be in an airport and a stranger would greet me.

"Leymah?"

"Yes? . . ."

"I knew it was you!"

And as the success of the film spread word of what the Mass Action had been about and accomplished, awards began coming—to me, to me as its leader, to me as representative of the women of Liberia. When I got a call telling me I'd been awarded the Blue Ribbon for Peace from the Women's Leadership Board of the John F. Kennedy School of Government at Harvard, I could hardly believe it. I could tell you that I got accustomed to such honors, but I didn't. Leaders for the 21st Century Award from Women's eNews . . . Golden Butterfly Award in The Hague . . . John Jay Medal for Justice from the John Jay College of Criminal Justice . . . . Refugee Women Peace Ambassadors . . .

They all touched me. "Big" prizes, like the John F. Kennedy Profile in Courage Award, and the Gruber Women's Rights Prize, which gave my family a measure of financial security, but also a humanitarian award from a New York high school and being named a "living legend" by a Seventh Day Adventist Church in Ashton, Maryland.

Each time my response was the same: *Me?*

So many years ago, I crouched in despair, dressed in a torn night-gown, in the bathroom of the apartment I shared with Daniel and opened my Bible. "God," I said, "give me a verse."

This is what I read: *"O thou afflicted, tossed with tempest, and not comforted, behold, I will lay thy stones with fair colors, and lay thy foundations with sapphires. . . ."*

I saw it as a promise—and it was. It all came true.

CHAPTER 20

HELPING MY COUNTRY

WRITE ALL YOUR TITLES on a sheet of paper! Lawyer, doctor, mother . . . Write them down and put them in here!" I picked up a small suitcase and sent it, passed hand to hand, among the hundred women in the room. When it was full, I closed the lock with a snap. "You see? I am locking them away. Right now, we have no titles. We are not lawyers, activists, politicians or wives. We will speak only as women and as Liberians."

It was August 29, 2010, and we were gathered in a meeting room at the cleaned and refurbished Samuel K. Doe Stadium, for Liberia's first President's Peer Review—female activists come together to sit in judgment of President Ellen Johnson Sirleaf's efforts to improve the lives of the nation's women.

It was the first time in our nation's history that a sitting president simply listened, for seven hours, to what women had to say; the first time the government made a deliberate decision to include us in its planning process and recognize the work that we do.

The review was my idea. I'd thought of it shortly after the president was first elected but couldn't get it through the layer of bureaucracy around her. Since then, I'd come to know Ellen. There are some striking similarities to our stories. At seventeen, she married a man seven years older than she, who abused her physically. She, too, had four children. There are some who still have not forgiven her early support for Taylor.

I've let it go. I think she has done quite well for Liberia, and that she has done things no one else could have. When I suggested the peer review directly to her office, she asked me to lead the session.

As always, it was thrilling to be in a room packed with so much female energy. Rural and urban women were there, Americo-Liberians and indigenous, women from every ethnic tribe, most of them dressed in brilliant African dresses and hair ties. The history of the Liberian women's movement was right before me—Sugars, Vaiba, Asatu, Varbah Gayflor, Lindora, MARWOPNET members Beatrice Sherman and Ophelia Hoff. I still love leading these kinds of meetings, speaking, challenging, telling stories. Telling jokes, too—over the years I've come to realize that when you make people laugh, they allow you to touch them in ways you ordinarily could not. I love the learning and continuity these gatherings bring.

We debated and talked for hours—what we'd done, what was left to do—then as the meeting was dissolving and everyone began to clear the room, a group of older women standing near me started to sing loudly:

You go to my house, you break down my door
You take everything, you chokla everything

You aaah-ohhh, aaah-ohhh, aaah-ohhh

Who run away? Aahh-ooohhh run away
Who run away? Aahh-ooohhh run away

They were dancing, slapping hands and laughing, and I had to smile myself. The song is from a long time ago, before the Mass Action. Sometimes, in the early days of the war, the Liberian Women's Initiative members would go to places where the rebels had gathered, for instance, a bridge, and stand there protesting. In the Liberian vernacular, "you *chokla* everything" means "you scattered everything." They were talking about what the rebels had done in their community. But for their own safety, the women had to be careful about what they said. "Aaah-ohhh" was code for "asshole."

So what they'd really been singing was, *You assholes, assholes, assholes. Who run away? Assholes run away*. That's what gave them such pleasure now. The assholes *had* run away. But these women—all of us—were still here and still in the fight.

LIBERIA STILL HAS a long way to go. Even in Monrovia, roads remain wrecked and many buildings are ruined and abandoned. Most neighborhoods don't have reliable electricity and running water; women and children walk by the road carrying buckets on their heads and used plastic water bottles create huge piles of litter. You can see exhaustion on the faces of those in the city center, crowded together and struggling to survive. Almost everyone is poor. Unemployment is around 85 percent, only half our population can read or write, and life expectancy hovers at fifty-eight years. Official corruption remains rampant and crime is a serious problem.

Because of all the moving and emigration, the extended family structure that was a base of our culture has disintegrated. I see it even in my own family. Recently, when I talked about buying baby things for a cousin in Monrovia who'd just given birth to twins, my daughters asked, "Who is *she?*"

Perhaps as a result, our society is fragmented, too. It's hard for young people to feel a sense of community unless they also believe in possibility. How can they? Few Liberians can afford to actively search for work opportunities or find out what's going on in the world. Buying local newspapers or getting access to the Internet at a wireless café costs around two US dollars; for a street vendor, that's two days' wages.

The desperation everywhere in Liberia can make it a hard place to visit. I give financial aid to cousins studying at a private university, and to Ma, and I've established a scholarship at St. Peter's to honor Geneva, but I'm careful when I make the trip. Some of my relatives have the crazy idea that I'm rich, which means I can't go home for Christmas or when school's about to open, because I'll be flooded with requests for school fees. June and July are bad, because those are the months of school graduation. When I go to visit Ma on Old Road, I go early in the morning and get out fast, because as soon as I'm spotted, her bedroom fills up with family members requesting, requesting, requesting. I don't even have a regular Liberian phone number for my mobile phone. I buy a SIM card when I come and throw it away when I leave; otherwise, my phone would be ringing nonstop.

And yet—my country has enjoyed eight years of peace. The university is open again. Some industry has begun to function and a few new hotels and office buildings have gone up. In some ways, the lot of women has improved. Under President Sirleaf, we've gotten the National Gender Policy to promote equality, a new sex crimes unit within the Ministry of Justice, and one of the strongest anti-rape laws in Africa. The National Girls' Education Policy provides free primary education (although unfortunately students have to purchase their own uniforms and textbooks, which makes school too expensive for some families). Parliament is considering affirmative action legislation that would mandate 30 percent female representation in government, and more women than ever are in key positions, including heading the Departments of Commerce, Foreign Affairs, Finance, Youth and Sports, and Gender and Development. Government scholarships are available for any girl who wants to study agriculture.

Oddly enough, the war did this for us—or rather, the widespread recognition that we helped bring the war to an end. We might have made progress anyway, but if we hadn't felt compelled to step into the public arena, it might have taken us a lot longer.

MANY OF THE PEOPLE I worked with during the war and Mass Action are still trying hard to bring peace and prosperity to our country and to the women of Africa. Sugars is mayor of the town of Edina in Grand Bassa County. She is as outspoken and radical as ever, with no regrets for the path she chose. Thelma Ekiyor is the executive director of a well-funded private foundation dedicated to increasing access to health care and education in Nigeria. She also remains vitally involved with WIPSEN.

Grace Jarsor is a social worker who has worked with the Ministry of Gender. The Mass Action changed her life forever. "I come from the bush!" she says. "And because of the work we did, I sit beside the president!" Grace had a daughter after the war, and named her for Geneva. Vaiba, whose lack of education was one of her thorns, is a professional counselor, running trauma-healing workshops. In 2009, she was made a peacemaker fellow at the Joan B. Kroc School of Peace Studies in San Diego, California. Ma Annie, whom I first encountered working with the pastors' wives, has addressed the UN on women's grassroots activism and is running for a district seat in Bong County.

BB Colley became the executive director of the Resource Center for Community Empowerment and Integrated Development in Monrovia. He still believes in "the people." Sam Doe received his PhD and is now a UN development and reconciliation advisor.

I still talk to Tunde now and then. I invited him to several screenings of *Pray the Devil Back to Hell*, but he never came. I have no contact with Daniel.

I occasionally get news of others. Christian Johnson, one of my ex-combatants, the tall boy who had lost both his legs, died in 2010 of AIDS. I never learned what became of his girlfriend and their child, nor of Cleo, the fierce female ex-fighter. But I did hear that Sam Brown eventually located his mother in Sierra Leone, and sent his child to live with her. For a long time, I saw Joseph Colley, drunk and living on the streets of Monrovia, but he managed to finally put up a little booth where he could fix shoes. When the government tore it down, I gave him the money to rebuild it.

The field near the fish market, where we protested, is once again a football pitch, and you can frequently see games in which some of the players are on crutches, because they are missing a leg.

The leaders and warlords who made all our lives such hell have met with varying fates. The former spokesperson for the rebel group MODEL went on to run an African food market in Philadelphia. A member of LURD's peace treaty negotiating team became an associate justice on the Liberian Supreme Court. Roosevelt Johnson and Foday Sankoh, the leader of Sierra Leone's RUF, are both dead. Prince Johnson became a Liberian senator and is running for president in the 2011 election.

In October 2008, Charles Taylor's son Charles McArther Emmanuel—"Chuckie"—who was born and raised in Florida, was convicted in the US for crimes he committed in Liberia as the head of the Anti-Terrorist Unit, known as the "Demon Forces." It was the first prosecution under the US's Extraterritorial Torture Statute, and Chuckie was sentenced to ninety-seven years in federal prison. More recently, five Liberians who claimed they had been tortured at the prison he ran filed a civil suit in Florida and were awarded $22.4 million in damages.

As of early 2011, the trial of Charles Taylor himself continues in The Hague. Taylor, the first African president to face prosecution by an international tribunal for war crimes, was charged with five counts of crimes against humanity (including murder, rape and sexual slavery); five counts of war crimes (acts of terrorism, murder, pillage); and for violating international humanitarian law (enlisting children under age fifteen into the armed forces).

I've seen moments from our former president's trial on television, such as when the model Naomi Campbell was called to testify about whether Taylor had given her a gift of "blood" diamonds. She said she'd been handed a bag of "dirty looking stones" by two men she didn't know, adding that she "had never heard of the country Liberia before." Even Western media paid attention. But when I watched the proceedings, all I could think of was how many individuals in Sierra Leone would have benefited from the enormous amount of money—$20 million by some accounts—being spent on the judicial process. I also believe that this trial should have been held in Africa.

Taylor has yet to be tried for the vicious crimes he committed against those of his own country or be called to account for the vast wealth he stole, the futures he wrecked, the land he destroyed. He has yet to answer to Liberia. To us.

CHAPTER 21

THE STORY DOESN'T END

ALWAYS KNEW that I would have another child, a last child, born in peace, whom I can cuddle and play and be with, for whom I can be a mother. In June 2009, I gave birth to James's and my daughter, in New York City. Abby was with me and later took me to her home. She and her husband brought me food and took the baby so I could rest. These are things that mean everything to an African woman. Things that money can't buy.

I named my new baby Jaydyn Thelma Abigail. But I have my own nickname for her. When I first got pregnant, I thought, If it's a boy, I'll call him Nehdeh, which in the Loma language means "my own." My female version is Nehcopee.

Nehcopee travels with me almost everywhere I go. At home, the other kids spoil her endlessly. They love to make her laugh. Her smile looks just like Geneva's.

I live in Ghana with my children, but family and work often bring me to Liberia. At the airport, I never have to wait in the immigration line, because the officials there remember me from the WIPNET days. The customs people never open my suitcase.

"This is the voice for peace," some official always announces, then he or she turns to me and smiles. "Step off the line. Come, collect your bags."

My family remains scattered. Josephine is still in France and Mala in Sweden. Fata lives in New York. But Ma, who is close to a hundred years old, remains in the old neighborhood, where one of her biological daughters lives with and cares for her. The plum tree and abandoned car are long gone. So are the empty spaces my friends and I played in.

Even old and poor, Ma retains an air of authority. I still love being with her. The last time I was in Monrovia, I braided her hair and it was a pleasure to do it. Her home, as shabby as it is, is a place where I feel loved.

My parents still live in the house in Paynesville. That area, too, is very different than before the war. I used to love its openness and being able to look out our big windows to the fields, but you can't see them anymore. The land is transformed, filled with shacks and shanties, and you can't live securely without a tall, locked fence.

My parents never restored their house. The yard is just dirt. They have a stove in the kitchen, but gas is expensive, so most of the time they cook over charcoal. Their well water's only good for bathing; they have to fetch drinking water from the Lutheran compound, a twenty-minute drive away.

My father is past seventy now. He's more religious than he used to be and has become dependent on my mother. He says that the war brought him back to his marriage and to God. He's told me he's proud of me. The day the WIPNET women and I took over the conference hall in Accra, it was televised in Africa, and people he knew ran to him. "'Wow!'" he says they marveled. "'It looks like your daughter is doing big things!'" My mother is still my mother, though I feel softer toward her than I once did. If I call her and say I have a headache, she'll call to check twice on me before nightfall. I remember that every time one of us girls fell flat on our faces, she was always there for us to go back to. She is not a happy woman. She still grieves her losses. "What was the war for?" she asks. "People in our family died—why?

"Sometimes I feel that all is useless," she will say. "You work all your life, saying 'Tomorrow, when I'm old, I will sit down with my children.' But I have no children or grandchildren here. Everyone is far away."

And me? As I write this, I am thirty-nine years old. The story I have just told you is only the first part of my journey. I am grateful to God for where He has brought me and what He's made me. I spend a great deal of my time on the road now—in Europe, the UK, Scandinavia, the US, throughout Africa—attending conferences, running workshops, and speaking. I see myself as a messenger; my job is to take the stories of the little girls from Bassa and Bong Counties, from Ghana and Congo and Sierra Leone, and make them heard on the global stage.

Once a year, WIPSEN's West African Women's Policy Forum brings together women from across the region. At the forum, women from civil society talk to those in government and members of the economic community; different women from different parties from different countries talking about the issues that unite us. We have a good time, too. We are establishing the first-ever women's elections observer team and plan to train thirty-two women, two from each country in West Africa, who can be deployed when a nation goes to the polls.

Just like in the old days, WIPSEN is working to bring ordinary women into the electoral process. In one Liberian community, for instance, we learned that when voter registration began, the male community leader put on public display the "country devil," a masked god of the Poro secret society. Traditionally, when the country devil was out, women had to go inside. In such communities, we help women speak up against these actions and for themselves; we also find those who would like to run for office, train them, and then match them with mentors.

Another priority is teaching activism to young women. WIPSEN has a project called the Peace Girls Leadership Dialogue, which was implemented by the minister of Gender and Development. We began by reaching out to younger women on issues of immediate concern, such as sexually transmitted diseases. But like the market talks during the Peace Outreach Project, that was just laying a foundation. We were looking for a spark of something special, looking for young women we can train. We may start with fifty girls, then decide to work more closely with half of them. Fill in the gaps in their education and then seek out a final ten whom we feel can become mediators, organizers, leaders. We are building a new generation of *us*.

I also strive to make young women's voices audible to those in power. Last December, we had a young girl's circle, a kind of "Shedding of the

Weight," for President Sirleaf and some cabinet ministers. One by one, the next generation told their stories.

"My mom and I came to town to look for greener pastures, but we didn't find them," said one young girl. "She decided to go back to the village. I wanted to stay. Now I sleep with men for fifty Liberian dollars. They bend me over a tree. Sometimes the back of a car." She was twelve.

"Madame President," said another girl, "I lost both my parents. I have two siblings to care for. I needed to finish high school, so I went to a teacher I knew who was in charge of sports, which I play very well. He gave me a scholarship to a local high school. At ten o'clock every morning, he took me out of class, took me to a local house and fucked me all day. I ran away, but when I went to another school, the same thing happened. I finished high school but I will not go to college. I will not be used for sex anymore."

President Sirleaf's face was very red. Every single female government official in that room was crying. Before this session, some of us viewed younger women who dropped out of school as flighty or foolish. Now we understood the realities of their lives. In our government, there is now public conversation about sexual harassment in school. The president herself is asking, "What can we do?"

Another project in rural Liberia is teaching young girls that they have more to offer than sex. That they don't know this is a sad legacy of war—and the peace afterward. Foreign workers who come to "help" countries after conflict often exploit the people they find there: wherever you see male aid workers, lonely and with cash to spend, you will see an increase in prostitution. No one ever takes serious action to address this problem. Requiring peacekeeping forces to take classes in "gender awareness," as sometimes happens, is hardly enough.

Liberia's peacekeepers taught our girls that their bodies were their biggest asset; an epidemic of teen pregnancy and a soaring school dropout rate was the result. In 2009, in one of the country's most populous northern counties, not a single girl graduated from high school.

The effort is painstaking and difficult, and success stories occur one by one. But they do occur. Last December, one of the girls I worked with told me she'd almost given up. "I didn't have the money to pay my school fees," she said. "I tried to reach you and couldn't. I tried the minister of Gender and couldn't. I thought of going back to selling myself. But I kept hearing your voice: 'Your body's not the only option.' I found a short-term job, and got the money I needed."

That girl now leads WIPSEN's Monrovia effort to register voters.

God has given me a lot. I have wonderful children. Nuku went through a teenage rebellion, but he's a good boy, super smart, artistically brilliant and makes friends easily. He is a student at EMU and hopes to be an architect. Amber wants to be a doctor. She's quiet, studious, highly spiritual and practical in a way I've never been; she's the one who managed our household budget. Before her junior year of high school, she won a full scholarship to a private school in New York. She now lives with my friend Abby. Neither Nuku nor Amber remember going hungry as children, for which I'm thankful.

Arthur is enormously affectionate and shy, except when it comes to expressing his opinions. He's a radical who hates to be disrespected, and a passionate football player whose dream is to go to the UK and visit Chelsea Stadium. Both my sons have worked for programs teaching boys about violence against women, and it makes me proud that they're feminists. Pudu is the glamorous one, a lover of fashion and makeup. She wants to be a designer and live in Paris. Malou is just beginning to blossom. Although she's been my daughter for seven years, I believe she was always afraid that one day I would send her back. Geneva's daughter, Leemu, lives in Ohio with her father, and I'm great friends with her just as I was with her mother. She wants to be a human rights attorney. Diamond, who still stays with me, is enrolled in a computer college in Ghana; Baby, who went back to live with her father, is completing university in Liberia.

All my children have their dreams, but none of them wants to do the kind of work I do. It hurts, but I understand. My work has given me a lot, but it has also cost us dearly. I wasn't there for Nuku's sixth-grade graduation. Every year, Amber and Pudu have gotten school awards, and every year I've missed the program. Arthur lives for football and I've never even seen him play a game.

There are other costs. Like most women in my field, I still feel I have to work twice as hard as a man to be good enough. I always have too much to do. I am always juggling. When I'm on the road, I call my parents every day. I call the kids at least once, and usually more. I used to be very conscious of my appearance. Now I'm just too tired.

God gave me an opportunity to change history and I wouldn't begrudge Him if I never had the chance to do anything else. But there is a lot that I want still to do. I hope to build WIPSEN into a powerful organization that can stand on its own, without me. My dream is to return to school for a PhD in public policy. I would love to spend time in the classroom with young people. To provide for my own financial future, I'm purchasing a few cars and opening a business in Liberia that will offer professional transportation services.

My deepest dream, though, is to go home. My heartbeat is Liberia; I sleep, eat and breathe Liberia. After everything that's happened, when I think of my country, I think of happiness.

When Geneva died and we brought her body home, a group of men I'd known for years from the Old Road neighborhood stopped by. They were poor boys who never finished school and now survived on odd jobs. They had come to help—to sweep and carry water, to dig my sister's grave. They offered us fifteen hundred very, very hard-earned Liberian dollars to help pay for the funeral. That's the depth of love that exists in that place. There is no way in the world that I can be successful and not go back to those people.

James has a house in Monrovia and when Nehcopee and I visit, we stay there. I've also bought two acres just outside the capital, and not far from a new branch of the University of Liberia. I want to build a house on one acre and some student housing on the other. In about four years, when my older kids are married or off in school, Nehcopee and I will move back. I'll continue to work with community girls, but I'll also be preparing for a political campaign: I want to run for a seat in Parliament. I'm aware that there will be talk about my private life, and I'm strengthening myself to answer those questions.

Reporters always ask me if what we WIPNET women achieved in Liberia can be replicated in other parts of Africa. I tell them that it's already happening.

In Zimbabwe, the Women of Zimbabwe Arise, whose leaders frequently end up in jail, continue their calls for political reform. When Jestina Mukoko, a Zimbabwean peace activist, was arrested in 2008, some Zimbabwean sisters got the judge's cell phone number and each sent him five text messages every day. The judge eventually had to change his number. A female supreme court judge threw the case out, and Jestina went free.

It's happening on the Internet, through organizations like the African Women's Development Fund, the African Feminist Forum, and the website Peace Is Loud. Women are mobilizing across ethnic lines and across national borders.

It's happening in Congo, where I went in the spring of 2009 to lead a series of workshops bringing together women's groups so they could understand each other and find a way to work together. For women, Congo is a work in progress, a place where change must come from within. It is possible. In this country, where civil war has killed over five million, displaced a million more, and spawned an epidemic of systematic, horrifically brutal rape, I did not meet helpless victims, but women of strength, bravery and determination.

During a meeting in Bukavu, I heard about a woman who fearlessly opposed a group of brutal rebels. When people from her community were arrested and threatened with death, she tried to get them released. She used a radio network to let her community know when and where fighting was about to break out, so they could escape. At one point, she accompanied a group of women who were going to visit a rebel leader, known for committing atrocities, to ask for peace. When they arrived, he stretched out his hand to her and she put her life in jeopardy by refusing to shake it.

This woman finally left the area and moved to Kinshasa. When I traveled to that city for another workshop, I told the story of this remarkable person. When I finished, an unassuming woman sitting in the meeting raised her hand.

"That was me."

Because of women like her, because of women like us, I believe that in the end, tyranny will never succeed, and goodness will always vanquish evil. Although I may not see it in my lifetime, peace will overcome. I believe, I *know*, that if you have unshakable faith in yourself, in your sisters and in the possibility of change, you can do almost anything.

The work is hard. The immensity of what needs to be done is discouraging. But you look at communities that are struggling on a daily basis. *They* keep on—and in the eyes of the people there, you are a symbol of hope. And so you, too, must keep on. You are not at liberty to give up.

Don't stop, echoes the older Liberian lady's voice. *Don't ever stop.*

My answer to her: I never will.

INDEX

ACKNOWLEDGMENTS

All praise, glory and honor to God for His unfailing love and favor toward me. Thank you to all my kids, Diamond, Leemu, Joshua (Nuku), Amber, Arthur, Nicole (Pudu), Malou and Nehcopee for your love and understanding. Thanks to my parents for being committed to me and my kids, to my siblings Mala, Josephine and Fata, to Thelma Ekiyor for being my true friend and to Abby Disney and her family (Pierre, Charlotte, Olivia, Henry and Eamon) for opening your hearts and home to me and my family. And thanks to Kess for your quiet support during these times.

Thanks as well to all the wonderful women and men that I have worked with over the years. This story would have been different without your support, strength and determination. And to Carol Mithers for making the book process comfortable and fun. It was a therapy.

ABOUT THE AUTHORS

Liberian peace and women's-rights activist **Leymah Gbowee** is Africa columnist for *Newsweek* and *The Daily Beast.* Her part helping oust Liberian ruler Charles Taylor was featured in the documentary *Pray the Devil Back to Hell.* She has received numerous honors for her work, including the John F. Kennedy Profile in Courage Award, Peter and Patricia Gruber Foundation Women's Rights Prize and African Women's Development Fund Woman of Substance Award. Gbowee is a single mother of six, including one adopted daughter, and is based in Accra, Ghana, where she is executive director of the Women Peace and Security Network—Africa and member of the African Women Leaders Network for Reproductive Health and Family Planning (AWLN).

Carol Mithers is a journalist and book author. Her work has appeared in a wide variety of newspapers and national magazines. She lives in Los Angeles with her husband and daughter.

Praise for *Mighty Be Our Powers*

" . . . a beautifully written narrative."

—Michelle Bachelet, under-secretary-general
and executive director of UN Women

"*Mighty Be Our Powers* reminds us that even in the worst of times, humanity's best can shine through."

—Archbishop Desmond Tutu,
Nobel Peace Prize Laureate, 1984

"One of the most inspirational and powerful books I've ever read. The story of one woman's struggle against the worst and what she can teach all of us about finding the courage and strength to change the world."

—Sheryl Sandberg, COO, Facebook

"An engrossing, fluently written story that anyone who cares about changing the world has to read."

—Reverend Dr. Calvin O. Butts, III, pastor,
The Abyssinian Baptist Church in the City of New York

"Leymah bore witness to the worst of humanity and helped bring Liberia out of the dark. Her memoir is a captivating narrative that will stand in history as testament to the power of women, faith and the spirit of our great country."

—Ellen Johnson Sirleaf, president of Liberia
and Nobel Peace Prize Laureate, 2011

"Searing war-torn memories from a visionary African peacekeeper and women's-rights activist. . . . Gbowee stands responsible for what began as a tireless vocal demonstration and soon escalated to a standoff on the presidential mansion steps demanding peace. This course of action facilitated the war's end in 2003 and the election of Africa's first female president, and ended the author's personal struggles with alcohol. With commanding charity, Gbowee celebrates Liberia's eight years of peace and continues teaching young women about the power of activism. A patriotic chronicle reverberant with valor and perseverance."

—STARRED Kirkus Review

"[*Mighty Be Our Powers* is a] larger, more universal kind of book that tells the story of both Leymah and an entire generation of girls-turned-women-turned-world-leaders. Read it—and be inspired."

—Oprah.com

A READING GUIDE TO
MIGHTY BE OUR POWERS

We are providing the following supplementary materials—an update on the author's life, discussion questions, suggestions for further reading and exploration, and the transcript of a recent interview with her—in the hopes they will enhance your reading of Leymah Gbowee's Mighty Be Our Powers. *We hope they will help you to engage with the text and will provide a jumping-off point for reading group discussions.*

About the Author: Update

Leymah Gbowee was awarded the Nobel Peace Prize in 2011—shared with Ellen Johnson Sirleaf, the president of Liberia, and Tawakkol Karman, Yemeni journalist and peace activist—"for their non-violent struggle for the safety of women and for women's rights to full participation in peace-building work." She cofounded the Women Peace and Security Network–Africa and is president of the Gbowee Peace Foundation Africa—the mission of which is to promote and facilitate activities and initiatives aimed at promoting peace and reconciliation through the holistic participation of local communities. The foundation envisions a peaceful and reconciled Africa that recognizes and utilizes the skills and talents of all, regardless of gender and ethnicity.

Gbowee is the Africa columnist for *Newsweek/Daily Beast*, serves on the board of directors of the Nobel Women's Initiative and the PeaceJam Foundation, and is a member of the African Women Leaders Network for

Reproductive Health and Family Planning. She holds an M.A. in Conflict Transformation from Eastern Mennonite University in Harrisonburg, Virginia. Based in Monrovia, Liberia, she is the proud mother of six.

Carol Mithers is a journalist and book author. Her work has appeared in a wide variety of newspapers and national magazines. She lives in Los Angeles with her husband and daughter.

. . . .

Questions for Thought and Discussion

1) The prologue to this memoir shows how women are traditionally left out of war histories. In just two paragraphs Gbowee questions violence, sexism, colonialism, the unequal distribution of wealth, and the classical genre of war histories. Does the prologue help you understand the overarching themes of the memoir? What are those themes?

2) Leymah's sense of herself changes throughout the book. In Chapter 1, at age 17, she is full of confidence and a sense of her own agency. How does she win, and then lose, this confidence, and what, finally, allows her to regain it? What do you have in common with the young Leymah? Is it possible to discuss her identity without reference to the brutal wars she and her family endure?

3) Talk about the relationships between the Congo People, the Americo-Liberians, and the indigenous people of Liberia. Who are Leymah's people, and in what ways does her heritage predict her options in life?

4) Leymah's graduation presents included a pair of Dexter boots. When she is forced to leave them behind as the family flees the civil war, she has a pang of regret. Two years later, on page 39, she returns to Paynesville and sees a neighbor on the way to the city, wearing her Dexter boots. What changes in that moment? What else did she leave behind in Paynesville?

5) Why does Leymah choose to be with Daniel? During her abusive relationship with him, there is a scene where she turns to the Bible and

discovers Isaiah Chapter 54. She reads this passage: "For the Lord has called thee as a woman forsaken and grieved in spirit. . . . O thou afflicted, tossed with tempest, and not comforted, behold, I will lay thy stones with fair colors, and lay thy foundations with sapphires. . . . " How do you interpret this passage as it relates to Leymah?

6) What is meant by the "cycle" of domestic violence? How does Leymah first learn to put a name to her experience of abuse, to recognize her own story? At what point does she learn to see the relationship between the personal and the political? What roles do her children and her work play in ending the terrible relationship with Daniel?

7) Describe Leymah's relationship with Tunde. What are the similarities and differences between her relationship with Daniel and her relationship with Tunde? How could Tunde be both deliverance and another trap?

8) Leymah's boss, BB, challenges her intellectually, calling on her to become "academically fit." He claims she is learning in a "naïve" way. How does he teach her to read critically? What questions does he ask?

9) After Leymah gets her associate's degree and teams up with Thelma Ekiyor, she has the opportunity to go to Accra in Ghana to help launch the Women in Peacebuilding Network (WIPNET)'s first conference. What were the most important results of this conference? What role did the WIPNET workshop practices called "Being a Woman," "The Shedding of the Weight," and "Crown and Thorn" have in bringing the women together? Were these therapeutic exercises or political exercises, or both?

10) How did Leymah and her fellow sisters in the peace-building movement set about to get an actual seat at the political table in April 2003? How did the Mass Action begin? Would you have been able to summon the courage to approach Charles Taylor? The LURD rebels?

11) After Charles Taylor is indicted by a UN war crimes tribunal and flees the peace talks in Ghana, he returns to Monrovia and the fighting begins anew. What was Leymah's next move, and how did Ellen Johnson Sirleaf help jumpstart the peace movement underway in Accra and in Liberia, where the women sat together in fields?

12) Discuss the moment when Leymah begins to remove her clothing in the doorway to the negotiating hall in Ghana. What is the power of humiliation, and who is humiliated in this scene?

13) Gini Reticker and Abigail Disney approach Leymah about doing a documentary film about the Mass Action and Leymah's role in it. What effect did this project initially have on the women of WIPNET? How does Leymah cope with the rejection of her peace-building sisters? What changed after the documentary's success?

14) On page 205, Leymah writes: "I know my children were angry at me. Later, when I asked if any of them wanted to grow up to be a peace-builder, Amber's response was, 'No. I want to stay home with my children.'" What do you think of Leymah's choice?

15) Leymah dedicates this memoir to her sister Geneva. What role does Geneva play in Leymah's life? What role does Leymah play in Geneva's life?

16) Discuss the subtitle of *Mighty Be Our Powers: How Sisterhood, Prayer, and Sex Changed a Nation at War*. Did this book change the way you think about people's power to achieve peace through non-violent action? How were the women of western Africa so successful?

. . . .

Suggestions for Further Reading and Exploration

Ellis, Stephen. *The Mask of Anarchy: The Destruction of Liberia and the Religious Dimension of an African Civil War* (New York University Press, revised edition, 2006).

- A cultural history of the role of religious and ritual expression in Liberia's civil war. Ellis discusses the child soldiers and teenage killers who were pressed into service by rebel fighters for the siege on Monrovia, and provides political background on the wars. This history provides excellent context for understanding Leymah Gbowee's early social work practice with disabled child soldiers.

Gandhi, Mohandas Karamchand (Mahatma), and Desai, Mahadev H. ***Gandhi, An Autobiography: The Story of My Experiments with Truth*** (CreateSpace, 2011).

- The classic autobiography of the leader of the struggle for the independence of India from Britain. Gandhi was author and practitioner of the philosophy of non-violence, non-cooperation, and peaceful resistance. These teachings helped to create the underpinnings of Leymah Gbowee's women's peace movement in Liberia.

Hetherington, Tim. ***Long Story Bit by Bit: Liberia Retold*** (Umbrage Editions, 2009).

- Hetherington was an award-winning photographer and filmmaker who spent four years photographing, collecting oral histories, and documenting his time in Liberia. He lived with a rebel army in the rainforest during the civil war, one of only two journalists to live behind enemy lines. His stories provide additional detail to Leymah Gbowee's accounts of Liberia's civil wars.

Kamara-Umunna, Agnes (with Emily Holland). ***And Still Peace Did Not Come: A Memoir of Reconciliation*** (Hyperion, 2011).

- This memoir of war in Liberia is an excellent companion book to Leymah's own. After a time of forced exile in Sierra Leone, Agnes returned to host the UN-run radio program "Straight From the Heart," in which she presented live on-air stories of the child soldiers, warlords, rape survivors, and others in their own words.

King, Jr., Martin Luther. ***Letter from the Birmingham Jail*** (HarperCollins, 1994).

- The definitive writing on racial injustice by Martin Luther King, Jr., architect of non-violent civil rights protest and inspiration to Leymah Gbowee.

Kristof, Nicholas D., and WuDunn, Sheryl. *Half the Sky: Turning Oppression into Opportunity for Women Worldwide* (Vintage, 2010).

- Essential reading by two Pulitzer Prize–winning journalists reporting on the oppression of women and girls in the developing world. The book recounts their time in Africa and Asia, offering portraits of women overcoming appalling odds. The authors come to see these women and their resilience as the key to economic development world-wide. *Half the Sky* calls upon readers to understand that the emancipation of women leads to freedom for all.

Sirleaf, Ellen Johnson. *This Child Will Be Great: Memoir of a Remarkable Life by Africa's First Woman President* (Harper Perennial, 2010).

- Sirleaf is the twenty-third and current president of Liberia, the first woman president on the African continent. Her memoir tells the story of a woman of great accomplishment and personal resilience and analyzes the recent political history of Liberia and the West African States. Sirleaf was a co-recipient of the Nobel Peace Prize, shared with Leymah Gbowee.

Taylor, Wendy Maragh. *This Part of the Sky: Building in Liberia* (CreateSpace, 2012).

- Wendy Maragh Taylor's chronicle of a journey to Liberia with her husband, a native Liberian. The couple takes part in the construction of a building now serving as a church and school, helping to rebuild a small piece of Liberia. As her culture shock subsides, she comes to see Liberia as a place of hope.

Waugh, Colin M. *Charles Taylor and Liberia: Ambition and Atrocity in Africa's Lone Star State* (Zed Books, 2011).

- The story of the destructive powers of the rebel leader who wanted to bring change to Liberia. At one time an elected president, Taylor later became an international fugitive, a warlord on the run. He was eventually brought to The Hague where he was sentenced to fifty years for war crimes. Excellent background on the figure Gbowee stared down and ultimately helped topple.

Yoder, John Howard. *The Politics of Jesus* (Wm. B. Eerdmans Publishing Company, 1994).

- An accessible study of the social and political teachings of Jesus by respected theologian John Howard Yoder. In this account, the author takes the traditional view of an apolitical Jesus and turns that view on its head. The book draws on the New Testament for its argument that Jesus was a pacifist and political ethicist.

For more information about Leymah's current projects, visit her website at http://leymahgbowee.com/wipsen.html.

Pray the Devil Back to Hell, the documentary about the women's revolution in Liberia, and Leymah's place in that movement, is available for viewing in streaming video in the United States at http://video.pbs.org/video/2155873888 and on Netflix. You can also purchase the DVD for personal use at amazon.com, barnesandnoble.com, and other retailers. If you are interested in purchasing a DVD copy of *Pray the Devil Back to Hell* for a public event in your community or on your campus, or if you'd like the DVD for use in your library, school, or research institution, please visit rocoeducation.com/film.

. . . .

Unlock the Intelligence, Passion, and Greatness of Girls

In a Talk she gave at the annual TED (Technology, Entertainment, Design) conference in Long Beach, California, in March 2012, Leymah spoke about the role of girls in the women's peacebuilding movement she founded in Liberia during two civil wars. These wars took an enormous toll on families, and especially on

*children and young women who were forced directly into the con-
flict by rebels and government soldiers who committed violent rapes
and murders as everyday war strategies. This Talk, transcribed below, is a testimonial to the courage of girls in conflict areas globally, and to the power they can unleash when working together. At
the end, Leymah converses briefly with TED conference curator
Chris Anderson.*

Many times I go around the world to speak, and people ask me questions about the challenges, my moments, some of my regrets. 1998: A
single mother of four, three months after the birth of my fourth child, I
went to do a job as a research assistant. I went to Northern Liberia. And
as part of the work, the village would give you lodgings. And they gave
me lodging with a single mother and her daughter.

The girl happened to be the only girl in the entire village who had
made it to the ninth grade. She was the laughingstock of the community.
Her mother was often told by other women, "You and your child will die
poor." After two weeks of working in that village, it was time to go back.
The mother came to me, knelt down, and said, "Leymah, take my daughter. I wish for her to be a nurse." Dirt poor, living in the home with my
parents, I couldn't afford to. With tears in my eyes, I said, "No."

Two months later, I go to another village on the same assignment and
they asked me to live with the village chief. The women's chief of the village has this little girl, fair color like me, totally dirty. And all day she
walked around only in her underwear. When I asked, "Who is that?" She
said, "That's Wei. The meaning of her name is pig. Her mother died
while giving birth to her and no one had any idea who her father was."
For two weeks, she became my companion, slept with me. I bought her
used clothes and bought her her first doll. The night before I left, she
came to the room and said, "Leymah, don't leave me here. I wish to go
with you. I wish to go to school." Dirt poor, no money, living with my
parents, I again said, "No." Two months later, both of those villages fell
into another war. Till today, I have no idea where those two girls are.

Fast-forward, 2004: In the peak of our activism, the minister of Gender Liberia called me and said, "Leymah, I have a nine-year-old for you.

I want you to bring her home because we don't have safe homes." The story of this little girl: She had been raped by her paternal grandfather every day for six months. She came to me bloated, very pale. Every night I'd come from work and lie on the cold floor. She'd lie beside me and say, "Auntie, I wish to be well. I wish to go to school."

2010: A young woman stands before President Sirleaf and gives her testimony of how she and her siblings live together, their father and mother died during the war. She's 19; her dream is to go to college to be able to support them. She's highly athletic. One of the things that happens is that she applies for a scholarship. Full scholarship. She gets it. Her dream of going to school, her wish of being educated, is finally here. She goes to school on the first day. The director of sports who's responsible for getting her into the program asks her to come out of class. And for the next three years, her fate will be having sex with him every day, as a favor for getting her in school.

Globally, we have policies, international instruments, work leaders. Great people have made commitments—we will protect our children from want and from fear. The UN has the Convention on the Rights of the Child. Countries like America, we've heard things like No Child Left Behind. Other countries come with different things. There is a Millennium Development called Three that focuses on girls. All of these great works by great people aimed at getting young people to where we want to get them globally, I think, have failed.

In Liberia, for example, the teenage pregnancy rate is 3 to every 10 girls. Teen prostitution is at its peak. In one community, we're told, you wake up in the morning and see used condoms like chewing gum paper. Girls as young as 12 being prostituted for less than a dollar a night. It's disheartening. It's sad. And then someone asked me, just before my TEDTalk, a few days ago, "So, where is the hope?"

Several years ago, a few friends of mine decided we needed to bridge the disconnect between our generation and the generation of young women. It's not enough to say you have two Nobel laureates from the Republic of Liberia when your girls' kids are totally out there with no hope, or seemingly no hope. We created a space called the Young Girls Transformative Project. We go into rural communities and all we do, like has been done in this room, is create the space. When these girls sit, you un-lock intelligence, you unlock passion, you unlock commitment, you un-lock focus, you unlock great leaders. Today, we've worked with over 300. And some of those girls who walked in the room very shy have taken bold steps, as young mothers, to go out there and advocate for the rights of other young women.

One young woman I met, teen mother of four, never thought about finishing high school, graduated successfully; never thought about going to college, enrolled in college. One day she said to me, "My wish is to fin-ish college and be able to support my children." She's at a place where she can't find money to go to school. She sells water, sells soft drinks, and sells recharge cards for cellphones. And you would think she would take that money and put it back into her education. Juanita is her name. She takes that money and finds single mothers in her community to send back to school. Says, "Leymah, my wish is to be educated. And if I can't be educated, when I see some of my sisters being educated, my wish has been fulfilled. I wish for a better life. I wish for food for my children. I wish that sexual abuse and exploitation in schools would stop." This is the dream of the African girl.

Several years ago, there was one African girl. This girl had a son who wished for a piece of doughnut because he was extremely hungry. Angry, frustrated, really upset about the state of her society and the state of her children, this young girl started a movement, a movement of ordinary women banding together to build peace. I will fulfill the wish. This is an-other African girl's wish. I failed to fulfill the wish of those two girls. I failed to do this. These were the things that were going through the head of this other young woman—I failed, I failed, I failed. So I will do this. Women came out, protested a brutal dictator, fearlessly spoke. Not only did the wish of a piece of doughnut come true, the wish of peace came true. This young woman wished also to go to school. She went to school. This young woman wished for other things to happen, it happened for her.

Today, this young woman is me, a Nobel laureate. I'm now on a jour-ney to fulfill the wish, in my tiny capacity, of little African girls—the wish of being educated. We set up a foundation. We're giving full four-year scholarships to girls from villages that we see with potential.

I don't have much to ask of you. I've also been to places in this U.S., and I know that girls in this country also have wishes, a wish for a better life somewhere in the Bronx, a wish for a better life somewhere in downtown L.A., a wish for a better life somewhere in Texas, a wish for a better life somewhere in New York, a wish for a better life somewhere in New Jersey.

Will you journey with me to help that girl, be it an African girl or an American girl or a Japanese girl, fulfill her wish, fulfill her dream, achieve that dream? Because all of these great innovators and inventors that we've talked to and seen over the last few days are also sitting in tiny corners in different parts of the world, and all they're asking us to do is create that space to unlock the intelligence, unlock the passion, unlock all of the great things that they hold within themselves. Let's journey together. Let's journey together.

Thank you.

(Applause)

Chris Anderson: Thank you so much. Right now in Liberia, what do you see as the main issue that troubles you?

LG: I've been asked to lead the Liberian Reconciliation Initiative. As part of my work, I'm doing these tours in different villages and towns—13, 15 hours on dirt roads—and there is no community that I've gone into that I haven't seen intelligent girls. But sadly, the vision of a great future, or the dream of a great future, is just a dream, because you have all of these vices. Teen pregnancy, like I said, is epidemic.

So what troubles me is that I was at that place and somehow I'm at this place, and I just don't want to be the only one at this place. I'm looking for ways for other girls to be with me. I want to look back 20 years from now and see that there's another Liberian girl, Ghanaian girl, Nigerian girl, Ethiopian girl standing on this TED stage. And maybe, just maybe, saying, "Because of that Nobel laureate I'm here today." So I'm troubled when I see them like there's no hope. But I'm also not pessimistic, because I know it doesn't take a lot to get them charged up.

CA: And in the last year, tell us one hopeful thing that you've seen happening.

LG: I can tell you many hopeful things that I've seen happening. But in the last year, where President Sirleaf comes from her village, we went there to work with these girls. And we could not find 25 girls in high school. All of these girls went to the gold mine, and they were predominantly prostitutes doing other things. We took 50 of those girls and we worked with them. And this was at the beginning of elections. This is one place where women were never—even the older ones barely sat in the circle with the men. These girls banded together and formed a group and launched a campaign for voter registration. This is a real rural village. And the theme they used was: "Even pretty girls vote." They were able to mobilize young women.

But not only did they do that, they went to those who were running for seats to ask them, "What is it that you will give the girls of this community when you win?" And one of the guys who already had a seat was very—because Liberia has one of the strongest rape laws, and he was one of those really fighting in parliament to overturn that law because he called it barbaric. Rape is not barbaric, but the law, he said, was barbaric. And when the girls started engaging him, he was very hostile toward them. These little girls turned to him and said, "We will vote you out of office." He's out of office today.

Reprinted courtesy of TED